The Odyssey
of Love

To Jess,

A pilgrimage across the
Great Books to commemorate
our meeting together at
By & By as I pilgrimage thru
the Shenandoah.

— Paul

The Odyssey of Love

A Christian Guide to the Great Books

PAUL KRAUSE

WIPF & STOCK · Eugene, Oregon

THE ODYSSEY OF LOVE
A Christian Guide to the Great Books

Wipf & Stock
An Imprint of Wipf and Stock Publishers
199 W. 8th Ave., Suite 3
Eugene, OR 97401

www.wipfandstock.com

PAPERBACK ISBN: 978-1-7252-9739-5
HARDCOVER ISBN: 978-1-7252-9740-1
EBOOK ISBN: 978-1-7252-9741-8

07/01/21

To my parents,
who taught me to read and instilled in me
a love of learning and stories.

Contents

Preface

SAINT JEROME SAID THAT "WHEN WE READ, GOD SPEAKS TO US." HE MEANT that in the context of reading Scripture, but it could just as easily be applied to all written works. This anthology of essays intends to have God speak to the reader in the form of essays.

One of the tragedies of our age is the lack of literary consciousness and love. Culture rises and falls on many things; language and a literary tradition are central to the rise and fall of culture. If the broadly Christian culture could have been defined by love, then it follows that the great works of literature from that culture would deal with love in their own ways. Furthermore, Saint Augustine said all truth, wherever it is found, belongs to God. In that spirit, I have endeavored to draw forth from the great wellspring of the Western humanities tradition the core truth contained in our civilization's writings.

This book is a collection of essays stretching back from Hesiod and Homer through to Dante, Charles Dickens, and Leo Tolstoy. Over forty books, plays, and poems are sampled and considered through the lens of the Christian faith, examining their shortcomings, insights, and implicit Christian themes. I had great joy composing the pieces and even greater joy in reading the works which are being reflected upon. Hopefully the reader will find great joy in being illuminated not by my work or ruminations, but by God's work in what is contained in these essays.

There are multiple goals for having composed this work. First is to show how great literature deals with the theme of love. Second is to highlight the general trajectory and pilgrimage of love in literature for nearly three millennia from Hesiod's *Theogony* and Homer's *Iliad* to Leo Tolstoy's *War and Peace*. Third is to inspire readers to return to these texts, or books more generally, and be enriched by the stories they tell that can lift the reader—like Plato's charioteer—to the celestial realm. Stories are the most personal things we have, and stories have the power to change the world, which is why they're being suppressed by the ideological guardians of literature who would rather deconstruct and destroy than inspire and uplift. Last, but not least, this work is also a defense of the humanities and its relevance to our lives and culture in a time when the humanities are thoroughly depreciated and oftentimes destroyed by the very teachers and guardians meant to transmit the wisdom and inspiration of our literary tradition to the next generation.

I hope this volume can bring the reader as much joy as they did me in writing them to communicate the great theme of love, which lifts our souls and eyes to the stars.

~ Paul Krause

Acknowledgments

I WISH TO FIRST ACKNOWLEDGE MATTHEW WIMER, EMILY CALLIHAN, AND all the members of Wipf and Stock who had a helping hand in bringing this project to fruition. Your generosity, kindness, and willingness to work with me are very much appreciated. Additionally, I would like to thank various editors, colleagues, and publishers, from whom the chapters of this book are derived. Special thanks are due to W. Winston Elliott III and Stephen Kluge-wicz, the publisher and editor respectively of *The Imaginative Conservative,* where I serve as a senior literary essayist. The opportunity to write for you has been one of the great blessings of my life. Thanks are also in order for Lee Trepanier, head editor of *VoegelinView,* where I serve as an associate editor and a frequent writer on religion, literature, and culture. I am also grateful to Erich Prince at *Merion West* and Jeffrey Bilbro at *Front Porch Republic* for the years of writing with them.

Introduction

In Defense of the Humanities

THERE IS A MAJOR REVOLUTION OCCURRING IN OUR SOCIETY, AND IT HAS been occurring for some time. No, I am not talking about the current state of political struggle. I am talking about the decline and fall of the humanities. The collapse of the humanities is not something with which readers here are unfamiliar. If the humanities are vital to the richness of human experience, why are they collapsing?

The name humanities has "human" as its basis. The humanities are about us. In a way, the humanities are the study of what it means to be human, along with the fruits of human genius and the creative spirit. The humanities range from philosophy—that most sublime and supreme queen—to literature, art, music, religion, language, and all the disciplines and topics that inform, build, and constitute what people have long called "culture." Humanist studies is not, however, an outright celebration of every aspect of the human spirit and endeavor. It can be just as critical as it is appraising. Its study can inform and instruct—pointing out errors, as much as pointing out goodness, virtue, beauty, and other such things for which to strive.

Everyone knows the first critique of the humanities: that it is not a viable or good investment—a waste of money to study such dull and dry topics, when one should invest in an education "to get a job." And we all know what that really means: becoming a cog in the increasingly digitized and mechanistic, economistic way of life. This mentality of obscene economism is itself rooted in the humanities. One need only look to English philosophers like Francis Bacon, Thomas Hobbes, and John Locke to see this conception of the human as a body of matter in motion with the goal of consumerism as the highest good in life, precisely because Hobbes and Locke denied the *summum bonum* in their works. For those interested in the genealogies of specific worldviews and outlooks on the eternal question *quid sit homo*, one would have to study the humanities. If Michael Corleone was taught by his father to "keep your friends close but your enemies closer," anyone who seeks to understand the other, or the enemy, will necessarily have to grapple with the humanities.

Additionally, the very idea of the university as a place to further bourgeois careerism is a product of only the last century, thanks to the progressive and pragmatic reformers who were influenced by the vision of an emerging urban, technological, and mechanistic society as the brave new world for which we were destined, and who thought education should reflect this new reality. But universities were first created in medieval Europe as places to study the arts and humanities: literature, theology, philosophy, and the coming canon created by the Renaissance humanists.

Part of the idea of the universities, and of the humanities more generally, was that the study of things human would awaken the mind and move it to seek after the good, the true, and the beautiful. Those seminal texts, now decried by some humanities departments, were chosen on account of their density, depth, and beauty. To study the humanities, in the eyes of the original mission of universities and their founders, was to make one a better human. The mission was not to spend half a decade of one's life learning the ins and outs of the skills necessary for a certain job. That is what apprenticeship was for.

The aim of the culture of the humanities is to foster an ethos of understanding—understanding what it means to be human but, more importantly, understanding what one has inherited. In this way, the humanities is profoundly conservative at its heart—which is among one of the reasons why the humanities are under assault by the external pressure of a growing mechanistic and economistic way of life, and by the internal pressure from those who preach the language of "consciousness," but mean it only in a political-economic-social context rather than a truly cultural and human one, thereby turning the humanities into a conduit for politicized social-sciences that destroys the humanities altogether. The humanities serve as a transcendental bridge, linking past, present, and future with destiny. And as we all know, man does not live by bread alone.

The human, the most exquisite of God's creation according to both ancient philosophy (Platonism, Aristotelianism, and Stoicism) and theology (Abrahamic), was always more than a consuming animal. Man was as much a cultural and social animal as he was consumeristic. Culture enlivens man, informs man, and helps to direct man to higher ends. Affectivity and relationality fed off one another. After all, when God saw Adam's loneliness in the garden, he fashioned woman from Adam's rib—his side—signifying their relational equality, and bound them together. As Saint Augustine so eloquently said in *City of God*, "The woman, then, is the creation of God, just as is the man; but her creation out of man emphasizes the idea of the unity between them." I would add that it is also important that, in the Genesis account, the first humans have a name and relationship with one another which invokes the importance of affectivity and intimacy—the thus-named and relational nature elevating humanity's social nature above a dry communitarianism that hopes to avoid the problems of bare life.

People once worried about book burnings. People still complain about the danger of censorship. There has not been a more successful book burning and censorship campaign than the assault against the humanities. The elimination from the consciousness of people of the very works, language, and culture that had informed communities and individuals for centuries— nay, millennia—is an achievement that would make Captain Beatty blush. And there is a certain irony that Ray Bradbury foresaw the day when (formerly) educated and literate individuals, such as Beatty, would be leading the destruction of the humanities because of the contradictory, obscene, and regressive views and writings contained in the great books, much like how esteemed faculty and professors take a culling knife to the classics of literature and philosophy with deliberately harmful intent.

It is said that we are increasingly living in an anxious age, an atomized and uprooted age, an age where culture is everywhere but, in reality, nowhere. We have become wanderers—strangers in a strange land—despite having, in most of our cases, been born and raised in a region that once breathed with the spirit of Homer, Sappho, Plato, Aristophanes, Aristotle, Virgil, Cicero, Moses, Augustine, Dante, Milton, Shakespeare, Bradstreet, Shelley, Melville, and Hawthorne. We are now Odysseus and Aeneas lost in the middle of their journey, but without the backstory and no destination toward which to aim.

One of the cornerstones of conservatism is humanism. One of the most basic aims of liberal arts studies is to familiarize students with the longstanding and inherited traditions of literature, philosophy, and theology. One's personal identification with a literary, philosophical, or theological school is not so much the point; rather, it is to inculcate the person with those who have come before us in dealing with those enduring questions. The death of the humanities is nothing less than the death of the human being and of human culture.

Is it any wonder, despite the most egregious of appropriations of the term "humanist" (especially by secular humanists—of whom they are among the most illiterate of the humanities, for they do not even realize the origins of humanist thought deep within the Christian religion), that people hate themselves, despite claiming to love themselves, and desperately seek to transform themselves to fill their restless heart? Is it any wonder that humans prefer to have their eyes glued downward on their phones, as if ready to embrace the pit of hell, rather than looking upward to the stars of the heavens and gazing upon the natural beauty of the earth? Is it any wonder that the dream of transhumanism is aggressively being pursued and discussed as if a reality? Dante looked to the stars to be moved, while we look to Instagram, Facebook, and Twitter.

People lament about the death of culture, but they know not what this entails and what the signs of that decline are. Where are the great men and women of letters? The fact that Ernest Cline is the savior of culture should be disconcerting to anyone who has read the likes of Chaucer, Shakespeare, Milton, or Melville. After all, where is the salvation of culture found in Mr. Cline's novel, now turned film?

In the first book of *Politics,* Aristotle makes a direct reference to the ninth book of Homer's *Iliad.* When Augustine penned *City of God,* he assumed his readers to be familiar with the works of the Platonists, Virgil, Cicero, Sallust, Varro, the Bible, and the great stories of Rome's founding mythology: Romulus and Remus, Lucretia, and Aeneas. Dante's *Divine Comedy* is not simply an allegory of his own tumultuous experiences in Florence; it is also a journey through the very soul of Western literature, philosophy, and theology from start to finish. Shakespeare is riddled with biblical and literary references that lessen the greatness of Shakespeare when missed by the reader. Jonathan Swift, that great satirist, was engaged in his own cultural criticism in satirizing the philosophies of Bacon, Hobbes, and Locke when Gulliver meets the Laputans.

This is, by and large, all lost to people today. Nostalgia and sentimentality, as Sir Roger Scruton has said, are underrated aspects of the human condition. Anthony Esolen has opined that we are not entering a new pagan age, for the pagans had great stories behind them and their consciousness, which is clearly not the case in the descent into the new mechanistic man: the consummation of the Baconian-Hobbesian man as a body of matter in motion or La Mettrie's *L'homme Machine.*

The culture war cannot be won without recourse to the great repository of culture. And there is a two-front war against culture: one from the outside (technology, economism, and globalism) and the other from the inside (who do so with quite deliberate intent). Any lover of culture, true culture, is a lover of the humanities at heart, because the humanities are the wellspring of culture—the very seeds and roots of culture. The joy of the humanities is that it cannot be bought (or should not be bought). True culture—much like Augustine's concept of "true religion" as worshipping the God where human desire finds its ultimate felicity—has the power to direct the soul to the good, the true, and the beautiful and to inculcate in man an appreciation of the good, the true, and the beautiful.

Any talk of saving culture or restoring culture begins with a defense of the humanities. Any hope of cultural revival equally begins with a re-emergence of the humanities. Any hope to truly celebrate—though not uncritically—the human person rests with being drenched in the dewfall of the humanities. The death of the humanities really does mean the death of the human. It represents the final destruction of the *Lebenswelt,* the great cultural inheritance that has moved man and earth. Our current metaphysical and ontological impoverishment is very much the result of our cultural impoverishment. Any revival of the human being, of culture, and of tradition, is tied to the resurrection of the humanities.

This essay was originally published in *The Imaginative Conservative,* 10 July 2018.

1

Reading Homer
from Here to Eternity

"Hey hey, ho ho, Western Civ has got to go!" That famous protest chant at Stanford University was the manifestation of, admittedly, a long deconstructive project aimed at eliminating the Western humanities from our civic and civilizational consciousness. "Old, dead, white, European males,"[1] we were told then, as we are told now, must go. There's no reason to study them, especially given their rank sexism, misogyny, and racism—so the argument goes. The humanities, the liberal arts, is a Western construction and uniquely so; therefore, the demise of Western civilization corresponds with the demise of the liberal arts as the pulsating heart that unites the disparate peoples that constitute Western civilization.

This is not an essay about Western civilization or what defines it. Instead, it is a defense of the Western humanities and why it still matters, by going back to the people whom Bernard Knox provocatively called the endangered species known as DWEM, or Dead White European Males.[2] More specifically it will go back to the most famous DWEM of all time, Homer. In so doing, this essay will also confront the incredible statement of Susan Sontag that Western civilization (and, by entailing relationship, Western humanities) is the "cancer of human history."[3]

---

1. See Knox, *Oldest Dead White European Males.*
2. Knox, 25.
3. Wasserman, "Author Susan Sontag Dies," para. 30.

Homer may be now long dead, but he still sings to us and touches our hearts. It is peculiar that a man who lived around seven hundred years before the birth of Christ is still the most widely known and read author after Saint Paul. Why is Homer such an eternal figure? Why do we still read Homer? Why should we continue to read Homer?

It is easy to say that the only reason why Homer is so well-known and read is because he was codified in the classical canon by those dead white European males. But so many others who were originally placed on that Renaissance list, men like Cicero, Plutarch, and Boethius, have now all but been forgotten, apart from specialists and generalist antiquarians. When I was at Yale, entering the dorm room of one of my friends, Homer was visibly seen on his bookshelf; Cicero, Plutarch, and Boethius, by contrast, nowhere to be found. There must be an allure and luster that Homer has, that most other writers do not.

Homer and the Humanities

The humanities are, fundamentally, about us. What makes us human? There seems to be a trinity that humanities students, scholars, and teachers can readily identify: rationality, language, love. We are the rational animal. We are the linguistic animal. We are the erotic animal. I do not mean to depreciate the others by elevating one, but I must do so in addressing the eternality of Homer.

We live in a time when individual greatness is mocked and scorned. "You didn't build that" has become a sort of consumeristic catchphrase used by people who deplore consumerism while having an iPhone in the back pocket of their designer jeans. The intent of the message, however, is clear. As such, Homer suffered from this collectivist and group identitarian craze; no individual can rise above the group unless through exploitation or oppression of others. Homer, certain people and their budding media allies inform us, could not have written the *Iliad* and the *Odyssey*. Rather, it was the product of an entire people, an entire group—again, no single individual could ever have such high genius to achieve greatness. One certainly mustn't aspire to be the next Homer, because there was no Homer as such. This assertion allows for endless rambling about the composition of the *Iliad* instead of wrestling with the text and the message itself. But that is precisely what the modern guardians—rather, executioners—of the humanities want.

I find it curious that no one attributes the same idea to Hesiod, Aeschylus, or Sophocles. After all, the Greek poet-dramatists who produced far more material than Homer ever did should equally qualify to this criticism. Yet no one argues that the works of Aeschylus, Sophocles, or Euripides are the product of an entire people over the course of many generations. Homer, more than any other figure from pre-Christian antiquity, is in the crosshairs of the philistines, iconoclasts, and nihilists. True, this anti-Homeric authorship issue is somewhat old: it goes as far back as Vico and Wolf in the eighteenth century. But it is now more prominent than ever due to self-evident ideological purposes. Indeed, it is rather courageous and ironically iconoclastic to assert the individuality and artistic creativity of Homer against those who see him as nothing more than a name attached to the *Iliad* and the *Odyssey*.

Why Homer gets the short stick is rather obvious. Homer is still the most famous and therefore needs to be knocked off his pedestal. One may have read a play or two of Aeschylus or Sophocles in high school or perhaps in university, but the dramatists are shortchange compared to Homer. Homer towers over all the DWEMs of antiquity. It is also the case that Homer is the most moving of the Greek literati. This is not meant to expunge the genius of Aeschylus, Sophocles, or Euripides; the satirical and critical insights of Aristophanes; the moving and erotically laced poetry of Sappho; or the sublimity of Homer's rival, Hesiod. This is simply to say that Homer still stands above them and still moves readers to tears nearly three millennia after his death.

It is undoubtedly true that the stories of the *Iliad* and *Odyssey* are rooted in oral culture. Moreover, the now lost epic *Cypria* implies a widespread familiarity with the Trojan War narrative and consciousness long after the supposed events transpired. Yet none of this entails the irrelevance of Homer, nor that Homer is just a name attributed to a collective process. Homer may have served as a sort of final redactor of the Trojan War story; even so, what Homer provided is what he undeniably wanted us to remember from this long and living oral tradition spanning generations and linking the present with the past. As such, we need to take Homer seriously instead of dismissing him; we need to take what Homer gave us, instead of speculating on what is missing or what was added. The few remaining fragments of the *Cypria* show, at the very least, that the Greek intelligentsia was familiar with the whole backstory of the Trojan War up to the enslavement of Lycaon. Furthermore, Hesiod's *Theogony* ends with a few short reflections on Achilles, Odysseus, and Aeneas, indicating familiarity with the aftermath of the Trojan War to the eighth-century poets as well.

Given this, it is curiously interesting that, with all the heroism surrounding the Trojan War, Homer's epic gives us only the final days of the conflict. As such, the story that Homer wants us to remember isn't what he left out but what we have from him. One might say that he took the backstory and aftermath for granted. If the emergence of literature was to preserve oral tradition as it was fading from memory, then Homer should have written down the backstory and aftermath; instead, he gives us a most moving poem concerned with only the final days of the war.

So why should we continue to read Homer? What does he have to say to us living today, us creatures with all the comforts of technology and wealth denied to Homer and his kinsmen?

The song of Homer is so moving because Homer's epic deals with the fundamental questions that we, as humans, still consider: What is our place in the cosmos, and what will lead us to salvation?

The Hesiodic Cosmos

To understand Homer, we must begin with his rival, Hesiod. The story goes that the two poets were bitter rivals and that Hesiod won first place in a poetry contest against the blind poet of the two defining epics of Western literature. Hesiod's surviving works, *Theogony* and *Works and Days*, are much easier reads than Homer's two monumental epics. Perhaps the brevity of the works allows for people to give Hesiod sole credit, while the breadth and scope of Homer's work demand collective credit—even though other authors have individually produced monumental works as long or longer than Homer's two masterpieces.

There remains a longstanding dispute over whether Hesiod's poems were written before Homer. In *La Scienza Nuova*, Giambattista Vico convincingly explained that the older tradition of poetry is that of sublime violence, even if his reading of Homer is often wanting at best (Vico famously said that Homer was primitive and couldn't possibly have written the *Iliad* and the *Odyssey*). Nevertheless, with this as our axiomatic foundation, it is quite clear that Hesiod's content is older than Homer's, irrespective of who penned their classics first. Anyone who has read *Theogony* knows that blood, lust, and violence run replete through its pages at a degree far greater than Homer, especially since Hesiod's poem celebrates violence, while Homer's epic subtly rebukes it. Moreover, Hesiod's poem is about the gods, and Homer's poem is about mortal men, even if gods feature prominently in it.

The writings of Hesiod and Homer are cosmogonic poems. They are, therefore, works of poetic metaphysics. The Hesiodic cosmos is entirely about the gods. Human actors do not appear, apart from the authorial voice asking the muses to sing praises to the violent gods of the cosmos who castrated their fathers and participated in patricidal usurpation to reign supreme over the stars. When the poem ends with the mentioning of Achilles, Odysseus, and Aeneas, it is just offhand; none of the human characters are actors and movers of the poem. The prime movers of Hesiod's poem are the gods. And it is Zeus, in particular, who wins the adoration of Hesiod and the muses.

The Hesiodic cosmos is an erotic and violent, strife-filled universe. Hesiod's poem opens with the infamous words, "From the Muses of Helicon let us begin our singing, that haunt Helicon's great and holy mountain, and dance on their soft feet round the violet-dark spring and the altar of the mighty son of Kronos. And when they have bathed their gentle skin in Permessos, or the Horse's Fountain, or the holy Olmeios, then on the highest slope of Helicon they make their dances, fair and lovely, stepping lively in time."[4] The erotic overtures are evident enough, and the erotic overture also prefigures the violence to come.

There are two lines of gods in the *Theogony*. The first line of gods is pre-existent. The primordial deities are the first gods to whom we are introduced. Some are named, others not. The two most important are Gaia (Mother Earth) and Uranus (Father Sky). These gods, most importantly, are not the product of violence or sex, though they do have sexual desires. The second line of gods, which includes the Titans and Olympians along with the other monsters of Greek mythological lore, is the product of violence and sex (and often violent sex, since the two are intertwined).

Hesiod details for us how Uranus came across the wide bosom of Gaia, and their marital union stemmed from Uranus's uncontrollable lust. Uranus preys upon Gaia and engages in predatory sex, which injures the Mother Goddess and results in the birth of the Titans. Worried that his children will hate him and usurp his authoritarian power, Uranus seals up the Titans deep in Gaia's fertile womb, which causes her much pain. As the Titans grow and move about, Gaia's belly expands and causes her to moan and scream in pain.

The birth of reason in the Hesiodic cosmos is through hatred; reason is the product of resentment and the desire to harm. Cunning Gaia, we are told, fashions a sickle out of the materials of the earth and implores one of her children to attack Uranus and bring forth their liberation. Kronos is the only Titan willing to take up the challenge. Kronos seizes the sickle not out of love for Gaia but out of hatred for his father. He then ambushes the Sky Father god in an act of patricidal usurpation that gives birth to the rest of the world and the Olympian deities: "[Uranus] came, bringing on night, and desirous of love, he spread himself over [Gaia], stretched out in every

4. Hesiod, *Theogony*, 3.

direction. His son reached out from the ambush with his left hand; with his right he took the huge sickle with its long row of sharp teeth and quickly cut off his father's genitals, and flung them behind him to fly where they might . . . for all the drops of blood that flew off were received by [Gaia]."[5]

The bloody drops from Uranus's castration, falling onto Gaia's fertile body, give birth to the monsters and furies. More graphically, however, is how this act of sexual violence and patricidal usurpation births the Olympians and sets the stage for the Titanomachy and the overthrow of the Titans by the Olympian deities. Hesiod writes in this most sublime moment of the poem: "As for the genitals, just as he first cut them off with his instrument of adamant and threw them from the land into the surging sea, even so they were carried on the waves for a long time. About them a white foam grew from the immortal flesh, and in it a girl formed. First she approached holy Cythera; then from there she came to sea-girt Cyprus. And out stepped a modest and beautiful goddess, and the grass began to grow all round beneath her slender feet. Gods and men call her Aphrodite."[6] The apple doesn't fall far from the tree. Those gods born of lust and violence have the spirit of lust and violence coursing through their veins.

Kronos is as vindictive as his father. Terrified by the prospects of losing his power, he eats his children to preserve his power. Just as Kronos alone rose to challenge his tyrannical father, so is Zeus the only Olympian to rise to challenge his tyrannical father. Zeus rallies the Olympians and launches the great war of the gods. Thunder and lightning reign over the earth, and the drums of war and violence sound forth to break trees, hills, and mountains: "The boundless sea roared terribly round about, the earth crashed loudly, and the broad sky quaked and groaned. Long Olympus was shaken to its foundations by the onrush of the immortals; the heavy tremors from their feet reached misty Tartarus, and the thrill din of the indescribable onset and the powerful bombardment. So it was when they discharged their woe-laden missiles at each other. The voices of the two sides reached the starry heaven as they called out, clashing with loud battle-cries."[7] After defeating the Titans, Zeus then slays the ferocious serpentine monster, Typhoeus, to solidify his place as the supreme god of the pantheon.

Hesiod's cosmos is one governed by strife. The *agon* is fundamental to the Hesiodic cosmos. There is, as the poem concludes, no hope in the Hesiodic cosmos of strife, violence, and war. The muses sing of the gods who are strong enough and willing enough to overthrow their parents and

5. Hesiod, *Theogony*, 8.

6. Hesiod, *Theogony*, 8–9.

7. Hesiod, *Theogony*, 23.

seize power for themselves. It is an unadulterated celebration of lust, sex, and war. The weaker gods who sat back, terrified at the prospect of engaging in bloodshed, are the gods whom the muses brush aside and forget.

Hesiod's *Theogony* is ultimately a praise poem to Zeus, but it is also—to a lesser extent—a praise poem to Kronos, the other god who warred with his father and set in motion the movement toward Zeus's triumph over the cosmos. In Hesiod's cosmos, we see the triumph of hatred, resentment, and strife. Furthermore, the *Theogony* is a heroic poem. It sings of the heroic deeds of Zeus. But what are the heroic deeds of Zeus celebrated by the muses and the poet? The deeds worthy of praise in the *Theogony* are militant deeds of conquest and usurpation. Zeus, and Zeus alone in the end, is worthy of praise for his courage in rebelling and defeating his father and slaying the most vicious monster of Greek mythological lore. In slaying gods and beasts, Zeus sets the heroic archetype with which we're familiar in the rest of Greek mythology: the hero killing monsters and vindictive supernatural entities.

This bleak and conflictual worldview is not just contained in epic heroic poetry. The *Histories* of Herodotus begin with the agonistic portrait of the world reminiscent of Hesiod. Herodotus quickly discusses the Persian account of the abduction of Io to Egypt, the Greek abduction and rape of Europa, then the story of Paris's abduction and rape of Helen which sparked the Trojan War. Throughout the *Histories,* we witness with Herodotus cycles of violence leading to vengeance or retributive justice (*tisis*), egoistic power and pride (*hybris*), ending in destruction (*nemesis*). This cycle then renews itself individually and collectively over the course of the work. While Herodotus rationalizes the mythological stories wherein human actors, rather than capricious gods, are responsible for these crimes, Herodotus's cosmos is still one of sublime violence just as much as Hesiod's cosmos is. Befitting the rationalizing tendency of Herodotus and the later Greek philosophic and historical tradition, the answer to the problem of human violence is the honoring of the law. Homer, however, offers us something far greater, more powerful, and more moving than the historians and philosophers.

The Homeric Cosmos

It is in this bleak cosmic reality that Homer enters the stage of world history. "Rage—Goddess, sing the rage of Peleus' son Achilles."[8] Homer's opening line is blasphemous and revolutionary. Hesiod's muses sing of the gods. Homer's muses sing of a man. This opening marks the great turning in

8. Homer, *Iliad*, 77.

human consciousness, the great turning that begins the Western tradition of humanism and the desire to understand man in the midst of the vast, dark, and often violent cosmos. The gods are present and capricious in Homer's epic, but the opening of the *Iliad* sets the tone that the grand song of Homer is dedicated to men rather than to gods.

The Homeric cosmos doesn't dispense with the Hesiodic cosmos, though it does subvert it. Rage, as the opening indicates, is very much part of the world. Strife governs the Homeric cosmos as much as it does the Hesiodic cosmos. The gods are as cruel and mischievous as they were in the *Theogony*. But Homer opens the cosmos to something new, something that has defined the human thirst for meaning ever since: redemption by love and the human agency to make it manifest.

The *Iliad* is not an epic of hypermasculinity and war, as it can easily and superficially appear to be at first glance. Rather, it is a grand love poem of cosmic scope and proportions. For the *Iliad* is not merely a love story like a romance between two individuals, but a love story that brings forth salvation in the cold and dark cosmos governed by lustful strife, war, and rape. The love story at the center of the *Iliad* isn't about saving two individuals in the midst of a torrential maelstrom, but a story about how love heals the very fabric and entirety of the cosmos. The epic, as we know, is the song of the metamorphosis of Achilles. But it is also the song of a growing consciousness in the cosmos, moving away from the purely agonistic cosmos of the older cosmogonic tradition recounted by Hesiod. The metamorphosis and redemption of Achilles is not just about Achilles. The metamorphosis and redemption of Achilles is also about us.

All the characters of the *Iliad* find themselves in two competing galaxies that divide the cosmos. The first galaxy is one of strife. The men and women who occupy it, or formerly occupied it, exude the Hesiodic spirit of lust, violence, and strife. They are moved solely by the spirit of conflictual lust.

Diomedes, to my mind, is the quintessential hero who occupies this first galaxy. Diomedes is introduced as we would expect Achilles to have been introduced. The great Greek warrior is a madman who thrives in the chaos of struggle. As the war wages, itself the manifestation of the *agon* governing the cosmos, Diomedes kills men left and right and injures the gods when he spears Ares and slashes Aphrodite. As Diomedes slays countless Trojans, Homer brilliantly subverts the hypermasculinity of the Hesiodic fantasy of militant and masculine men.

The men that Diomedes kill are men with names, men with families, men with faces. Homer's painstaking description of the death process is not a gory celebration of violence but a subtle subversion of the Hesiodic ideal.

In naming the men who die and giving us their lineage, we are reminded that these men who have their entrails spilled out over the sands and beaches of Troy are sons, husbands, and fathers. Alongside the descriptions of death are human images of men reaching out to their beloved comrades in agony and brief backstories of their birth and childhood, of being raised in serene green pastures by tender and loving parents.

We also see the rage-filled Diomedes in his pure form during the funeral games held for Patroclus. The funeral games held for Patroclus reveal Diomedes as the man who thrives on chaos, conflict, and strife. Apollo intervenes in the chariot race, allowing Eumeleus to overtake the strife-filled killer. Diomedes begins to cry in rage. What should have been a moment of honor for a hero turns into a chaotic and strife-filled event with men and gods alike clawing at one another and conniving for top prizes. What should have been the grand moment of unity, love in honor of a fallen comrade, becomes a moment of division as Greeks quarrel with one another on the racetracks and hurl insults at each other. Eumeleus and his charioteers stumble and fall, cutting their flesh and causing blood to spill out on the sand. Diomedes eventually triumphs. Rage is what leads to victory for those sad and sorry souls trapped in the galaxy of strife.

Paris is the other notable character who occupies this galaxy of strife. Unlike Diomedes, who thrives on conflict, Paris thrives on lust (just another manifestation of strife, to be honest). He is even more primeval than Diomedes in this respect. Paris cannot control his urge to dominate a beautiful woman, the quintessential object of his fantasy and desire. The sight of Helen causes him to shirk his duties to family and fatherland during his duel with Menelaus. Whisked off by Aphrodite, the lustful shepherd prince of Troy has his eyes full of fear turn into a gaze of fantastical sexual desire when he sees Helen in front of him. He retires to his bedchamber to have sex with the very woman he abducted, which sparked the most famous war in Western history. What we find in the character of Paris, just as we find in the character of Diomedes, is how civilization—duty and responsibility—cannot exist in this first governing galaxy of the cosmos. Only strife and lust reign supreme.

The second galaxy is represented by civilization and the love that accompanies it. Homer undeniably has prejudicial favoritism for this dim star in the cosmos. Troy is the physical embodiment of the world of order, an order premised on love (specifically, devotedness). In contrast to the spirit of lust, violence, and strife, this second galaxy is governed by love, order, and devotion. The uncontrollable passions that spur the chaos of the Hesiodic cosmos are given an ordering that allows for the finer things in life to consummate and flourish.

Hector is the essential hero who occupies this second galaxy. Hector is introduced as a family man, a man of faith and fatherland. When Hector's brother Helenus implores him to return to Troy, Helenus instructs him to give thanks to the gods upon his return and perform his public duties for the city and its citizens. Hector complies, and when he enters the city of Troy, his first words to the wives and guards are, "Pray to the gods."[9] Hector's patriotic heart also "races to help [his] Trojans" throughout the poem.[10] Hector is a man moved by devotion to the gods, his father, family, and fatherland. The Romans eventually invented a word that we are all familiar with to describe such devotion: *pietas*, piety.

The very name Hector, in Greek, also testifies to this ordered love that the Prince of Troy exudes. Hector means one who holds, or to possess. The name is not insignificant. Hector is portrayed as the conduit that holds the two worlds together. He takes his passion and orders them to the products of civilization: family, duty, and religion. Everything he does is out of love for his father, his family, his fatherland. He holds the realms of the divine and temporal together as much as he holds back the Greeks from conquering Troy.

The most touching moment of Hector's life is recounted when he disrobes himself before his infant son, Astyanax. Standing on the walls of Troy, surrounded by strife, the impressive and hidden figure of Hector terrifies the young babe. Astyanax clings to his mother for comfort. Hector, however, provides a quasi-incarnational moment of revelatory face-to-face love. Seeing his son in distress and understanding that it is because he is donning his battle armor, the great prince takes off his armor to reveal his face and tender body and then cradles his son in his arms. The cries of Astyanax fade away as he falls asleep in the soft arms of his father who offers up a prayer to the gods for protection. This most moving scene of the great warrior-prince is subversive because Hector's greatest moment is an act of love rather than an act of war. (Achilles will also follow this pattern by the epic's conclusion.)

Other characters fall into these two galaxies, but there are also individuals who oscillate between the two. Helen finds herself being pulled into the orbit of order and civilization, but not without regret and consequences for her prior life in the cosmos governed by lust. Agamemnon and Menelaus also occupy the cosmos of strife. Achilles, that other raged-filled killer, starts off in the first galaxy, but over the course of the song, he comes to embrace the galaxy of ordered love. And this is what the poem is about: How love redeems and heals the world, brings forth our immortality, and

9. Homer, *Iliad*, 203.
10. Homer, *Iliad*, 207.

allows human nature to flourish. Indeed, Homer goes as far as to suggest true virtue, true happiness, true peace, are found in acts of love.

Achilles and the Homeric Revolution

We already know that Achilles is the greatest warrior, the greatest killer, in the Greek army. But what starts the standoff between Agamemnon and Achilles is the theft of Briseis, his bride-to-be. Briseis reveals this information when she weeps over the body of Patroclus, another character who exuded the power of the galaxy of calming and ordered love, "But you, Patroclus, you would not let me weep, not when the swift Achilles cut my husband down, not when he plundered the lordly Mynes' city—not even weep! No, again and again you vowed you'd make me godlike Achilles' lawful, wedded wife, you would sail me west in your warships, home to Phthia and there with the Myrmidons hold my marriage feast. So now I mourn your death—I will never stop—you were always kind."[11] Briseis here reveals to us something very important about Patroclus. Patroclus may have been a great warrior, but he was even a greater man in his kindness and love. Patroclus is the ideal man, not Achilles (at least at this moment in the epic), and we even witness Patroclus tenderly heal wounded soldiers out of love for them.

The abduction of Briseis intentionally mirrors the abduction of Helen that sparked the war and now sparks the war between Achilles and Agamemnon. Achilles sulks in his tent like an infantile adolescent, upset that Agamemnon has stolen his bride-to-be. It is easy to be put off by Achilles when we are introduced to him because of his refusal to aid his comrades. As we should. But the animosity we hold toward Achilles allows for his most powerful redemption at the poem's conclusion.

The fury of Achilles is unleashed through a series of events beginning with Hera's seduction of Zeus. Zeus has intervened, at least temporarily, on the side of Hector and the Trojans, who are pushing the Greeks to the brink of breaking. Achilles refuses to enter battle but allows Patroclus and his Myrmidons to help the Greeks in this time of crisis. Patroclus nearly single-handedly turns the tide—even slaying the great warrior Sarpedon—until he is cut down by Hector. In the maelstrom of war and petty divine sexual fantasies and plotting, the death of Patroclus unbalances the cosmos. The world burns and bathes in blood due to the skulduggery and the triumph of the Hesiodic cosmos. Love needs to restore the disorder wrought by strife's expansion over the world.

11. Homer, *Iliad*, 498.

Patroclus's death takes away the calming and ordering spirit he provided over Achilles during his prior sulking. Patroclus was a bringer of orderly love to Briseis when her city had been conquered, and he also served as a force of orderly love over Achilles during his refusal to fight after Agamemnon seized Briseis. The rageful Achilles, in his tent beside the calm of Patroclus, was outwardly at peace, though he was inwardly at war with himself. It is as if Patroclus served as the orderly body constraining the rageful spirit of Achilles crashing and turning about inside him. With that body gone and the spirit of rage unleashed, Achilles ventures forth into battle and turns the tide of the war, but the world suffers and bleeds as a result. Patroclus, as the incarnate manifestation of love, kept the peace. With that love removed, rage and hate consumed Achilles in totality.

As Achilles slaughters Trojans left and right, by which Homer again subtly subverts this hypermasculine archetype in reminding us of the lineages of the fallen, one of the sons of Priam throws himself at the feet of Achilles. Lycaon defenselessly begs, weeps for mercy. Achilles, in this domineering position, raises his sword hand and cuts open the young prince whom he had previously captured tending Priam's orchard and sold into slavery during an earlier moment in the war. After slaying Lycaon, Achilles vows to wipe out the seed of Priam from the earth. Then, as we know, he duels and kills Hector and begins to defile Hector's body.

The terrible rage of Achilles has been unleashed and fully manifested for us. The goddess of Rage has seemingly triumphed. Achilles subsequently helps to arrange funeral games for Patroclus and holds Hector's body as if it were a trophy carcass. In his slaughtering of Hector, Achilles quickly devolves into a barbarous and ravenous dog. He is no longer the handsome Argive prince and Myrmidon leader that he once was. The animalization that is brought on by war consumes Achilles in full. This animalization has also consumed the whole world, as we witnessed in the fire and bloodshed consuming the land.

Here the great triumph of Homer begins. We have witnessed the full-throated and bloody return of the Hesiodic cosmos in terrible vengeance, with a sword of rage spilling blood over the earth. The galaxy of orderly love, of civilization and filial piety, has been burned over by strife. Moreover, with Hector's death, there is no holder of the two worlds together. The torch of love, that unitive force that binds the cosmic galaxies together, lies extinguished on the ground. The world burns as a result. Chaos reigns supreme.

Priam is the other great character who embodies the values of the galaxy of love which Homer is constructing. He is a good king, a gentle and loving father, and a man devoted to his son. Priam's love for Hector compels him to enter the tent of Achilles against his better senses. In fact, Hector had thought Achilles could be reasoned with before losing his nerve, only to accept his fate by turning back to die at the killer's hand. Furthermore, we know that Achilles has vowed to wipe the seed of Priam off the face of the earth. With a defenseless Priam in his tent, Achilles literally has the opportunity to consummate his vow of rage. Strife, rage, and hate have every opportunity to triumph with Priam in the tent of Achilles.

When Priam throws himself at the feet of Achilles and begs for the return of Hector's body, we witness the recapitulation of the same image of Lycaon throwing himself at the feet of Achilles and begging for mercy. In this domineering image and position, we fully expect that Achilles will slay Priam. After all, we have seen this image before and know what Achilles did. This is compounded by the fact that Achilles has sworn to kill Priam and all his sons and daughters.

But that most famous and fitting conclusion to an unfinished work manifests itself at this moment. Achilles empathizes with the grieving father. Memories of Peleus's love for Achilles are sparked deep within the ravenous and rage-filled killer as he witnesses the tears and love of Priam for Hector. Instead of lifting the sword to slay his archnemesis, Achilles lifts Priam up in dignity, and the two men weep together in a tender and loving embrace that doesn't lead to violence as the faux embraces of Paris and Helen and Hera and Zeus did. It is in this moment that Achilles inherits the torch once held by Hector as the man who holds the two worlds together. The metamorphosis of Achilles is complete. He has learned love and is saved by love.

Love, for Homer, is a uniquely human experience and reality. The gods do not love. The gods are filled only with condemnable lusts to satiate their egos. Humans, however, have this most precious gift. The *Iliad*, then, is a long and arduous movement to the manifestation of love in the world. Love entails relationships. Love entails empathy. Love leads to the forgiveness, and forgiveness gives way to healing. Love is what divinizes human nature and makes life meaningful and purposeful.

This is where Homer is most ingenious and radical. In the contrast between Hector and Achilles, Homer has shown the limits of the filial love, piety, and devotion that Hector embodied and represented. For all the virtues Hector exuded, he died. And with the death of Hector, the cosmos is torn apart by lust, strife, and war. No amount of filial love, piety, or devotion can restore the wounded cosmos. Instead, Homer offers an even more radical solution: forgiveness. The highest reality of love isn't devotion but forgiveness. Forgiveness as the highest reality of love is what Achilles learns and what we all learn through the metamorphosis of Achilles. In this way, Achilles is, as Homer says, greater than Hector. With Achilles, we witness the true birth of the galaxy of love in its fullest totality.

It is also important to note that it is the memory of a father's love for his son that becomes the triumphant spirit at the conclusion of the work. The memory of love helps to rekindle the heart of love that had been hardened over the years inside Achilles. It is the memory of love that rekindles the lost spark of divinity residing deep inside humans. Without the memory of love that Priam's actions sparked, Achilles would likely have killed his Trojan adversary in the final act of the triumph of the Hesiodic cosmos of rage, resentment, and strife. Instead, we witness the subversion of the Hesiodic cosmos through loving forgiveness.

The conclusion of the *Iliad* is perfect and moving, even though we know Achilles is going to die and Troy burn. Despite this, we do not feel cheated. Love has conquered hate and triumphed over the cosmos of strife.

Love, particularly in the form of forgiveness, heals the fractured and burning world; a peace, albeit temporary, is the outcome of the love shared between Achilles and Priam. That peace is a foretaste of the serenity of the cosmos of love that Homer is painfully advocating over the course of his epic. That peace is a roadmap for rebuilding in the ruins wrought by war. For a cosmos of love would be a cosmos at peace.

The greatest deeds of the greatest heroes of the *Iliad* are deeds of love. Hector's love for his son; Andromache's love for her husband; Hecuba's tearful lament for Hector to stay in the walls of Troy; Priam's love for his son; Achilles's forgiving love for Priam; these are the greatest deeds of the greatest heroes who populate the epic. The heroes who live eternally etched in our memories despite the fires of sublime violence are Hector, Priam, and Achilles, among others, who manifest these moments of loving intimacy bound up with the consciousness of tragedy and mortality. The most moving moments of the *Iliad* are often these brief, intimate, and personal manifestations of love in the midst of war. Thus we see our heroes as mortal humans just like us. Lovers. Husbands. Fathers. Sons. The truly heroic deeds celebrated by Homer are not deeds of the sword and spear but deeds of intimacy, compassion, and comforting love. Love is what makes a man heroic, not how many men or monsters he has killed.

Homer's Humanism

Homer's revolution is a humanistic revolution. Homer is the first humanist in the Western tradition. Rather than locate the nexus of moral healing with the capricious gods of Olympus, he finds it within the human agency for empathy and forgiveness. Love binds together what we previously thought impossible. Homer also begins the dialectical refinement of the pathological cosmos that the Greeks inhabited before Plato.

Hesiod's cosmos of strife, moved by hate, ends in patricide, war, and divine rape. Hesiod's cosmos is a sublimely violent cosmos. Homer turns the Hesiodic cosmos on its head by going beyond the strife and hate-filled cosmos about which Hesiod's muses sing praise.

Yet Homer doesn't discard the Hesiodic cosmos as much as he refines it. He takes the rage that governs the Hesiodic cosmos and opens the door to the possibility of love. In doing so, Homer also carves out the redemptive and powerful quality of human agency in his work. Yes, the will of Zeus is satisfied in the end. But how the will of Zeus is satisfied is left to human choice. Achilles could have returned the body of Hector to Priam any way he liked. That is all that the will of Zeus stipulated. The manner in which Achilles fulfilled the will of Zeus is, then, the greatest expression of human magnanimity; it was the highest manifestation of the love which Homer sings will heal the world. This love manifested by Achilles surpasses the petty nobility of the capricious and unpredictable gods of the poem. The true heroism sung of in the poem is found in the human act of forgiveness, an act freely undertaken by Achilles at the close of the epic.

There is no indication that Homer didn't believe in the Greek gods. But he certainly didn't think the gods existed for our salvation. If the richly developed mythology of Pseudo-Apollodorus existed in Homer's day, then the destruction of Troy and the death of Achilles were inevitable. Yet we do not need to be the puppets of the gods. Achilles finds it in his heart to weep with Priam and forgive him. There is nothing in the *Bibliotheca* of Pseudo-Apollodorus that indicates Achilles's metamorphosis from killer to lover was what the gods intended. Instead, Achilles achieves this for himself, sparked by a concrete encounter with a father's love for his son that breaks his own heart of iron. Homer, therefore, argues that the true nobility of the cosmos is the agency of moral and loving human beings. In the love expressed by the Homeric heroes, especially the loving forgiveness expressed by Achilles, the voice of Homer appears and sounds triumphantly.

Homer is eternal because he begins the pilgrimage of Western literature as a journey through the battlefield of love and meaning. Homer inaugurates a near three-millennia-long art project that sees the human will and heart expressing itself in songs and poems that strike at the very essence of what it means to be human. Rather than take up the sword to find meaning, Homer exposes the futility of meaning in an agonistic, conflictual cosmos and instead offers us meaning through the raw power of human sentimentality through the serenity of the lyre or, for those of us today, the enchantment of reading. Yet Homer also reveals to us the reality of love; love is the product of strife, struggle, and hardship. Love is not a printable slogan to tape onto a car or stake into your yard.

Will love save the world? Homer certainly thought so. And he wrote the grandest epic showing how love can move mountains, heal a wounded world, and bring salvation to the worst of killers.

The great exceptionalism of Western civilization is that our salvation will not be political but something far deeper, more powerful, and perhaps more mysterious than kings and mass political movements. Homer begins the entire Western tradition of literature, which articulates the most splendid vision of how love and forgiveness heals our injured world, a vision which we see carried onward from the gospels to Dante to Shakespeare to Austen to Dumas to Tolstoy. Only those blinded by their commitment to destroy the humanities and kill Homer are incapable of seeing this magnanimous vision of hope. Love is the exception. And it is the exception that gives life to our literary tradition, which began in that most sublime and beautiful work that remains unrivalled three thousand years later.

Reading Homer gives us a glimpse of eternity, that eternal image of love and how it brings serenity to the cosmos and human soul. Homer's final image in the *Iliad* is a city finally at peace, a peace brought forth by an act of forgiveness. Forgiveness brings peace in its wake: peace to Achilles as an individual and to all the Greeks and Trojans as a collective whole. Loving forgiveness touches more than just the self.

In many ways, we have journeyed through hell and ended at the city dreamt of by three millennia of succeeding theologians, philosophers, and poets. Considering that Homer leaves us with the image of a cosmos at peace, the song and meaning of Homer become clear to us at the end of this long and arduous journey. The *Iliad* ends with the star of the galaxy of love at the center of the dark cosmos brightly shining in the midst of the darkness which surrounds it. And shine ever so brightly it does.

This essay was originally published in *Voegelin View*, 1 June 2020.

2

Homer's Epic of the Family

THE TROJAN WAR, FOR OUR HOMERIC HEROES, BEGINS WITH MARITAL INFI-
delity and succumbing to temptation but ends with marital fidelity and
overcoming temptation. While the gods are ever present in the *Iliad* and
Odyssey, I wish to examine the otherwise purely human aspect of Homer's
two great epics and how they relate to family, and the role of marital infidelity and fidelity as it relates to wholeness and life. After all, family is one of
the great Homeric concerns.

The *Iliad* and *Odyssey* can be read as stand-alone works. However, the
two great poems should be read together. Both works revolve around the
Trojan War. Both stories are intimately tied together as one story, especially
through the person of Odysseus, who is a major character in the *Iliad* and
the namesake of the *Odyssey*.

Pseudo-Apollodorus presented Odysseus's hand in the origins of the
Trojan War through Odysseus's fostering the compromise which would lead
all of Greece to go to war against Troy. The suitors of Helen would swear an
oath to support the eventual husband of Helen, irrespective of who would
become her husband. Thus, Odysseus's legacy as a family man is continued
well after Homer. And if Pseudo-Apollodorus's chronology of Odysseus is
to be accepted simply on literary grounds, Odysseus was considered to be a
family man prior to the Trojan War.

The place of family in finding the meaning of life is best reflected
by the two heroes of the *Iliad*, Achilles and Hector. Achilles abandons his
mother and out-of-wedlock son to win his immortality through the fame
that will come in war. The sword decides all, and the idea that fulfillment

in life can be found by the glory of conquest and war is all too well known to the ancient world. Nevertheless, Achilles was torn by his desire for the battle-cry and his weeping mother; he eventually sides in favor of the call of the battle-cry, but not without some consideration of his family.

By contrast, Hector is the tragic hero of the *Iliad*. Hector is an upstanding father and family man, a patriot, reverent to the gods, an honorable man. Before Virgil depicted Aeneas as the upstanding figure who embraced filial piety to the uttermost, Homer casts Hector in a truly pious light; Hector is devoted to his family, faith, and fatherland (and Aeneas is often by Hector's side, inheriting Hector's virtues). Who cannot be moved by his teary goodbye to Andromache and his comforting actions to his newborn son, whom he cradles in his arm as he prays to Jove? Hector is not only physically present with his wife and son; he is emotionally and spiritually present with his wife and son before going off to battle. The intimate moment between Hector and his family is moving precisely because of its humanness; the love reflected by Hector to his wife and son, the ultimate expression of the sublime.

It was Hector, not Achilles, who was considered one of the nine worthies of the medieval age and one of the virtuous pagans according to Catholicism. Hector was remembered for his honor, Achilles for his savagery. Hector fights to defend his family and fatherland; Achilles fights for himself and his own vanity. The man worthy of praise was the man counted among the worthies and immortalized in the song "The British Grenadiers." Hector dies looking at his beloved city—his fatherland—for which he gave his life, a fateful yet glorious death, if there ever was one in the midst of the carnage that was the Trojan War.

While the story of pious Hector ends outside the walls of Troy, the story of Achilles and his revelation concerning the importance of family (and life) reaches fruition in the *Odyssey*. Homer reveals his hand that the family is the highest good to be had in life when Odysseus descends into the underworld and reunites with the heroes of the Trojan War. Odysseus's descent into the underworld also leads him to see the many beautiful and free-loving queens and princesses of Greece, their beauty a temptation for which lesser men would fall (as Paris did for Helen). The fact that beauty is presented so loosely as Odysseus comes across Antiope, Alcmena, Megara, Epicaste, and Chloris, among others, cannot be lost on the reader, given the location of where Odysseus is currently journeying—the abode of the dead. Homer presents beauty as the *femme fatale* in his works, thereby equating beauty with a form of control—not that beauty should be shunned, but that there is a fine line between beauty as an allure bringing about salvation and beauty as a controlling force that ultimately brings about death and destruction. Homeric beauty is related to the family, the false hope of beauty found in the individual cut off from filial relationships.

In his encounter with Agamemnon, Odysseus is shocked to see the ghost of the great king who led the Greek army to conquer Troy. Agamemnon answers that it was not misfortune decreed by the gods that brought his death, but marital infidelity that led to his murder. "Odysseus, mastermind of war, I was not wrecked in the ships when lord Poseidon roused some punishing blast of stormwinds, gust on gust, nor did ranks of enemies mow me down on land—Aegisthus hatched my doom and my destruction, he killed me, he with my own accursed wife."

Agamemnon continues to recount his murder by Aegisthus and betrayal by his own wife, Clytemnestra. It is interesting to observe that Agamemnon was killed at a banquet. The literary theme of death by eating is something that should be well familiar to a Christian readership, as well as to readers of ancient folktales.

It is at the dinner table where betrayal or poison occurs—the place where humans are to feel at ease and comfortable, merry and drunk, loosening their fears and embracing the joy of company. The association of hedonism with destruction, for it is in a moment of pleasantry when we are easily caught off guard, is an ancient trope that begins with Homer. Agamemnon should have been home, safe and secure, but instead is more vulnerable than ever because of Clytemnestra's infidelity, ultimately leading to his death.

Euripides's tragedy *Iphigenia in Aulis* presents Agamemnon in his naked vanity (while also casting Odysseus in a more negative light than Homer does). Agamemnon sacrifices his lovely daughter Iphigenia to the gods to procure safe passage to Troy. Agamemnon's own bloodline is expendable if the glory of victory in battle is secured. Agamemnon's wanton and willful sacrifice of his daughter is but another example of filial destruction—something Yahweh forbids in Genesis, establishing the principle of the sacredness of life in the Abrahamic tradition. Again and again, whether it is in the *Iliad*, the *Odyssey*, or even other Greek plays and poems, the dissolution of the family is always accompanied by death.

Agamemnon's murder which was in part caused by Clytemnestra's infidelity, leads to a collapse of trust in Agamemnon when he tells Odysseus not to tell his wife Penelope the total truth in all matters. The betrayal of trust in relationship is the worst of sins in Christian tradition. Dante placed such traitors in the ninth circle of hell: those who betrayed their friends, their countrymen, and, more horribly, their family. While Homer foreshadows Odysseus's triumph when Agamemnon quips that Penelope will never betray him, the damage to Agamemnon is complete and irreversible. Not only is he dead, he cannot trust anyone, as indicated in his dialogue with

Odysseus; moreover, he cannot trust the person who should be trusted most (one's spouse). The relational animus of man's social nature is destroyed, and fulfillment through a relationship can never be consummated for those who have trust issues.

Upon leaving Agamemnon and meeting Achilles, Odysseus showers the great warrior with praise. Achilles, however, scoffs at Odysseus's praise. Achilles rebuffs the laurels bestowed on him by declaring he would rather be alive as a poor slave tenant farmer with his mother and his son, than be the lord of the dead. In fact, family is the only thing on Achilles's mind upon meeting Odysseus, as he asks about his son: "I'd rather slave on earth for another man—some dirt-poor tenant farmer who scrapes to keep alive— than rule down here over all the breathless dead. But come, tell me the news about my gallant son."[1]

Homeric irony is on full display here, especially if the *Odyssey* is read after the *Iliad* as a companion piece. Achilles, the man who didn't concern himself with life and chose war (death) over family, comes to understand the importance of family and therefore of life only when he is in the abode of the dead. This revelation for Achilles comes too late for his soul. He is trapped forever as master over the "breathless dead." As Achilles's lament goes on, he weeps to have the opportunity to return to his father's home and to teach men the ways of life rather than lust and conquest.

Grieving, Achilles is comforted by Odysseus as he informs him what has become of his son (Neoptolemus). This is a touching moment, the contrast to Hector's goodbye in the *Iliad* that brings about the completion of the contrast between the two heroes of that work. But Hector held his son in his arms and comforted him in all his feebleness, the strength and courage of Hector giving strength and courage—comfort—to Astyanax. The scene of Odysseus telling Achilles the fate of Neoptolemus is touching, because it is the revelatory moment for Achilles about the importance of family. Achilles eagerly waits to hear the news of what has become of his son, because he cannot watch his son to know himself. With tears coming down his eyes, he had begged Odysseus to tell him what any father wishes to know: what has become of his son.

While undoubtedly moving, this scene stands in stark contrast with Hector. Hector, as mentioned, was physically, emotionally, and spiritually present with Andromache and Astyanax in an unforgettable human moment. Achilles does eagerly wait to hear the news of his son. But he is detached, a gnostic ghost without a body who cannot provide warmth and comfort to his son; neither can he help nor congratulate him. Achilles is left

---

1. Homer, *Odyssey*, 265.

in anguish with his newfound knowledge of what is truly important in life and where the desire of man is made whole.

Achilles left his mother and son to win immortality in war. It was this immortality to be won in war that Achilles thought would satiate his desires. Only in death does Achilles see through the veil that no amount of death and conquest can satisfy man's yearnings. Instead, it is the simple life—the family life—a life spent in relationship with spouse, children, and friends (and countrymen) where desire is contented.

This revelation of the meaning of life comes roughly at the half-way point of the *Odyssey*, thus setting the stage for the rest of the journey home. And home is where the family is. Agamemnon should have been safe at home. Reuniting with his wife and kingdom, Agamemnon's *parousia* is turned against him as he is lured into a trap set by a scheming usurper and unfaithful wife. In death, Achilles learns that the glory he sought in war was vain and that the life of happiness is found in the practical wisdom and love of the simple life, with family of whom he is now deprived. The fates of the other heroes of the *Iliad* are a sharp contrast with the forthcoming fate of Odysseus.

The *Odyssey* is a tale of a journey home. More importantly, the journey home is not merely to a piece of land to settle and call home. It is a journey to an already established home and to a family. Home for Odysseus is not simply (or merely) Ithaca. Home is where Penelope and Telemachus are; home is where Odysseus's family resides. Home is where Odysseus's roots are.

Penelope and Telemachus are not simply characters afar referenced by Odysseus in his musings but are given important roles in the story. They are humans to whom the reader can relate, just as Odysseus relates to them as husband and father. That is to say, they are real. Penelope and Telemachus have names and faces attached to them. Odysseus's love for Penelope draws him ever closer to her and gives him the strength to persevere through temptation and imprisonment, while Penelope's love for him keeps her faithful to him against the myriad of suitors who regard Penelope as an object of social advancement by which they may inherit Odysseus's kingdom and secure their own standing in Greek society.

Odysseus's captivity to Calypso is the prototypical false heaven offered to men: eternity with endless sex, comfortable pleasures, and bliss through objectified beauty (in the form of Calypso herself). Calypso, for her part, also treats Odysseus as an object of desire and merely seeks to utilize Odysseus as an instrument of her divinity. However, it is the love of the real and the fidelity that draws man and woman together that allows Odysseus to overcome his shackling to Calypso, as Hermes comes to his rescue. Odysseus is married to Penelope, is the king of Ithaca, and the father of Telemachus; people depend on him, and he has duties and obligations to fulfill.

In overcoming the temptations of Calypso's (false) paradise, Homer also explicitly informs us that man is a social and relational animal and not a solitary, isolated, and atomized individual seeking simple physical pleasures. No atomized individualistic hedonist could turn down what Calypso offers. And what did Calypso represent, other than the life of pure self-pleasure? Odysseus's love for Penelope and Telemachus, as well as his duties to his countrymen as king, wins out. He breaks the constrictive power of the divines for the love between humans.

While Odysseus slept with Calypso and Circe, there are several things to remember before rushing to condemn the supposed infidelity of Odysseus. Both women are not really women at all but goddesses, nymphs, who are not equals with Odysseus but his superiors. Gods and goddesses interfere in human affairs all the time in the Greek (and Roman) myths because humans are not sovereign persons as in Abrahamic anthropology, but the fated playthings of the gods. Their love is no love at all, given that Odysseus grows ever colder toward Calypso and ever warmer in his want to be with Penelope over the years. As with Circe, notwithstanding the threats involved in their encounter, Odysseus's actions toward another goddess—who is not a human woman—are aimed at saving his fellow countrymen, whom he loves as their patriotic king.

Odysseus feels a duty to try to protect them and see them home. It is all the more impressive that Odysseus overcomes Calypso and Circe for Penelope. Everything that Odysseus does is motivated by his love for Penelope and his love for his fellow countrymen.

Furthermore, Calypso and Circe represent figments of the imagination—imaginary desire and lust, producing the most sublime of objects of the human mind. Their divinity is their unreality. They are, to the human imagination, perfect. They are everything that fallen man wantonly craves—beautiful, sexual, and vivacious objects of desire.

Odysseus overcomes both Calypso and Circe, and his love for Penelope grows ever stronger. Odysseus's overcoming the temptations of Calypso and Circe are not moments of weakness or hypocrisy, but moments of triumph and fidelity. Not even the most perfect of beings can keep Odysseus away from Penelope.

The fact that Odysseus overcomes the temptations of Calypso and Circe should not be lost upon the reader. The warm and mutual love of two humans in the reciprocating bond of marriage is superior to the false love between an object of perfection with which one cannot have an authentic relationship. This is represented by the fact that Odysseus is a man, and Calypso and Circe are nymphs.

Odysseus is in a different category than Calypso and Circe—an inferior one at that. From Odysseus's perspective, Calypso and Circe are objects of desire rather than relational subjects of healing and wholeness. They do not represent the liberation of Odysseus's longings but represent the enslavement of Odysseus's yearnings. From Calypso and Circe's perspective, Odysseus is an object of their fantasies and lusts. Odysseus is an object whom they want to control—which is precisely what would have happened if Odysseus had fallen for them. He would have been an object of their enslavement. (Here, I think, Homer is also reflecting upon man's enslavement to the passions.) In comparison, the relationship between Odysseus and Penelope is unbreakable. The men seeking Odysseus's throne cannot break Penelope, and the woman whom Odysseus loves is the only woman who can call him home. Calypso and Circe cannot call Odysseus home but only prevent him from returning home.

Whereas Agamemnon returned home only to be murdered because of marital infidelity, this fate does not befall Odysseus because of the fidelity and genius of Penelope. Penelope is just as cunning as Odysseus, as the story makes clear. Penelope is not just a faithful wife, she is a perfect companion to Odysseus—as Eve was meant to be for Adam—and together the two are made whole, indivisible. Astute Christians should also see the nature of the love between Penelope and Odysseus, since their marriage is an indissoluble bond. Their togetherness in love, sanctified through their marriage, cannot be broken by man or the gods. They truly are indivisible. From the perspective of marital fidelity and the life-giving spirit it entails, Penelope is the heroine of the *Odyssey*. If she had not been faithful to Odysseus, he would have returned home and suffered a fate similar to Agamemnon's.

The broken marriages in Homer's epics lead to war and death at a scale never seen before. Homer seems to emphasize the cruelty and bloodshed, because this is a story of what happens to man and society when family and marriages break down. Paris betrays his father and country in seducing Helen, and Helen breaks the bond of marriage between her and Menelaus in escaping to Troy with Paris. Agamemnon is betrayed by Clytemnestra, which allows Aegisthus to murder him. Achilles abandons his family to seek glory in war, only to realize in death that family is the most important thing that matters in life—for family is what gives life, and where life is found.

This is the ultimate message of Homer's two epics: Where family is found, life is found; where family is found, true beauty is found; where family is found, piety is found; where family is dissolved, only death and destruction follows. Homer's message of the meaning in life couldn't be clearer.

Odysseus does not find peace until he returns home and reclaims his home from intruders. Duty to family is the highest call of men and women in the *Iliad* and *Odyssey*. It is fitting that the *Iliad* and the origins of the Trojan War starts with the dissolution of family, while the *Odyssey* ends the Trojan War with the reconciliation of a family. The reconciliation is made even more triumphant given the trials and temptations that beset both Penelope and Odysseus.

Homer's epic of the family is profoundly traditional in its advocacy. It is unsurprising that Christianity, the religion of love and family, took a liking to Homer's works and themes. Furthermore, Homer's Odysseus is a profoundly conservative figure. Odysseus is moved by love for family and fatherland, the love of the real, and desire to be reunited with Penelope, with whom he shares an indissoluble bond, despite the interference of goddesses and other women. Odysseus's odyssey began because of the dissolution of a family; it comes to an end—finally bringing him the happy rest he seeks—when he reunites with his family. Home, according to Homer, is where the family is.

This essay was originally published in *The Imaginative Conservative*, 16 October 2018.

3

Aeschylus and the Struggle for Justice

AESCHYLUS IS CONSIDERED THE GREATEST OF THE GREEK PLAYWRIGHTS. His *Oresteia* remains one of the few tripartite classics of Western literature, a play and its threefold movement serving as a stirring window into the progression and development of afntique literature and consciousness. C.J. Herington argued that the *Oresteia* includes "a gradual climb from torment, through testing, into the light."[1]

Why is Aeschylus the acme of the Greek playwright tradition, and why is he so important? On one hand, Aeschylus is great because his work is the manifestation of a long literary-philosophical tradition that was wrestling with the cosmogonic idea of strife. On the other hand, it is because his works represent the ideal movement of humanity from strife, rage, and hate to justice, love, and persuasion, which is the very spirit of civilization after all these millennia.

The World Before Aeschylus

Hesiod's *Theogony* is a sublimely violent poem where the muses sing praises to the gods who engage in patricide and usurpation. The gods, who were conceived in lust and hatred, have nothing but lust and hatred toward their fathers (Uranus among the Titans, Cronus among the Olympians). Cronus castrates Uranus, and his blood and phallus fall to the earth and sea, giving

---

1. Herington, "Aeschylus," 397.

rise to monsters and birthing Aphrodite from the open womb of Thalassa, the primordial goddess of the sea. Strife reigns supreme in Hesiod's grand epic and is that of which the muses sing in praise.

Giambattista Vico argued that sublime poetry is the first—and primitive—instantiation of logos in human life. While Homer may have composed his grand epics before Hesiod or around the same time, it is without question that Hesiod's cosmos is the older one. Homer's cosmos, while retaining much of the strife of Hesiod, is radically subversive. In this respect, Homer was the radical altering the Greek understanding of the cosmos, while Hesiod was the reactionary trying to preserve—if not return—to the more ancient cosmos of strife, blood, and guts.

Homer's *Iliad* is a majestic epic of love. Whereas Hesiod's muses sing of tyrannical gods, Homer's muses sing of a rage-filled man in faraway Ilium who, over the course of the epic, learns something new about the meaning of life through the ingenious pen of Homer. Achilles is initially moved by his passions but, by epic's end, comes to learn love by ordering his passions to something new and grander than rage.

The defining image of Homer's *Iliad* is the shield Achilles receives after the death of Patroclus. The shield is emblazoned with two images. The first is a seemingly peaceful city celebrating a wedding day, which, upon closer inspection, is filled with strife. Surrounding that first image is the second image of a city at war. Though strife is more apparent in the second image, the strife experienced from war has led all persons—young and old, male and female, soldier and non-combatant—to be focused in a collective endeavor. In strife, Homer subtly informs us, there is the possibility of ordering our passions to something good, something beautiful, something productive.

When rage-filled Achilles goes on his killing spree after the death of Patroclus, he slaughters the sons of Priam with his destructive hand and spear. Lycaon throws himself shamelessly at the feet of Achilles and begs for his life. Achilles refuses to show pity and mercilessly cuts open his bowels, as his intestines spill out onto the sand and his feet. After slaying Hector, he attempts to defile his body, but the gods prevent Hector's bodily destruction.

In that most remarkable conclusion of Homer's, Priam enters the tent of Achilles and throws himself at the feet of Achilles, just as Lycaon did. Homer inverts the image and outcome in this recapitulation of images (and Homer plays on and pays homage to many images of Greek mythological lure throughout his love epic). Rather than brutally cut down Priam, as he did many of Priam's sons, Achilles learns to love and weeps with Priam. They shed tears together. Homer takes the strife-filled cosmos of Hesiod and his predecessors and turns it on its head by arguing that the cosmos is filled with strife and love, and that love may heal the strife-filled world, if even for a brief moment. That is why Homer's *Iliad* ends so fittingly, even though we know Troy is still to be sacked and Achilles killed.

Aeschylus's Transformation

Enter Aeschylus. The *Oresteia* includes the conclusion of Agamemnon's life. The first play in his trilogy opens with a lookout guard restless and as if imprisoned because of his duties and the restlessness that he feels. He is completely on edge and disordered. Though he looks up at the stars, the stars he knows "by heart,"[2] the starry skies cannot guide him to the gods, because he is an imprisoned watcher, and his disquietude sets the ominous stage for the rest of the play.

We quickly learn that Clytemnestra, Agamemnon's unfaithful wife, is conspiring with Aegisthus to kill her husband as an act of revenge for killing their daughter Iphigenia (which Euripides treats in naked detail in his play *Iphigenia in Aulis*), and for leaving her to be alone and worried for ten years. She feels betrayed by Agamemnon. Agamemnon's love for her was less than his lust for power; as such, the world of *Agamemnon* is one that is restless and cold, as if a prison cell of torment. The chorus hauntingly chants on the eve of Agamemnon's murder: "The lust for power never dies—men cannot have enough!"[3]

The play ends in murder. It concludes with Clytemnestra recapitulating the old cosmogonic world of strife and power as she stands over the dead bodies of Agamemnon and Cassandra, whom she cut down in cold blood, "Our lives are based on pain . . . . You and I have power now. We will set the house in order once for all."[4] Order, in this bleak and ancient outlook, is brought about by power and not love or persuasion (at least in the first movement of Aeschylus's trilogy).

But this is not where the *Oresteia* arc ends. It continues. The *Libation Bearers* opens not with a restless imprisonment but with a prayer to the gods and a plea for salvation. The opening sets the tone for the play, and this second act of the trilogy captures Orestes in pain and needing purgation but also dependent on the gods, who were largely absent in the brutal world of politicking and murderous scheming. It is true that Orestes will murder his mother and Aegisthus, thus standing over their dead bodies just as Clytemnestra had stood over the murdered bodies of Agamemnon and Cassandra;

2. Aeschylus, *Oresteia*, 103.

3. Aeschylus, *Oresteia*, 158.

4. Aeschylus, *Oresteia*, 171–72.

but where Clytemnestra killed Agamemnon and Cassandra out of hatred and spite, Orestes kills his mother and scheming lover out of devotion to his father and to the gods (or so he claims). This sets up the third and final play, the *Eumenides*.

Orestes is haunted by Clytemnestra's furies, who hound him into exile and pursue him to Apollo's temple because of the murder of his mother. But before those haunting images of a man pursued by the furies of conscience, Pythia opens the third act by discussing piety, destiny, free will, and the importance of love and family. Again, the opening of the play sets the tone and themes for the rest of the play, and the third play opens with the most optimistic imagery and language.

The furies are not just the spirits of Clytemnestra; they are the link between the dead and the living. The furies act as intermediaries of sorts between the realm of the breathless dead and the pulsating living. That the furies hound Orestes also signifies that they are more than just Clytemnestra's ghosts: they are the psyche of Orestes, who is haunted over his deed. The furies are the unconscious moral law written on the hearts of humans, which reminds us of our misdeeds and gross violations. The furies are awakened by Clytemnestra's wrath and pursue Orestes to Athena and Apollo (straight to the gods of reason and justice, incidentally).

It is the court case before Athena and Apollo that is the enduring achievement of Aeschylus. The furies demand justice for murder. Orestes appeals that he did what he did because it was the command of Apollo and because he loved his father. No wife—and certainly no mother—would ever do what Clytemnestra had done—or so Orestes appeals. The showdown pits instinct against reason or persuasion, that supposedly high and noble ideal that finally enters Greek literature through the pen of Aeschylus. Athena says to the leader and the furies: "But if you have any reverence for Persuasion, the majesty of Persuasion, the spell of my voice that would appease your fury—Oh please stay."[5]

The furies cry out for justice in the form of revenge, which would just continue the lustful and bloody cycle of death. Athena convinces the furies that she has not supplanted their authority or prestige. On the contrary, she makes them realize that what they desire—justice—is something good and rational. The manner in which they sought to manifest justice, however, was the problem. The furies cry and wail at first but suddenly join with Athena. Love conquers hate and brings healing. "Give joy in return for joy, one common will for love, and hate with one strong heart: such union heals

5. Aeschylus, *Oresteia*, 270.

a thousand ills of man,"[6] the furies chant after being persuaded by Athena and receiving a name change, a sort of baptism to represent them as a new creation. So the furies sing with Athena at the trilogy's end, "Cry, cry in triumph, carry on the dancing on and on. This peace between Athena's people and their guests must never end. All-seeing Zeus and Fate embrace, down they come to urge our union on—Cry, cry in triumph, carry on the dancing on and on!"[7]

Aeschylus's cosmos is not without bloodshed, violence, or torment. He has not completely shed the reality of patricide, filicide, and bloodlust which characterized the Hesiodic cosmos. Nor is Aeschylus's cosmos the first instantiation of love penetrating the dark and fatalistic abyss of struggle; Homer achieved that (within the scope of Greek literature). But Aeschylus's cosmos goes beyond Homer's in presenting reason, persuasion, as an integral aspect of the cosmos that was otherwise absent in Homer.

Furthermore, the house of Atreus, which represents humanity as a whole, also goes through a metamorphosis over the course of the trilogy. The human actors were imprisoned, restless, and lustful in *Agamemnon*. The human actors are moved to passion and force in the *Libation Bearers*, as the end of their restless lust displayed in the previous play. The human actors are finally moved to reason, persuasion, and justice when it comes to the *Eumenides*, as Aeschylus completes the threefold movement from restless lust to persuasive justice.

It is struggle and conflict, struggle and conflict with flesh and blood and with conscience, that cause the great leap forward, according to Aeschylus. In wrestling in the muck, mud, and blood, we do not remain there. We lift ourselves out of it. We proceed from restless passion to directed rage, and finally to ordered reason and the birth of civilization, premised on persuasion, love, and justice. The *Oresteia* is a window into the sad and sorry trials and experiences that pushed Orestes (i.e., us) to seek persuasion, justice, and the joy that is found in persuasion and justice. Moreover, Aeschylus is a window into the development of the tension between instinct and strife with reason and order in the larger context of ancient Greek literature.

By the time we reach Euripides, we see the destruction of Aeschylus's synthesis from the cosmogonies of Hesiod and Homer (where the gods are central characters in all three). The gods and humans depicted by Euripides, the great cynic, are a return to the insufficiency of the pantheon and the ideal of persuasion. In trying to understand why Medea slaughters her children, why the depraved and enslaved women of Bacchus rip Pentheus

6. Aeschylus, *Oresteia*, 274.

7. Aeschylus, *Oresteia*, 276–77.

limb from limb, and why the women of Troy or even the daughters of men (Iphigenia) are brutally objectified and sacrificed, we must have Aeschylus in mind when reading the horror stories of Euripides.

Was the union of love and persuasion, as entailed by Aeschylus, really the gateway to the eradication of love in the name of persuasion? Were the furies in the right and Athena in the wrong all along (as Euripides implies in his cynical and often brutal depiction of the gods in his plays)? Can love and persuasion coexist? Are we doomed to fatalistic strife? Aeschylus is essential for anyone wrestling with these questions, as well as being a prophet in the darkness or a demon masquerading as an angel of light—depending on how one peers into the sacristy of the Greek gods wrestled with by Hesiod, Homer, Aeschylus, Sophocles, Euripides, Socrates, Plato, Aristotle, Saint Paul, Saint Cyprian, and Saint Augustine, among many others.

Aeschylus's cosmos is one where love and persuasion, order and freedom, justice and punishment are all tied together. The world that we often strive to achieve is the same world that Aeschylus hoped to achieve more than two and a half millennia ago. As such, Aeschylus remains the enduring playwright—perhaps laughing at us or weeping with us in our struggle, like the furies and Orestes, to seek justice, to do justice, and to love without hatred or rage. Isn't this the enduring pursuit of human civilization?

This essay was originally published in *Merion West* under the title "Why Aeschylus Still Matters Today," 15 August 2019.

4

Sophocles and the Necessity of Family

Sophocles, like his slightly younger contemporary Euripides, lived in exciting and transformative times. But where Euripides blasphemously ridiculed the gods and showed their callous cruelty, Sophocles—at least among the handful of plays that have survived—leaves the gods conspicuously absent from his dramas. Instead of the gods being our deliverance, the family is the instrument of salvation and the bulwark against tyranny in his surviving plays—but not without descending into darkness, before ascending into the light.

The Sophoclean Spirit

Sophocles was closer to Aeschylus than Euripides in his content and message. Like Aeschylus, Sophocles was also more frequently honored at the festivals and playwright competitions than the younger and more impetuous tragedian who exposed the hollowness of the dark sacristy of the Athenian pantheon. This bears out in his plays where love and filial piety, themes that were present in Aeschylus, become the major themes in Sophocles. However, unlike Aeschylus, who located filial piety as congruous with the gods, Sophocles located the nexus of filial piety purely between humans. Electra's deliverance with the advent of Orestes; Antigone's heartbreaking devotion to Polyneices which awakens Creon, the ruler of Thebes, to his failures; even the sympathy the reader has for isolated Philoctetes—all point to the importance of family life in providing meaning, comfort, and civilizational stability in Sophocles's works.

Beyond filial piety and deliverance, the other great theme that concerned Sophocles was the tyranny of the state. Creon embodies statist tyranny in *Antigone*. Even pitiable Oedipus is the strongman of the state in *Oedipus Rex*, going as far as boldly eulogizing himself as the "ruin that saved the state."[1] Clytemnestra and Aegisthus in *Electra* are equally statist agents who are interested in the lust for power that characterizes the naked reality of human politics.

Athens had slipped from the open democracy that it was when she led the defense of Hellas against the Persians. Though the Athenian delegates and Pericles in Thucydides's *History of the Peloponnesian War* proclaim in an open-air forum the greatness of Athens, that greatness was waning prior to the war and was subsequently extinguished during the conflict when Sophocles was composing his late works. The backdrop to the tragedy of *Electra* is the Trojan War, a war every bit the equivalent of the Peloponnesian War in its brutality.

Likewise, *Philoctetes* has the Trojan War as its immediate context. *Philoctetes* was written during the final decade of the Peloponnesian War; the loneliness and desolate isolation that Philoctetes embodies is the same loneliness and isolation that drove Clytemnestra to plot to kill Agamemnon—the difference being that Philoctetes was mercilessly abandoned for his smelly foot and left for dead on an island all alone. Philoctetes survived but is taken advantage of by returning Greek heroes (Odysseus and Neoptolemus). Poor Philoctetes is robbed of a life, a family, and the happy ideal of life with others.

In this respect, Sophocles is amending the same wisdom imparted to the world from the pen of Homer and Aeschylus. Love, especially as directed to the family or for family, is what makes life worth living in the rage-filled and dark cosmos that the ancient Greeks inhabited. That filial love, however, was rapidly dissipating during the time of Sophocles. (And this is what caused Euripides to present love as potentially dangerous.) Sophocles lived through the rise and decline of filial piety, which corresponded, in his mind, to the rise and decline of Athens.

Oedipus Rex and Antigone

It would be wrong to maintain that Sophocles—or any of the Greeks for that matter—had an understanding of natural law in the same way that scholastic

1. Sophocles, *Complete Plays*, 229.

Christians did. In fact, reading back onto the Greeks the high moral law is, ironically, part of the Christian inheritance of the West. Apart from Aristotle and Cicero (especially the latter), it is hard to ascertain anything resembling Saint Thomas Aquinas's *Summa Theologiae* and its ruminations on the natural law, which was also developed through centuries of Catholic thinking and encyclicals. Nevertheless, we do see the faint glimpses of the natural law in Sophocles, a law which was more fully developed—if we can say that—than in Aristotle and Cicero (who still pale in comparison to their Catholic successors).

The closest revelation to Sophocles's natural law (and the centrality of the family to it) comes through the person of Creon, especially as connected through *Oedipus Rex* and *Antigone*. Patricide and incest are objects of shame in *Oedipus Rex*. Such crimes—though Oedipus is fated by the gods to commit such heinous acts—are the focus of scorn from Sophocles's pen. Blinded and ashamed, Oedipus prepares to leave Thebes, but not without talking to Creon one last time. In the final dialogue between Oedipus and Creon, Oedipus implores Creon to nurture Antigone and Ismene and bless him before his exile.

Prior to this touching moment, the closest thing to a resolution in the play, Oedipus was filled with pride and the lust for power. Accompanied by Jocasta, his mother whom he took as his wife, the two coldly asserted that to be liberated from one's parents makes one happy. Moreover, we are informed that Oedipus's foster father, Polybus, loved him ever so dearly. Upon hearing the news of his supposed father's death, Oedipus rejoices, which exposes his hollowness. "You were a gift. He took you from my arms," the shepherd messenger tells Oedipus. "A gift?" Oedipus retorts, "But he loved me as his own." The messenger replies, "He had no children of his own to love."[2] Jocasta, overhearing the conversation, is overcome with guilt and shame and leaves to commit suicide.

Oedipus and Jocasta had mocked the gods and scorned fathers and mothers in their lust for self-power and gain. Although we know the gods had fated them to misery, one cannot help but feel a certain rage at both in celebrating the death of parents. Their celebratory emptiness was of their choosing, Sophocles seems to hint, which makes their crimes worse than if they had simply played out the lot that fate had dealt them. As such, the family is utterly destroyed, except for Antigone and Ismene, who mature under Creon's watchful and loving arms.

However, in *Antigone*, with Creon suffering from political challenges, Creon's relationship with Antigone changes for the worse. He condemns

2. Sophocles, *Complete Plays*, 247.

Antigone for wanting to bury the body of her traitorous brother. Creon had decreed civically that none of the enemies of Thebes were to be honored. Polyneices is to be left on the blood-stained field of battle; his body to be the food of vultures for his rebelliousness. Antigone, by contrast, affirms the law of filial love in wanting to bury the body of her brother. (Burial was one of the most important of rites in ancient Greek society.)

Creon and the loving, not necessarily strong-willed (as usually interpreted) Antigone clash over how to react to the death of Polyneices. Creon has ordered, with the authority of the state and law, to let traitors rot and be consumed by rats and vultures. Antigone, on the other side, exhibits the spirit of love by burying the body of her brother in a dignified grave. Creon's tyrannical actions sever his bond with Antigone. Ismene's submission to civic tyranny instead of the moral law equally destroys her relationship with her sister.

It is not until Antigone and Haemon flee to the bloody fields to bury and honor Polyneices, thus making themselves enemies of the state, that Creon—in his loneliness—realizes his errors. He cries out as if to the heavens, "In the end it is the ancient codes—oh, my regrets!—that one must keep: To value life then one must value law."[3] Creon's tearful statement is ironic. The law he associates with life is not the civil law that he had been forcibly promoting but the moral law of the family, which brings and nurtures life. He rushes to the field. Too late. Antigone and Haemon are both dead. Creon realizes his sin and repents. But the tragedy has has now fully manifested itself, though we have learned something important from Creon's claim that to value life one must keep those "ancient codes" of filial piety.

Electra

In the midst of Sophocles's works is the struggle between the family and state tyranny. Aristotle maintained that family served as the basis of all civilization. Aristotle wasn't onto something new. He was restating something ancient that had been forgotten in Athens's descent into imperialism and, eventually, tyranny. In starting over, Aristotle began again with the basics.

The Athens of Sophocles's time was a morally degenerate and anti-filial place. The place of the family in Athenian life had been dethroned. The dissolution of family and the crisis of agnatic relationships are not only visibly presented in the tragedians; they are also the focus of the comedic wit and commentary by Aristophanes in the *Wasps*. Likewise, Plato treats

3. Sophocles, *Complete Plays*, 379.

the subject of the dissolution of filial bonds and the supremacy of the state in his dialogues, especially the *Euthyphro* and *Crito*.

In calling for a return to the "ancient codes," Sophocles was advocating a return to the stability and order of the family as the most effective buttress against state power and the chaos unleashed in a society obsessed with self-pursuit and power (which ultimately destroyed Athens in the Peloponnesian War). *Electra* is the great play that showcases the theme of filial deliverance. Electra has been living under the tyranny of her mother Clytemnestra and Clytemnestra's adulterous lover Aegisthus. She is alone and tormented. She loathes her mother for her actions and doesn't consider Clytemnestra her mother, based upon her actions. No mother would murder her husband and coldly celebrate the news of the death of her son.

Deviating from his great master and teacher, Sophocles rewrites Electra's deliverance. Aeschylus had Electra meet Orestes at the tomb of Agamemnon in the *Libation Bearers*. Electra fully knows of Orestes's plan to execute vengeance or justice (depending on your perspective) upon Clytemnestra and Aegisthus. In Sophocles's version, our heart agonizes and weeps for Electra. She is abused and distraught. When Clytemnestra celebrates the news of the death of Orestes, Electra proclaims that her world has been taken from her and that she has no will—or reason—left to live. "Did the callous woman cry and mourn for her dead son? Was there an ounce of grief or pain? Not a bit of it. She left us laughing. O my poor dearest Orestes, you have snuffed my life out by your death," Electra bitterly cries.[4] Her cries are a testament of her love.

Without family, and suffering the burden of tyranny, Electra informs us that life is unbearable. "This is she—a most unhappy woman," she weeps in front of Orestes (not yet knowing that it is he). Orestes, in seeing his sister in this state of agony, is moved to pity, a testament of his love for her. "I cannot bear to think of your wretched un-wedded life," he says.[5] In this exchange, Sophocles is telling us that life without a family is miserable but is also indicating that life with a family is plentiful and joyful.

When Orestes reveals himself to Electra, she is moved to joy and bliss, knowing that her brother is still alive. "O day of bliss," she proclaims. "Pure bliss indeed," Orestes lovingly answers.[6] Love, family, and deliverance are bound up together in *Electra*. The love of a brother and sister, the reunification of a family torn apart by murder and the lust for power, brings about not only earthly deliverance in the form of blissful joy, but also deliverance

4. Sophocles, *Complete Plays*, 83.

5. Sophocles, *Complete Plays*, 94.

6. Sophocles, *Complete Plays*, 96.

from the hand of cruel and petty political power. *Electra* is not a tragedy like *Oedipus Rex* or *Antigone*. *Electra* is a play of deliverance and the triumph of the bonds of love that comes through the tribulations of tragedy.

Unlike in Aeschylus, there is no indication that Orestes kills Clytemnestra and Aegisthus out of fidelity to the gods. Instead, he is an oracle of reckoning and an angel of deliverance. The real story is not revenge or justice. It is Electra's liberation—her salvation, if you will—and her liberation from the tyranny under which she suffers. This libration takes love and family, according to Sophocles. Without love and family, life is unbearable. With the arrival of Orestes, love and the reconstitution of a family bring deliverance and the end of tyranny. One can only hope that life with others, with a family, is that which also awaits Philoctetes as he leaves his Robinson Crusoe-like state of existence behind him.

Sophoclean Wisdom

If Aeschylus saw strife and love being superseded by persuasion and justice through the ancient divinities—and if Euripides exposed the hollowness of those divinities that Aeschylus piously venerated—Sophocles offered the *modus vivendi* between the two. After all, Aristophanes pits Aeschylus and Euripides against each other in the *Frogs*. But in that play, Aeschylus favors Sophocles as his heir apparent.

While Aeschylus offers a vision of laboring with the gods for a better world of reason and justice, and while Euripides seems to suggest that man alone is in control of his fate and actions, Sophocles humanizes the hopeful vision of Aeschylus. The gods are never central characters in Sophocles's dramas in the way that they were in Aeschylus. The gods are conspicuously absent, at least in the plays that have survived for posterity. Instead, we see love and deliverance between humans. The gods remain at a distance.

Sophocles then was a traditionalist and a humanist. Sophocles understood the place of love and the family as the cornerstone of civilization and the good life, thus standing in stark contrast to the dangerous love of Euripides. The dissipation of the family had led to the forgetting of those "ancient codes" and ways of life that make civic life possible and fruitful. When the family dies or disintegrates, state tyranny emerges to take its place. Yet Sophocles's advocacy rests on filial piety instead of divine piety.

Moreover, and more scandalously, if not darkly, redemption in Sophocles is born only in—and through—tragedy. Without tragedy, there can be no redemption. We must plunge into the abyss of death and tyranny before being lifted out of the darkness. The light in Sophocles is surrounded by a cesspool of blood, corruption, and murder. Indeed, the light flows out of that drowning darkness of gore, revenge, and sorrow.

Sophocles was not sacrilegious or irreligious. He honored the gods like a good Athenian. Yet he didn't seem to think, as Aeschylus did, that the gods are integral players in human development and deliverance. That, he left to us. In some respects, a world where we are responsible for moral action and loving deliverance is just as daunting and haunting a prospect as standing before Athena and Apollo in trial and being melded as a co-laborer with Reason and Justice.

The light is brightest when it is surrounded by the darkest cloud trying to suffocate it. And the light of Sophocles reveals many deep truths about the importance of love and family amid the darkness ensnaring it. To journey and stand at the top of Mount Parnassus is a gritty and grisly struggle. Despite the darkness surrounding us in this journey, Sophocles guides us up the mountain with a dim light, only to reveal a grander light at the peak.

This essay was originally published in *Merion West*, 26 August 2019.

5

Yearning for Eden

On the Poetry of Horace

QUINTUS HORATIUS FLACCUS, BETTER KNOWN TO US AS HORACE, LIVED through the decline and fall of the Roman Republic, Julius Caesar's assassination, and decades of civil war leading to the rise of Octavius Augustus as emperor. Despite the turbulent waves in which he swam, he also lived in the golden age of Latin poetry and is remembered, alongside Virgil and Ovid, as one of the three resplendent Roman poets who could rightly be said to have been a triumvirate of their own. A praise poet and poet of sensual love, Horace, it seems to me, is also the first romantic poet: his poetry decries the horror of war, mourns the burdens of urban civilization, and opines for a return to the idyllic agrarian and rural way of life.

In his great introductory exposition on existentialism, *Irrational Man*, William Barrett described Romanticism in part as the "protest of feeling against reason" and "the protest on behalf of nature against the encroachments of an industrial society."[1] Entailed throughout Barrett's description of the romantic antecedents to existential philosophy is the emphasis of the agrarian ideal, of nature, against mass mobilization, industrialism, and the organization of man for the end of war. Insofar as a definitive trait of romanticism is the agrarian ideal, Horace's poetry almost certainly fits the description of being romantic.

Horace was a hedonist. He was a sensualist who enjoyed the pleasures of wine and the body. As Suetonius reminds us in his *Life of Horace*, "It is said that he was immoderately lustful; for it is reported that in a room lined

1. Barrett, *Irrational Man*, 123.

with mirrors he had harlots so arranged that whichever way he looked, he saw a reflection of venery. He lived for the most part in the country on his Sabine or Tiburtine estate, and his house is pointed out near the little grove of Tiburnus."[2] It isn't surprising that much of Horace's poetry deals with the blurred lines between love and lust, feast and sex, companionship and friendship. Here too Horace is a forerunner to the Romantic poets of England and Germany. Men like John Keats, Percy Bysshe Shelley, Lord Byron, Novalis, Goethe, and Friedrich Hölderlin were also notorious womanizers, sensualists, and hedonists, along with being the founding fathers of the Romantic movement still so influential and important today as it was some two hundred years ago.

Yet Suetonius also informs us that Horace spent much of his life in his countryside estate, an estate situated in the rolling hills and pastures of central Italy—the same Italy that the Romantics of near two millennia later would travel and oftentimes die in. Horace then lived in the middle of old Italy. More precisely, he lived in the Italy untouched by the burdensome urbanization of Rome and other cities drowning in a population "not trained to stay on a horse" and "afraid of hunting."[3]

Horace lived from 65 to 8 BC, and for the first thirty or so years of his life, there was not a moment without war. This is captured in his lyric poetry, which often talks of war, civil war, strife, and the exploits of Julius Caesar and of Augustus. The fratricidal bloodshed of Romans slaughtering Romans was something that shook Rome to its core and something that Horace equally derides as impious: "Surely if any man shall wish to put an end / to impious slaughter and the madness of civil strife, / if he shall wish his statues / to be inscribed 'Father of Cities', let him have courage / to rein back our wild license."[4]

There is a certain irony when reading Horace. Given his wild license in his own life, often bordering on adultery and anything but chastity, it seems odd when he derides some of the very practices and lusts which gripped him. But Horace's traditionalism makes sense given that his poetry was written in the aftermath of the Augustan settlement, something which he praises thoroughly and repeatedly in his poetry.

After emerging victorious in the battle to control the fate of the world, Augustus embarked on an ambitious traditionalist moral campaign to rejuvenate the decaying Roman establishment, institutions, and people, infusing them with the moral virtue needed to sustain the Roman civilization. After

2. Suetonius, *Suetonius*, 489.

3. Horace, *Complete Odes*, 101.

4. Horace, *Complete Odes*, 101.

all, Horace rightly says, "Laws are useless without virtue."[5] Augustus and his poets and writers promoted what we can readily identify as traditionalism: duty toward the gods and parents, duty to country, and respect for law and order. It suffices to say that in a world ripped open by chaos, Augustus and his intellectuals, from Livy and Virgil to Horace, upheld *pietas* and embedded its ideals in their works.

But Horace's romanticism is what is most interesting, for it is in the agrarian ideal that we see a fuller and livelier traditionalism than the mundane *pietas* to God, father, and fatherland. It is in nature that Horace finds the source of the divine order that the Augustan poets thought was necessary for a peaceful and joyful life.

"Back to war, Venus, after all / these years? Spare me, spare me, I beg you." Horace is astute to the bleak realities of war and the lust to dominate. Not only does he beg Venus to spare him from war, he goes on to call her a "cruel mother."[6] The constancy of war, its horrors and destruction, has destroyed Horace's life: "As for me, I no longer take pleasure in a woman / or boy, nor in the fond hope that my love might still / be returned, nor in drinking bouts, / not in binding my brow with fresh flowers."[7]

As a poet Horace does not comprehend the "mad rush to join . . . wicked war."[8] Though a patriot with no love for Rome's great enemy, Carthage, Horace nevertheless opines that war must have some explanation beyond the gods' thirst for blood: "Your swords / were sheathed. Why do you draw them now? / Perhaps too little Latin blood has poured upon the plains / and into Neptune's sea, / not so that Rome could burn the lofty citadels / of Carthage, her great enemy."[9] In trying to understand the mad rush to war, Horace does stumble upon a deep psychological truth: "Is it blind madness, or some deadlier force? / Some ancient guilt? Give answer now."[10] (Though he poses rhetorical questions about war being the product of insanity or blood guilt, demanding an answer from the gods, the questions he poses strike at the heart of war and man's depravity—the mad love of disorder, chaos, and the guilt of fratricide.

What war has destroyed is the autumn fields "with fruit so richly crowned" that provide the peaceful and joyful life. As Horace aptly sings, "Fortunate the man who, free from cares, / like men of old still works / his

5. Horace, *Complete Odes*, 101.

6. Horace, *Complete Odes*, 112.

7. Horace, *Complete Odes*, 113.

8. Horace, *Complete Odes*, 11.

9. Horace, *Complete Odes*, 11.

10. Horace, *Complete Odes*, 11.

father's fields with his own oxen . . . . When Autumn raises in the fields
its head / with fruit so richly crowned, / with what delight he plucks the
pears he grafted / and grapes that challenge any purple dye."[11] Thus we see
Horace's image of peace: an idyllic farm. Moreover, it is a family farm, a
family farm owned by several generations, where sons plow the land that
their father had tilled. A rooted heritage lies at the core of Horace's idyllic
image of peace and joy.

Additionally, the peace and pleasure afforded in the simple agrarian
life is precisely what Horace's deracinated contemporaries have forgotten.
Horace sings of the pleasure and joy in the hunt:

> But when the thunder of Jove's winter season
> musters the rains and snows,
> with all his dogs on every side he drives
> wild boar into his ring of nets,
> or stretches wide-meshed toils on twigs he's smoothed
> to trap the greedy thrushes,
> and hunts the timid hare and crane migrating
> to his snare—delicious prey.
> Amid these pleasures who would not forget
> the miseries brought on by love?[12]

Horace's beautiful, if not otherwise romanticized, vision of the good life is
shown being superseded by the urban life of aimlessness and antagonism
to nature. Horace laments how the old ways are being forgotten: "The free
young Roman is not trained to stay on a horse. He is afraid of hunting."[13]
Horace's romanticism, however, has a very real alternative: the destruction
of war.

And this pivots Horace to his praise of Augustus. Augustus is the embodiment, real or imagined, of the romantic ideal conceived of by Horace.
Augustus is the figure who allows for a return to the past, a return to the
farm and villa, a return to peace and therefore pleasure. Augustus comes as
a god, a shield, to end the mad wars and civil strife that have plagued Rome
and dominated Horace's life:

> I was eager to sing of battles and defeated cities,
> But Phoebus struck his lyre and forbade me
> To sail my little boat
> Across the Tyrrhenian sea. Your Augustan age,
> Caesar, has given rich crops back

11. Horace, *Complete Odes*, 4.
12. Horace, *Complete Odes*, 5.
13. Horace, *Complete Odes*, 101.

To our fields, has brought the standards back to our Jupiter,
Tearing them from the proud door posts
Of the Parthians . . .
While Caesar is guardian of the state, neither civil war
Nor civil madness will drive away our peace,
Nor will anger beat out its swords
And set city against unhappy city.[14]

The high-water mark of Horace's praise poetry comes with a string attached. It is the string of romanticism. For Horace's praise of Augustus Caesar, in nearly all his poems, sings of his bringing of peace, which restores the agricultural prosperity, permitting song and sumptuous feast: "This holy day will truly drive away / all my black cares: I shall have no fear / of war or violent death while Caesar / is master of the world. Go, boy, and bring me fragrant oils, and garlands, / and a cask of wine."[15] We see then that it is not Augustus who is the subject of Horace's praise, but that which Augustus allows to manifest—the Edenic ideal with its tranquility, organic fertility, and pleasure.

That Horace sings praise to Augustus for restoring agricultural prosperity shouldn't come as a surprise. After all, Suetonius said that Horace spent much of his life in his countryside estate. Moreover, the mobilization of the masses for war—civil war, worst of all—meant the depletion of the land, as well as the disintegration of the family with the many hundreds of thousands of Roman men slaughtered on the fields of battle. War destroyed the agricultural calm in which Horace clearly indulged and which he enjoyed. Peace provided the restoration of that countryside ideal with wife, mistress, children, dogs, horses, and glowing sun.

Horace's praise of Augustus then is unmistakably reactionary and romantic but is tied to the romance of agrarianism. Augustus is not a bringer of progress and advancement but a force of restoration and return, specifically, the return to a garden. Yet Horace's poetry also captures the realities of historical cataclysm and supersession, what Hegel would later call *Aufhebung*.

We weep with Horace because he is a man lost in a sea of change. Though Augustus brings peace and a certain restoration of the countryside and rural way of life, that life is vanishing and cannot last. Population migration has depleted the countryside and made Rome, Ravenna, and other cities the new centers of power. The family farm, that ideal image eulogized by Horace as being the foundation of the fortunate life, is being abolished by the winds of history. Horace's life of pleasure, and the life of

14. Horace, *Complete Odes*, 130.
15. Horace, *Complete Odes*, 93.

the hunt—animal and woman—was catching fire and dissolving before his very eyes.

The family-owned farm of generations was soon replaced by the slave-run latifundia system that was itself a manifestation of Rome's imperial war policies. Conquest of land and peoples meant the state needed to do something with these newly conquered lands and masses of people. Those Roman elites fortunate enough to have escaped the sword of war and power politics soon reaped the reward. The small-scale family farm found itself overwhelmed by the Roman equivalent of contemporary large-scale agribusiness, which swallowed up centuries of rooted history. Horace's lament for a return to the ideal rural way of life and his praise of Augustus for allowing this restoration was short-lived.

Though there is an unmistakable tragic ethos affiliated with the romantic impulse—which I would argue begins with Horace and remains a deep part of the Western psyche and tradition—this impulse is nonetheless awe-inspiring and truly moves the heart of man. The agrarian ideal for which Horace pines, that "enchanted" image of nature that "we shall wonder at," is something familiar and moving:

> So let us seek the Blessed Fields and Wealthy Isles,
> where every year the land unploughed gives grain,
> and vines unpruned are never out of flower,
> and olive shoots unfailing bud, and set their fruit,
> and dusky fig ungrafted graces its own tree,
> the honey flows from hollow ilex, and from hills
> the streamlet lightly leaps with sounding footfall.
> There to the milking pails unbidden come the goats,
> and friendly flocks their swollen udders bring.
> when evening comes no howling bear patrols the pens,
> no viper heaves its mound of earth.
> Enchanted, we shall wonder at it all.[16]

One of the major reasons why Horace is an Augustan poet isn't his praise for Augustus. The Augustans may have offered praise to Augustus, their patron and noble ruler, but the real heart of the Augustan poets is a belief in a divinely instituted order that governs nature. The heart of the Augustan poets is set on discovering this divinely instituted order, thereby bringing the joy and peace that humans seek. Horace's romantic poetry captures this Augustan yearning perfectly and beautifully. Against the chaos of war, the rise of the city, and the general drift away from nature, Horace calls us back to nature to find our home.

16. Horace, *Complete Odes*, 19.

"Enchanted, we shall wonder at it all" indeed. So let us seek the blessed fields where milk and honey flow and humans can relate to creation as God intended. Horace's romanticism is enduring because the call of return is enduring. Deep within the Western psyche and tradition is this yearning for return. Horace, more than any other of the grandiose poets of antiquity, captured that call, that cry, for return—a yearning for a restored Eden, where the peaceful harmony of life in a garden would be our eternal home.

This essay was originally published in *Front Porch Republic* under the title "Yearning for Eden: Horace and the Romance of Agrarianism," 14 February 2020.

6

Metamorphosis by Love

OVID WAS ONE OF THE GREAT POETS OF ANTIQUITY AND STANDS ALONG-side Virgil and Horace as the trio of immortal Latin poets of Augustan Rome who wrote about the intensity of the passions. Ovid's *Metamorphoses* is a grand poetic epic, yes, epic, of the transformation of history and truth into poetry. As he concludes, "Wherever through the lands beneath her sway / The might of Rome extends, my words shall be / Upon the lips of men. If truth at all / Is stablished by poetic prophecy / My fame shall live to all eternity."[1] But deep within the collection of stories that serve as the pulsating heart of Ovid's finest accomplishment, there is a sparkling truth that his prophetic poetry does reveal: divinization, metamorphosis, by love. The fame which permits Ovid to live for all eternity is through his being a prophetic poet of the power of love.

By the medieval period, Ovid was one of the canonical writers studied and was one of the pillars of what we now call classical education. Ovid's sensualism and violence were allegorized under the new Christian regime. Ovid's devotion to love was approved under the revelation of the Christian truth of love's transformative power and of love being the highest good in life, while the naturalistic overtures were shown to be the shortcomings of the pre-Christian world; his writings on violence and lust were taught by negative example as what is not proper love and how various acts of impiety lead to consequences (as they do throughout the poem). Although Ovid was baptized into Christianity and therefore bequeathed to the rest of the

---

1. Ovid, *Metamorphoses*, 379.

world, he was not without his detractors then (most prominently and espe-cialy, the English Puritans), as he still is now.

The length of Ovid's epic poem of the creation of the world to the apo-theosis of Julius Caesar includes many myths and stories, some bleak, some uplifting. I wish to treat three of the stories contained therein to highlight one of those truths "stablished by poetic prophecy."[2] The stories of Perseus and Andromeda, Pygmalion and the statue, and Acis and Galatea undoubt-edly reveal the power of love and our metamorphosis by it.

One of the issues of understanding the pagan world and psyche was the dark cosmos they inhabited. Chaos is the oldest of the gods in Ovid's ac-count, not too dissimilar from Hesiod's cosmos of strife, rage, and war. Hu-mans were often the puppets of the gods and the fated objects of divine lust, rape, and control. Pious fatalism is often the best one could hope to achieve. Yet in the midst of this often dark and violent cosmos of thunderbolts and skulduggery, these three stories in Ovid's *Metamorphoses* illuminate our world and give a great deal of hope to humans

The *Metamorphoses* opens with the usual act of invoking the gods or muses: "Of bodies changed to other forms I tell; / You Gods, who have yourselves wrought ever change / Inspire my enterprise and lead my lay / In one continuous song from nature's first / Remote beginnings to our modern times." In describing the creation, we are witness to the dark and chaotic cosmos: "No sun as yet poured light upon the world, / No waxing moon her crescent filled anew, / Nor in the ambient air yet hung the earth, / Self-bal-anced, equipoised, nor Ocean's arms / Embraced the long far margin of the land . . . . Cold essence fought with hot, and moist with dry, / And hard with soft and light with things of weight." Ovid's creation account, with Chaos as the "one, well named" god, begins with chaos and emerges through strife.[3] The chaos of the cosmos is tamed by hard labor and energy, toil and sweat; in other words, strife begets strife and is countered by an alternative form of strife—the arduous strife of work, *laborem*.

Although the creation is not the product of love, the stories contained in Ovid's *Metamorphoses* often deal with love or lust (or often both) and capture the essence of the human struggle and condition, that struggle in which humans hope for their own divinization and salvation through love. We are exposed then to two competing outlooks as how to transform ourselves: through struggling strife or through the tenderness of love. The creation myth might be through hard conflictual labor, but by the poem's

2. Ovid, *Metamorphoses*, 379.

3. Ovid, *Metamorphoses*, 1.

end, Ovid achieves a very subtle and radical transformation in understanding the spirit of the cosmos.

Perseus and Andromeda

The story of Perseus and Andromeda is a tale of faith, hope, and love triumphant. There is much darkness that clouds the grand story. Cassiopeia, Andromeda's mother, is a vain and haughty woman who causes her beautiful virgin daughter to be endangered by exuding vanity in claiming that Andromeda is more beautiful than the naiads. Challenging the divine hierarchy in such a way, Neptune (Poseidon) is enraged and enchains Andromeda to be eaten by the sea-monster Cetus. Medusa, the Gorgon whom Perseus slays, was also a vain woman—a feminine Narcissus—enraptured by her beautiful hair. Medusa seduces Neptune, and they consummate their sexual lust in the virgin temple of Minerva (Athena). This outrages Minerva and causes her to turn Medusa's beloved prize into a nest of disgusting and repulsive snakes. Phineus, Andromeda's original prospective husband, loves not her charm and feminine mystique but the political utility that she brings; Phineus's lust for political power is the basis of his relationship with Andromeda.

Despite all the skulduggery, vanity, and impiety that is interwoven into the tale, it is important to note that those who are metamorphosized are sinners deserving punishment. Medusa must be killed for her violation of a divine temple alongside her vanity. Phineus must also be slain for his lust for powerful and political ambitions which wreak havoc during the wedding banquet. Though these transformations are due to just punishment for sin, the metamorphosis of Perseus and Andromeda is with what the story principally concerns itself.

Perseus is the son of Jove and therefore a demi-god, a sort of godman who is part human and part divine. While he is an instrument of divine judgment against sinners, he is also transformed through his deeds of heroic love and faith to the gods. It is, after all, his *fides*, his faith, that allows him to overcome all the monsters and other obstacles that stand in his way.

Minerva has instructed Perseus how to defeat Medusa. Do not look into her eyes, the goddess implores the hero-son, and subsequently gives him a shield to protect himself. Coming upon a sleeping Medusa, Perseus uses the shield—rather than his naked eyes—to line up the culling blow. After decapitating the gorgon, he places the head in a pouch to keep himself and others safe from her tremendous powers, which remain even after death.

As he soars overhead on Pegasus, he comes across the innocent and beautiful Andromeda enchained on the rocks. As Ovid makes clear, her innocence and purity demand saving: "There, innocent, by Jove's unjust decree / Condemned to suffer for her mother's tongue, /Andromeda was pinioned on a rock."[4] Because Andromeda is free from any affront, any sin, she cannot be punished.

But what causes Perseus to rescue her? It is evident that Andromeda is not deserving of the fate of being eaten by Cetus, but it is not her innocence that is the instrument of her deliverance, as much as it is Perseus's love upon seeing her: "When Perseus saw her, had a wafting breeze / Not stirred her hair, her eyes not overflowed / With trembling tears, he had imagined her / A marble statue. Love, before he knew, / Kindled; he gazed entranced; and overcome / By loveliness so exquisite, so rare, / Almost forgot to hover in the air."[5] It is love that delivers Andromeda from her enchainment. Moreover, it is important to recognize that it is sight of her face, rather than her body, that allows Perseus to recognize her as human.

The face is the seat of the soul and subjectivity. The human face brings liveliness and personality to the lifeless, soulless material world. It is not incidental then that it is the face that reveals Andromeda's beauty and personality. After turning Cetus into stone, Perseus asks for the fair girl's name: "Reveal, I beg, your name and this land's name."[6] That Perseus asks for her name indicates his interest in her subjectivity and not just her carnal beauty (though this is certainly included with her subjectivity and soulfulness).

In Andromeda's rescue, she becomes Perseus's bride-to-be. Love here consummates itself in marriage. The two begin telling their stories to each other, thereby enlarging their lives through the intertwining of the stories that define their persons.

Returning home and grateful for Andromeda's deliverance, Cepheus and Cassiopeia arrange for their daughter's marriage to Perseus. The wedding banquet is disrupted by Phineus, a "rash ringleader of war."[7] Phineus, as we've mentioned, was the original promised suitor of Andromeda. However, his interest in Andromeda was moved for purely political reasons; he never loved her and doesn't love her as Perseus does. This is revealed in Cepheus's rebuke: "Is this / Your thanks for such great service? This the dower / You pay for her life saved? / It was not Perseus / Who took her from you, if you want the truth: / It was the Nereids and Neptune's wrath, / It was

4. Ovid, *Metamorphoses*, 94–5.
5. Ovid, *Metamorphoses*, 95.
6. Ovid, *Metamorphoses*, 95.
7. Ovid, *Metamorphoses*, 99.

the horned Ammon, it was the sea-monster / Who came to feast upon my flesh and blood. / You lost her then, then when her death was sure, / Unless her death indeed is what you want / And mean my grief to ease your cruel heart."[8] With or without her breathing soul by his side, Phineus could claim his legitimacy to power through his betrothal to Andromeda; it mattered not if she lived or died on that rock.

Lust, specifically the lust for power, brings chaos to the political realm. After all, it is in a palace and a social environ that this part of the tale takes place. Love brings serene harmony to politics. The many lords and ladies, bards and citizens, are in attendance, enjoying the fruits of love in marriage. This is disturbed, as Ovid's recounting of the story implies, through the lust for power and the ambition that comes with it. Love nevertheless triumphs. In the maelstrom of battle, Phineus and his band of marauding warriors are defeated. Perseus turns them into stone.

After defeating Phineus, Perseus and Andromeda seal their love for each other in a bountiful and fertile marriage. Perseus and Andromeda wed; their marriage brings forth many children. The metamorphosis of Perseus and Andromeda is through love. In the midst of sin and darkness, chaos and war, love emerged triumphant and brought forth the greatest transformation of all: the bonding of two flesh as one in marriage.

Pygmalion and the Statue

One of the most charming, if not peculiar, stories contained in Ovid's *Metamorphoses* is the tale of Pygmalion and the statue. Pygmalion is a sculptor, and a damned good sculptor. What he creates is almost life-like, the closest stone, marble, and ivory can be to living flesh and blood.

When we are introduced to Pygmalion, he is suffering from loneliness and general resentment of the female sex. "Pygmalion had seen these women spend / Their days in wickedness, and horrified / At all the countless vices nature gives / To womankind lived celibate and long / Lacked the companionship of married love."[9] We can infer from the introduction to Pygmalion's plight that he had been spurned by love and was aghast at the degenerate morals of the people, women especially, around him. With his love spurned, Pygmalion descends into a celibate and lonely isolation where he crafts female statues as a coping mechanism for his plight.

During his plight, he crafts a statue so beautiful and lifelike that it almost appears to be alive. "Meanwhile he carved his snow-white ivory / With

8. Ovid, *Metamorphoses*, 99.
9. Ovid, *Metamorphoses*, 232.

marvelous triumphant artistry / And gave it perfect shape, more beautiful / Than ever woman born. His masterwork / Fired him with love. It seemed to be alive, / Its face to be a real girl's face."[10] Beauty's face lit a fire deep inside the cool and tempered heart of Pygmalion, and he raced to the festival of Venus to say prayers.

Pygmalion's admiration of beauty, the power of beauty, literally brought new life to him. Beauty also pushes him to Venus to offer up pious prayers: "Vouchsafe / O Gods, if all things you can grant, my bride / Shall be . . . / The living likeness of my ivory girl."[11] It might be easy to condemn Pygmalion as a young boy going through puberty, but that misses the gentle introduction where his prior love seems to have been spurned, leading him into the pit of despair and loneliness in which he is. Nay, rather than mock Pygmalion for his flurry of passion, we should understand how the new life in Pygmalion came to be: love discovered and mediated through beauty.

Moreover, Pygmalion is a pious man. His prayers to Venus serve as a testament to his piety. Because Pygmalion is pious, his prayer shall be granted.

After saying his prayers, Pygmalion rushes home and grasps the statue once more. In a dazzling display of rhetorical and linguistic skill, Ovid describes the scene:

incumbensque toro dedit oscula visa tepere est;
admovet os iterum, manibus quoque pectora temptat:
temptatum mollescit ebur positoque rigore
subsidit digitis ceditque.

(Where she lay he kissed her and she seemed warm to the touch;
so kissing her again and caressing her breasts,
the ivory grew soft in his fingers
and its hardness vanished into flesh.)[12]

As the statue transformed to warm, living flesh and blood, "she [became] alive!"[13] With the statue now a woman, Pygmalion "poured his thanks to Venus, and, at last / His lips pressed real lips, and she, his girl, / Felt every kiss, and blushed, and shyly raised / Her eyes to his and saw the world and him. / The goddess graced the union she had made, / And when nine times the crescent moon had filled / Her silver orb an infant girl was born."[14]

10. Ovid, Metamorphoses, 232.
11. Ovid, Metamorphoses, 233.
12. My translation from the Latin.
13. Ovid, Metamorphoses, 234.
14. Ovid, Metamorphoses, 234.

This short and admittedly amusing story is one of the most power-ful and deep in the *Metamorphoses*. The story of Pygmalion communicates how beauty and love bring life to a cold and lonely world. Beauty and love resurrect Pygmalion, if you will, and lead to a marriage with the ultimate life-giving event as its culmination: childbirth. Pygmalion's salvation and the humanization of a cold, empty statue (representative of the cold, empty, loveless matter) are through the life-giving power of beauty and love. Beauty and love go together; if beauty is to save the world, then this entails that love will save the world—just as it did Pygmalion and Galatea.

The Tragic Love of Acis and Galatea

Galatea became the traditional naming of Pygmalion's statue, though Ovid leaves the statue turned beautiful snow-white woman unnamed. The story of Acis and the river nymph Galatea is another one of the great love stories contained in Ovid's epic. By now it should be apparent that many of the stories that Ovid tells are tales of love. While Acis and Galatea is a far more somber story, we still get a foretaste of divinization in Acis's rebirth into a god.

The tragic love story of Acis and Galatea is sandwiched within the pil-grimage of Aeneas; it begins an aside of stories that provide basic contextual background to the places that Aeneas and the pilgriming Trojans venture. Our story begins with Scylla combing Galatea's hair before inquiring why she continues to turn down various suitors. Galatea explains by talking of the memory of her love with Acis: "He was sixteen, the down upon his cheek / Scare yet a beard, and he was beautiful. / He was my love, but I was Cy-clops' love, / Who wooed me endlessly and, if you ask / Whether my hate for him or love for Acis / Was stronger in my heart, I could not tell."[15] The ending of the story, however, reveals that her love for Acis was more power-ful than her hate for Polyphemus.

Polyphemus, the one-eyed cyclops, is the undeniable villain of the story. The shepherd giant is described as a vile and monstrous creature, as most shepherds were, indicative of the Roman (and Greek) distrust of no-madic peoples (known as the barbarians). Polyphemus is also described as a lustful giant and maniac; he has coursing through his veins a "wild urge to kill" and a "lust for blood."[16] Polyphemus is no beautiful, handsome, and tender suitor as is Acis.

15. Ovid, *Metamorphoses*, 318.
16. Ovid, *Metamorphoses*, 318.

The love of Acis and Galatea is one of rich and deep purity. Acis and Galatea are gentle and honest lovers who embrace one another in their subjectivity; unlike many tales where the love of mortal and divine is usually the lust of the divine to control the mortal, there is no indication that Galatea lusted to control Acis as Circe or Calypso did to Odysseus or Zeus to Ganymede. Instead, the love between Acis and Galatea is pure; they share their joys and personalities with each other, which enrages Polyphemus.

The lament of Polyphemus could have been the episode of redemption for the giant but instead turns into the catalyst for his rage. "I'll gauge his living guts, I'll rend his limbs / And strew them in the fields and in the sea," the vicious cyclops screams. Chancing upon them as a predator waiting to ambush, Polyphemus's coldness comes to the fore when he says, "I see you; now I shall make sure / That loving fond embrace shall be your last." Polyphemus springs upon them like a lion. The attack startles Galatea, who dives into the sea and causes Acis to run up the mountainside.

In despair, Acis calls out, "Help, Galatea! Father, mother, help!" All to no avail. Polyphemus continues to chase the young man until he crushes him with a rock. Polyphemus retreats back to his blood-soaked cave a murderer. But the gods, the fates, take pity on Galatea and Acis. As Galatea recounts, "But I (it was all the Fates permitted me) / Caused Acis to assume ancestral powers." Acis is subsequently resurrected as a divine river spirit: "Acis there himself / Changed to a river-god; and still the same / His waters keep that legendary name."[17]

Acis overcomes death because of love. As his blood spills out over the countryside, his blood is transformed into a divine river spirit precisely because he loved and was beloved. Furthermore, the memory of love is the driving spirit of the story. In a rare instance of first person-third person blurring, this particular story is told from the persona of Galatea rather than the poet Ovid. The memory of love, we realize, is what prevents Galatea from taking on new suitors. The memory of love is what also ensures Acis's immortality. Acis's love for Galatea, and her receptivity to that love, is the unbreakable bond that brought Acis back from the grave—in the form of a river god—and keeps Galatea forever his, despite the many suitors now pursuing her.

The story of Galatea and Acis, while somber and dark, reminds us that love conquers death. Though Acis is killed by Polyphemus, he is resurrected, if you will, and takes on a new (divine) form. The only reason why Acis takes on a new form is because of the love he shared with Galatea; without love, Acis would have remained sinking into the ground—for dust he was and to

17. Ovid, *Metamorphoses*, 321–22.

dust he would have returned, if not for the salvific power of love. Additionally, the story communicates the power of love through memory. Love does not die with the mangling and rotting of the body. Love endures forever in the blessed realm of memory. The memory of love ensures that love never dies. A certain bishop of Hippo would later have much to say on this topic.

Ovid's Cosmos

It is true that there is extensive violence throughout the *Metamorphoses* (consider the violence in two of the stories we have just sampled). In part, this is the reality of Ovid's understanding of the world. Love and violence often did go together (and do go together). This too is a great achievement of Ovid, because he lays bare the gratuity and violence that accompanied his world. He doesn't hide the fact that sex and violence are widespread. Nevertheless, Ovid also reveals how love—sweet and tender, caressing love—breaks through in this bleak and violent cosmos. There are stories of transformation that lead to shock and revulsion and stories of transformation that lead to ecstatic endearment and tears. The stories of metamorphosis by love, especially that tender and compassionate love, are the tales that stick.

Ovid's *Metamorphoses* is many things. In its most fundamental form, Ovid's epic love poem of many stories reveals deep truths in its poetic proclamations of the transformative power and spirit of love. The truth revealed by Ovid's grand love epic is how love transforms us, love renews us, and love constitutes the pulsating heart of life. Despite all the chaos and flux we deal with, despite all the violence and objection, despite all the cruelty and even death, love remains the one constancy of the cosmos standing alongside all the various manifestations of strife. Love manages to creep into the cosmos that was, as the creation myth retells, not the product of love but of chaotic strife. Thus Ovid achieves the poetic metamorphosis of the creation story; he transforms the cosmos of chaos and strife into a cosmos of love with the possibility, however brief, of serenity in love, even if it is engulfed in the darkness of violence and bloodshed.

The *Metamorphoses* does not offer anything new in detailing a cosmos in a state of perpetual flux, strife, and change. Heraclitus and Lucretius had already posited this notion. What Ovid's *Metamorphoses* does offer as new in comparison to prevailing Greek and Roman views of the world is how love is the one constant in this cosmos of flux and violence. Love, as we have seen, brings life into a world of death and sin; love, tied with beauty, renews the world; love endures even after death and is the spirit of transformation over the grave. When Pythagoras speaks of the constancy of the soul in Book XV, Ovid reveals his understanding of the soul as the constancy of love which has permeated throughout the poem.

To integrate Pythagoras and Ovid, as I think is the message of the *Metamorphoses*, love is the same forever but adopts new migrations in ever-varying forms. The pilgrim souls of whom Pythagoras speaks are nothing less than loving souls on a pilgrimage of love through the cosmos who toss and turn about in its chaos and violence. When Ovid concludes the poem with the word *vivam*, "[I] shall live,"[18] he lives eternally through the love about which he came to prophesy—for he was a pilgrim soul hoping to be transformed by love. No fire can destroy, no sword can cut, no age can forget, the truth that love is the constant guiding spirit of the cosmos, no matter how much darkness, violence, and bloodshed surrounds it.

This essay was originally published in *The Imaginative Conservative*, 13 February 2020.

---

18. Ovid, *Metamorphoses*, 379.

7

The Shield of Aeneas

THE GRANDEST IMAGE OF VIRGIL'S *AENEID* IS THE SHIELD FORGED BY THE god Vulcan in the eighth book of Aeneas's adventure to "Lavinian shores and Italian soil." Virgil pays homage to Homer, his master and mentor, who also describes a grand image on a shield forged by the gods for Achilles. But where Achilles's shield is filled with the images of mythos and pathos, Aeneas's shield is filled with the spectacle of history and triumph. In the two shields from the two poets, we see the supersession of mythos and pathos with historical memory.

Poetry as a medium for history is quintessentially Roman and is the enduring invention of Virgil. The Greeks had poetry, and Homer wrote poetry. But Homer's epic is not filled with the memory of history as is Virgil's *Aeneid*, and Greek poetry doesn't rely on the recourse to history to move the story forward as Virgil's *Aeneid* does. The *Aeneid*, in many ways, is self-conscious of history. Even the supposed mythological stories that lie at the heart of the epic are filled with the imagery of Roman memory and prefigure the memory of Roman history.

When Aeneas makes landfall in the safe harbors of Carthage and is introduced to the erotically charged and voluptuous queen of the land, Dido, he sooths her with his voice in retelling the destruction of Troy. When Aeneas weeps for Priam, "the monarch who once had ruled in all his glory the many lands of Asia, Asia's many tribes. A powerful trunk lying on the shore. The head wrenched from the shoulders. A corpse without a name,"[1] Virgil recourses to imagery and the memory of Pompey in describing the

---

1. Virgil, *Aeneid*, 94.

55

tragic fate of the king of Troy. As the great classicist Bernard Knox says, "Any Roman who read these lines in the years after Virgil's poem was published or heard them recited would at once remember a real and recent ruler over 'the many lands of Asia,' whose headless corpse lay on the shore. It was the corpse of Gnaeus Pompeius (Pompey), who had been ruler of all the lands of Asia."[2]

Priam and Pompey are therefore associated together as tragic figures. Both men represent the old, the past, hewn down by the fires of war and the birth of the new. Indeed, this dynamic relationship between past and present, between old and new, is a major theme throughout the poem. Both men situated themselves, at least in death, in the Orient. Both men, at least in death, were cut down by warriors from the West. Of course, this Occidental-Oriental tension is also played out through the epic, just as it was playing out in the real lives of the Roman readers and listeners of Virgil, which is somewhat ironic given Rome's geographic position in the Occident. (We'll return to this subject in a bit.)

The relationship between Aeneas and Dido is heartbreaking, to say the least. Dido's previous husband had been killed, which forced her and her attendants to flee across the Mediterranean. Being a migratory people, she opens herself to fellow migrants. Aeneas is enraptured by Dido and Dido by Aeneas. Had Aeneas not been the chosen vessel to "found a city, bring [the] gods to Latium, source of the Latin race, the Alban lords and the high walls of Rome,"[3] he would have stayed in Carthage to consummate their love. But the gods, as we know, had other intentions; and history, as we know, cannot stop.

Dido's death is filled with the memory of the Punic Wars. Dido's death-devoted heart thrusts her atop a pyre to kill herself while cursing eternal vengeance on the children of Aeneas. Dido's curse, of course, provides a mytho-poetic justification for the three Punic Wars that Carthage and Rome fought for supremacy over the Mediterranean and, as such, for the future of Western civilization. Moreover, Dido's death in an immolating flame would have been something Virgil's Roman audience knew well. The death of Dido in an all-consuming fire evokes the memory of the burning of Carthage and Cato the Elder's famous proclamation "*Carthaginem esse delendam.*"

During the Third Punic War, the Romans had laid siege to the once great city and jewel of the Mediterranean. After a three-year-long siege, the Romans stormed the city and put an end to the Carthaginian threat once and for all. Scipio Africanus the Younger, the commanding general of the

2. Virgil, *Aeneid*, 25.
3. Virgil, *Aeneid*, 47.

Roman army, torched the city to prevent Carthage from ever being a thorn in the side of Rome's ambitions again. The city burned and burned, leaving not a single stone atop another.

The death of Dido by fiery immolation as she thrust Aeneas's blade (a symbol of war) into her breast, only to collapse in the engulfing flames, is nothing more or less than the haunting memory of the Punic Wars which nearly laid waste to Rome and the violent destruction of the North African city by sword and fire. Carthage became for Rome what Sodom and Gomorrah were to Abraham and Lot. Carthage was laid waste and became a city of burnt ash and salt, just as the image of Dido's death reminds us.

The culminating battle between Aeneas and the Latins, led by Turnus, is also filled with the repository of Roman history and consciousness. Rome, we must recall, started out as a single city among many cities in the Italian Peninsula. The Latin race was not yet united under a single political banner. The Latins were diverse and the peninsula reminiscent of Hellenic Greece in being a collection of city-states and colonies. As Rome expanded outside of her seven hills, she came into a series of deadly conflicts with the neighboring peoples. And the war between the Trojans and the Latin shepherds and hunters, who formed a substantial portion of Turnus's army, reminds the Roman reader of the three centuries of the Latin Wars fought to bring unification to the Italian Peninsula under those "high walls of Rome."

Additionally, the fact that Turnus is the leader of the Latin armies also represents the complicated legacy of Greek colonization and the Roman-Hellenic Wars where Rome eventually triumphed over the sons of Achilles and Alexander. Prior to the Latin Wars, the Greeks were the most powerful and advanced people on the Italian Peninsula. The Etruscans may have been tyrannical, but the Greek colonies on the southern portion of the peninsula were always a mark of embarrassment for the Romans. The Romans were not Greek. And they took no pride in Greek subversion of Roman culture. Cato the Elder went as far as to expel the Greek playwrights and intellectuals for subverting the martial and manly virtues and values of the Roman people.

It is fitting that the triumph of Rome comes at the expense of a great warrior who has Greek blood coursing through his veins. Turnus is the Achilles of the West. Like his Greek forebear, Turnus is a man who cannot control his passions. Enraged that Lavinia is now promised to Aeneas, he gathers his allies and armies to make war in the name of Eros and Thanatos. Yet this image is also reminiscent of another man who brought the world to war because of his lust for a woman, a man who would appear in the culminating image of the shield of Achilles, though on the losing side. Turnus is not only the Achilles of the West and the specter of Greece over Italy, he is also Mark Antony and the specter of his passion, which brought Rome further down the hole of war.

In fact, the conflict between laboring and dutiful Aeneas with erotic and pathological Turnus is the great clash of civilizations. Cato the Elder wrote the first Latin history of the Romans and, as mentioned, was famous for his anti-Greek views. Cato believed that Greek softness would destroy the traditional values of the Roman people. The pathological nature of the Greeks, especially as contained in their literature, led Cato to conclude that if Greek ideas infiltrated Roman culture, they would lead to the moral degeneration of the Romans—hence why he expelled the Greek playwrights and intellectuals when he was consul. Cato defended the laboring nature of the Romans and their dedication to filial piety against the erotic and self-centered conceit of the Greeks. This is recapitulated in Aeneas as the model Roman, hard-working and dutiful to the gods and his father, and Turnus, the model Greek (as imagined by Cato), who is pathological and moved by emotion more than duty or rationality.

The real reason that Turnus is slayed by Aeneas is because Rome had emerged victorious in the unification of Italy, expelled the Greeks from the peninsula, and defeated the Greeks in the Roman-Greek wars. Turnus—who "track[ed] down [his] roots [to] Inachus and Acrisius, Mycenae to the core!"[4]—had to die at the hand of the founding father of Rome, because Aeneas's killing of Turnus prefigures the Roman subjugation of the Greeks and the extirpation of the Mycenaean counterweight to Rome. The slaying of the Achilles of the West reminds the Roman reader of the long and arduous struggle against Greece.

In killing Turnus, Aeneas throws off the dark specter of Greece haunting Rome and vindicates Cato the Elder. (We mustn't forget that the enemies and murderers of Julius Caesar took refuge in Greece and were assailed as Greeks rather than as Romans.)

But before Aeneas could slay Turnus, Vulcan had to forge a shield so that Aeneas could wield it into battle. The shield is composed of many of the great images of Roman history. Virgil describes the shield forged in the laboring fire of Vulcan's forge:

> There is the story of Italy,
> Rome in all her triumphs. There the fire-god forged them,
> well aware of the seers and schooled in times to come . . .
> the mother wolf stretched out in the green grotto of Mars,
> twin boys at her dugs, who hung there, frisky, suckling
> without a fear as she with her lithe neck bent back,

4. Virgil, *Aeneid*, 225.

stroking each in turn, licked her wolf pups
into shape with a mother's tongue.
Not far from there
he had forged Rome as well and the Sabine women
brutally dragged from the crowded bowl . . .
And here in the heart
of the shield: the bronze ships, the Battle of Actium,
you could see it all, the world drawn up for war,
Leucata Headland seething, the breakers molten gold.
On one flank, Caesar Augustus leading Italy into battle,
the Senate and people too, the gods of hearth and home
and the great gods themselves . . .
And opposing them comes Antony leading on
the riches of the Orient, troops of every stripe—
victory over the nations of the Dawn and blood-red shores
and in his retinue, Egypt, all the might of the East
and Bactra, the end of the earth, and trailing
in his wake, that outrage, that Egyptian wife![5]

The very shield that Aeneas carries into battle bears the stamp of Rome's mastery of the world. There is no mistaking that Aeneas will prevail as the victor over his rivals. The central masterpiece of Vulcan's laborious effort is the great battle of Actium, the final victory of Rome over the Oriental barbarians (or so conceived in the mind of the Romans) and the Romanization of the world. The Battle of Actium, on the shield Aeneas carries with him into battle, is presented as the culminating triumph of Rome, of civilization, of duty and labor against the spirit of pathos and eros that enslaved the Orient (including the Greeks) and needed slaying by its contrasting spirit of *laborem* and *pietas* (embodied by Aeneas and the Romans).

That Aeneas marches off to war with a shield telling the story of Rome ensures that the shield also reminds Roman readers of the hardship of civilization and the labor involved in producing *Romanitas*. The story of Rome, which Virgil's readers and listeners would have known well, thus began with Aeneas and the story which Virgil was now telling. The hardship of civilization is the very seed of Rome. Additionally, the unity between *laborem* and *pietas* in the epic is bound up in the shield itself. The shield is a product of labor that was forged through hard work and is the instrument of Italy's civilizing. Turnus, by contrast, plunders and steals; after killing Pallas, Turnus takes his battle belt as a trophy. Aeneas's duty, his laboring duty, is to bring civilization to Italy (and the world) through the sword and shield.

5. Virgil, *Aeneid*, 262–4.

The shield, then, bearing in it the labor of Vulcan and telling the story of Rome's triumph over the world, entirely foreshadows and prefigures the subsequent thousand years of history up to the time of Virgil and Augustus Caesar. Aeneas's battle against Turnus, the Latins, and the barbarians who aid him, is nothing less than a mytho-poetic recapitulation of the memories of Rome's historical battles against the Latins to unify Italy, her conflicts with the Greeks, and the final destruction "of the Orient" and its "troops of every stripe," which marked the triumph of civilization and the will of the gods. The triumph of Augustus Caesar at the Battle of Actium and the restoration of order to a disordered world is therefore the continuation of what Aeneas had begun in bringing order to the disordered world of Italy.

The war with Turnus and his allies calls to mind the very culminating battle for civilization itself: the Battle of Actium with the forces of labor, duty, and order arrayed against the forces of pathological eros and disorder. The "troops of every stripe" that constituted Antony's army are the same diverse multitude of troops who fight with Turnus. "Men in their prime from Argos, ranks of Auruncans, Rutulians, Sicanian veterans on in years, Sacranians in columns, Labicians bearing their painted shields . . . topping off the armies rides Camilla, sprung from the Volscian people."[6] As Virgil described the brilliant and shining gathering of the armies, and especially Turnus, "his build magnificent,"[7] the Roman audience would have been instantly reminded of that grand glittering of bronze ships and armies that is the central image on Aeneas's shield of war, which also marked the end of Hellenism and the beginning of *Romanitas*, just as the death of Turnus symbolized the same throwing off of the Greek specter over Rome and the world.

While Homer was providing a new poetic metaphysic in his epic, Virgil's project was just as ambitious, if not grander, in reaching into the wellspring of memory and Roman self-consciousness to fill his epic with allusions and direct references to the very images and stories which moved the Roman heart and soul, indeed, the soul of the West, precisely because Aeneas's triumph over Turnus and his "troops of every stripe" was the victory of Western civilization over its competitors. Virgil was interested in telling the story of Rome by going back into its past and relating how the seed of the past will blossom into the flower of the future. Instead of drawing on mythological consciousness and imagery, as Homer did, Virgil tapped from the living memory of history and the personages that had moved history forward to its bloody climax at Actium.

6. Virgil, *Aeneid*, 239.

7. Virgil, *Aeneid*, 239.

Just as part of the Roman understanding of themselves was bringing order to a disorderly world—or at least that is how Augustus Caesar understood his place and role in history—the story of Aeneas is very much of a princely warrior bringing order to a disordered world as hitherto mentioned—an image that Virgil's readers would have all too readily equated with Augustus Caesar, about whom is prophesied during Aeneas's descent into the underworld. When Aeneas and the wayfaring Trojans make landfall in Italy, we get a foreshadowing of this long and arduous struggle for civilization: "That sight was bruited about as a sign of wonder, terror: for Lavinia, prophets sang of a brilliant fame to come, for the people they foretold a long, grueling war."[8] War is how order is brought about in the Roman psyche. And war certainly dominated the recent memory of the Roman people. There was rarely a decade without war, especially in the century leading up to the coronation of Augustus Caesar. Thus, it isn't surprising that the climax and culminating chapters of the *Aeneid* deal with war.

The war that Aeneas wages is necessary to bring us up to the present day (Virgil's present day) with Augustus Caesar as the new Aeneas. All history, Virgil informs us, had been moving to the glorious victory of Augustus at Actium and the extension of those "high walls of Rome" over Europe and Asia. As Virgil says, "How Fate compelled the worlds of Europe and Asia to clash in war! All people know the story, all at the earth's edge, cut off where the rolling Ocean pounds them back and all whom the ruthless Sun in the torrid zone, arching amidst the four cool zones of the earth sunders far from us."[9]

That clashing of Europe and Asia, so recent in the memory of Romans as men like Crassus, Pompey, and Julius Caesar all ventured into the Orient, is thus placed back as the very founding movement of Roman history. The clashing of Europe and Asia in the *Aeneid* evokes the exotic adventures and "grueling war" against Parthia, Egypt, and the Jews, which had recently transpired. Again, in reading or listening to these words, the Roman reader would have instantly known what Virgil was describing and deliberately evoking.

Virgil's ability to draw from such a diverse and extensive wellspring of memory and consciousness testifies to his genius and the importance of story, memory, and consciousness to the Roman people. Every sentence of Virgil's grand epic touches the memory of his readers. It awakens and enlightens the mind and moves the soul to pity, compassion, and anger, all at the same time.

8. Virgil, *Aeneid*, 216.
9. Virgil, *Aeneid*, 220.

This reaching into the wellspring of consciousness, of memory, of history, is the leitmotif that Virgil employs to push his story forward. As he needs, he taps into the living memory of the Roman mind to produce the grandest of imagery drawn from the reality of Roman history. In fact, from Dido to Turnus—the Punic Wars to the Greek Wars—we see the progression of the epic as contingently tied to the memory of Rome's chronological history, culminating, of course, with the Battle of Actium and the triumph of order and civilization. And that is precisely how the epic ends, with a grand battle and the triumph of order and civilization in a strange and disordered land. The closing of the *Aeneid* is the image of the Battle of Actium and the defeat of Antony and Cleopatra.

In an age when other histories of Rome were being written, Virgil had the audacity to tap into the living wellspring of the Roman psyche and tell a tale that T.S. Eliot rightly called "our classic." Virgil's epic will remain the quintessential Western epic, so long as there is a West whose patrimony runs through the same history and personages that moved the *Aeneid* from start to finish. Virgil draws on the consciousness of memory and history to fill his story with the particular consciousness of a particular people and their particular patrimony. Yet it wasn't until the twentieth century that the memorialized historical consciousness on which Virgil drew, and from which the West drew in teaching art, music, and poetry, began to be discarded. The memorialized historical consciousness from which Virgil drew was the same from which Pascal drew when he wrote in his *Pensées*, "How fine it is to see, with the eyes of faith, Darius and Cyrus, Alexander, the Romans, Pompey and Herod working, without knowing it, for the glory of the Gospel!"[10]

To construct the past, the mystic seed of Rome's origin, Virgil dipped into the living consciousness of the present. In doing so, he united past and present together. Indeed, he offered a comforting future from this union of past and present in challenging and changing times. The liveliness of the *Aeneid*, its blushing and passionate characters and their actions, were drawn from the realities of history and Rome's lived experience.

The *Aeneid* was only possible because the Roman people had the memory and consciousness to make it possible. Virgil's well of memory was living when he wrote his masterpiece. It is up to us to ensure that its living well of memory doesn't dry up. Without it, the *Aeneid* will pass into the dustbin of history like the corpses of Priam and Pompey.

10. Pascal, *Pensées*, 99.

This essay was originally published in *The Imaginative Conservative*, 1 October 2019.

8

From Diotima to Christ

Augustine's Visionary Ascents in *Confessions*

SAINT AUGUSTINE'S *CONFESSIONS* IS RIGHTLY CONSIDERED A CLASSIC OF Western literature as much as it is a masterpiece of theology and philosophy. The Latin prose is remarkable. Most vernacular translations are equally poetic and unforgettable. Over the course of Augustine's odyssey to conversion, he experiences two visionary ascents and hints at numerous failed attempts earlier in his life.

The odyssey of Augustine's soul in *Confessions* has been much discussed in academic and theological literature. Suffice it to say, there is a beautiful double paradox in Augustine's journey. On the one hand, the odyssey of Augustine's soul is an interior journey to find himself. As he reflects before and after his conversion, *mihi quaestio factus sum*: what am I?

On the other hand, the odyssey of Augustine's restless soul manifests itself in physical potentiality leading to movement. It is as much an interior as an exterior journey, a journey of the soul but also one which affects the body. Not only is Augustine's restless heart burning within him, but his restless heart is leading to the journey of his soul to real places, where he suffers real temptations and struggles. The movement to God takes him from Thagaste to Carthage—that "region of destitution."[1] From Carthage, a literal Babylon in Augustine's mind, to Rome, and eventually to Milan. In Carthage, that bubbling cesspool of sin in which Augustine's disordered heart pleasured, his attempts to ascend to God fail and fail miserably.

---

1. Augustine, *Confessions*, 34.

While Augustine has fallen into a life of sin while a professor of rhetoric at Carthage, Saint Monica, his mother, has dreams of his eventual conversion. Augustine rebuffs the visions of which she tells him. However, it
seems that Augustine was not totally convinced by his own protests.

After having the conversation about Monica's dreams, Augustine informs us that he was in a deep mire of darkness and falsehood. "Despite my
frequent efforts to climb out of it, I was the more heavily plunged back into
the filth and wallowed in it."[2] Augustine tells us here, almost immediately
after discussing with Monica her dreams, that he was attempting an ascent
out of the abyss that he was in, implying that he was unconvinced by his
own explaining away of his mother's dream. Augustine's restless heart was,
indeed, restless in its sin; it was most frenzied in its state of sin, which is
what compelled Augustine's then wicked will to engage in the acts it did.

Later, while he was still shackled to sin in Carthage, Augustine states
that he again tried to approach God in his inquisitiveness and burning restlessness. Where as before his weakness led him to sinker deeper into sin,
this time it was his puffed-up pride that kept him from ascending to God. "I
tried to approach you, but you pushed me away so that I should taste death,
for you resist the proud," he says.[3] As before, he failed in this quest to ascend
to God.

It is interesting to note that these early attempts to ascend to God are
not so much described as hinted at. They end in failure, and Augustine's
reflections on these failed early attempts to ascend to God focus only on the
disastrous consequences rather than on the weak and prideful attempts to
ascend. He merely hints at the climb and informs us of his miserable failures
rather than going into detail about the failure of his attempts to ascend to
God.

Moreover, these failed early attempts at climbing the ladder to God fail
when Augustine is in that province of barren destitution. Devoid of truth,
wallowing in spiritual darkness, and living a life according to the wicked
will, Augustine's attempts to ascend to God are not only held back because of
his spiritual state; they are held back because of the physical place in which
he is sinning. The emptiness of Carthage leads to empty attempts to ascend,
whereby he falls back into the crackling and burning frying pan of his illicit
loves. Carthage is not just a spiritual barrier but also a physical barrier to his
journey with God. Augustine needs to leave this region of destitution before
he can glimpse the beatific vision. It is while he is in Carthage that he makes
constant references to slavery and law; Augustine depicts Carthage not only

2. Augustine, *Confessions*, 50.
3. Augustine, *Confessions*, 68.

as a spiritual bondage which he is unable to overcome but also as a physical bondage from which he must be freed, like a slave, before he can glimpse truth and journey to God's heavenly fragrance and abundance.

The first of Augustine's detailed visionary ascents is described in Book VII during his famous discourse on the nature of evil. Having traveled from sinful Carthage to a godlier place in Milan, Augustine's odyssey to God is now freed from the bondage of sin that was his lust and from Carthage itself, which indulged his lusts. As mentioned, Augustine's two visions do not occur in that region of destitution to which he was handed in his state of sin. Though not yet having found Christ, Augustine has now been freed of many of the temptations and errors that constrained him while in Carthage. In a deeply poetic sense, Augustine has been freed from sin in his deliverance from Carthage to Milan. It should not be a surprise to us then that Augustine's glimpse of God and conversion to him who is life occurs in Milan rather than in Carthage.

While in Milan, dithering away his time, being uncommitted to Catholicism, Augustine comes across the "books of the Platonists." With the vestiges of his Manichean faith shattered, Augustine's reading of Plotinus leads him to return to himself. Having physically traveled to a godlier place, Augustine is ready to travel inwardly to a godlier place too. While not yet having been cleansed by the water of baptism, Augustine is cleansed by Plotinus of his Manichean mindset, of only being able to think in terms of corporeal substances. "By the Platonic books," he informs us, "I was admonished to return to myself."[4]

Cleansed from the pollution of Manichaeism, but not yet saved by Christ and his sacraments, Augustine's ascent by introspection is a thoroughly Neoplatonic one. By his own will and through the guidance of Plotinus, Augustine lifts himself up, transcends his mind, and enters into himself, which was also a penetration into the invisible God from whom he strayed but who never strayed from him. "I entered and with my soul's eye, such as it was, saw above that same eye of my soul the immutable light higher than my mind—not the light of every day, obvious to anyone, nor a larger version of the same kind which would, as it were, have given out a much brighter light and filled everything with its magnitude."[5]

Here, Augustine catches a glimpse of the sublime. Having done so on his own account, however, he is too weak to sustain it. He comes crashing down in spectacular fashion. "When I first came to know you, you raised me up to make me see that what I saw is Being, and that I who saw am not

4. Augustine, *Confessions*, 123.

5. Augustine, *Confessions*, 123.

yet Being. And you gave a shock to the weakness of my sight by the strong radiance of your rays, and I trembled with love and awe. And I found my-self far from you."[6] Again, we encounter a beautiful paradox in Augustine's writings.

Augustine does not yet know the name of Christ, but he later admits that he hears the voice of God in this visionary ascent. Having glimpsed the strong radiance of God's rays, like a blinding and sublime light, Augustine trembles with love and awe at this sight of absolute sublimity which is deadly to the mortal soul without the armor of Christ. In this glimpse of the beatific vision, he ends up reflecting not at how close he was to God but how far away he was. "I found myself far from you 'in a region of dissimilarity,' and heard as it were your voice from on high: 'I am the food of the fully grown; grow and you will feed on me.'"[7] For the first time in the text, Augustine's intellectual prowess is not polluted by pride but graced with humility.

Having glimpsed the eternal light from a distance, Augustine recogniz-es how far away he truly was. His soul was wasting away like a spider's web. From this ascent, he subsequently falls back to earth as he is not cupped in the hands of God. He did not gain salvation, but his mind was purified from the putridity of Manichaeism and was now able to think correctly about the nature of good and evil.

It is interesting to note at this point that Augustine's ability to now reflect on the nature of good and evil was not wholly from this Neoplatonic ascent up Diotima's ladder. In this ascent, far away from God as he still was, he also heard the spoken Word. He will hear the spoken Word again in Milan in a far more powerful fashion too. In that duality, Augustine's mo-mentary ascent to the fearful yet spectacular sublime allows him—upon his crash back to earth—to write about the nature of evil. It is only after several scriptural injunctions, the hearing of God's voice, and the Platonist books which freed his mind from the errors of Manichaeism, that Augustine can write about the nature of evil. This vision serves as a prefiguration of his hearing words and reading scriptural injunctions, which lead to his conver-sion in the garden at Milan.

This ascent, as mentioned, is not one that leaves Augustine in a state of pride. If anything, he is still a burning mess, and his heart is still frenzied. In a certain sense, the odyssey of his soul is just beginning. Rather than being convinced of the truth of Platonism, which does not contain the name of Christ, he becomes convinced of the limits of Platonism, precisely because these books do not contain the saving name of Christ. It is another moment

6. Augustine, *Confessions*, 123.
7. Augustine, *Confessions*, 124.

of delicious paradox in Augustine's pilgrimage. Moreover, it is because this ascent was prompted by the books of the Platonist that Augustine was too weak to see anything but the distant but splendid rays of light.

"I sought a way to obtain strength enough to enjoy you; but I did not find it until I embraced 'the mediator between God and man, the man Christ Jesus,' who is above all things, God blessed for ever . . . . To possess my God, the humble Jesus, I was not yet humble enough."[8] Augustine, far from puffed-up pride as a strictly non-Christian Platonist might have received in glimpsing such an awe-inspiring vision (like Porphyry), falls away from the very Platonism that pushed him up the ladder to catch sight of eternity from a faraway distance. The books of the Platonists, Augustine informs us, may have opened his mind to seek immaterial truth, but the books of the Platonists did not contain the name to whom every knee should bend and every tongue confess as Lord.

Nevertheless, Augustine sees God's providence in having him delivered over to the Platonists first before coming to absolute truth. "I believe that you wanted me to counter them before I came to study your scriptures. Your intention was that the manner in which I was affected by them should be imprinted in my memory, so that when later I had been made docile by your books and my wounds were healed by your gentle fingers, I would learn to discern and distinguish the difference between presumption and confession."[9] The growth of Augustine to see the sacramental reality of God's sovereignty and providence is an important development in his odyssey. He was broken down by God in a manner appropriate to him. He was humbled intellectually by being so far away and recognizing how far from God he was.

The second great visionary ascent in Augustine's masterpiece comes after his conversion and baptism, on his return trip to Africa. Departing from Milan, Augustine, Monica, and his friends arrive at Ostia, where Monica falls ill and eventually dies. With Monica ill, Augustine bonds with her in a way never seen before. While Augustine was clearly a mama's boy in between the lines—which is why he wanted to escape from her presence in the first place—he depicts himself as often being at a distance from his mother. She prays and weeps for him. Now, however, they have a bonding and binding vision together. Instead of being apart, they are now side by side.

This is also the second vision containing the two of them; the first was Monica's dream about Augustine's eventual conversion. The difference

8. Augustine, *Confessions*, 128.
9. Augustine, *Confessions*, 130.

between that vision and this one was that the first was to Monica alone; Augustine was a phantom vision in her dream, rather than a flesh-and-blood son beside her. Now they have a vision together in each other's arms, rather than a vision of the other in one's dreams.

There is a beautiful dialectical contrast in the visionary ascent at Ostia with the one Augustine experienced at Milan. As with Monica's dream where Augustine was absent (present only in dream form), his vision at Ostia includes Monica by his side, whereas his previous vision in Milan was by himself. There is a beautiful movement in how the loose-ended visions that Augustine and Monica had earlier in the work are tied up at Ostia. From loneliness to loving company, the vision at Ostia is one of relationality.

Because this ascent is relational, the ascent is also the product of a dialogue. Traces of Diotima's speech and ladder from Plato's *Symposium* are readily recognizable here. However, the vision at Ostia is not only explicitly Christian; it is also born from an explicitly Christian conversation and binds the conversation of Monica and Augustine to the power of the spoken Word in biblical revelation. Throughout the Bible, from creation to the patriarchs to the prophets, to Christ commanding the dead to rise and the blind to see, God's transformative wisdom and power come about by acts of speech—acts of *diálogos*. True wisdom is found in having a conversation, because conversation is deeply intimate and personal.

As Augustine confesses:

> The conversation led us towards the conclusion that the pleasure of the bodily sense, however delightful in the radiant light of this physical world, is seen by comparison with the life of eternity to not even be worth consideration. Our minds were lifted up by an ardent affection towards eternal being itself. Step by step we climbed beyond all corporeal objects and the heaven itself, where sun, moon, and stars shed light on the earth. We ascended even further by internal reflection and dialogue and wonder at your works, and we entered into our own minds. We moved up beyond them so as to attain to the region of inexhaustible abundance where you feed Israel eternally with truth for food. There life is the wisdom by which all creatures come into being, both things which were and which will be. But wisdom itself is not brought into being but is as it was and always will be. Furthermore, in this wisdom there is no past and future, but only being, since it is eternal . . . . And while we talked and panted after it, we touched it in some small degree by a moment of concentration of the heart. And we sighed and left behind us the 'firstfruits' of the Spirit bound to that higher world, as we

returned to the noise of our human speech where a sentence has
both a beginning and an ending.[10]

The ascent begins by dialogue. The ascent advances through dialogue: "We
ascended even further by internal reflection and dialogue and wonder at
your works."[11] Even the descent back to earth is accompanied by dialogue.
The ascent that Monica and Augustine have together is an ascent pushed by
their love for each other, which is a manifestation of God's love, which fuels
their climb.

As before, there are several wonderful paradoxes and closures that
are brought about in this Neoplatonic, to be sure, but also explicitly Christian ascent. First, the ascension begins through conversation and advances
through conversation before both "entered into [their] own minds."[12] Yet
Augustine continues to speak in the plural, implying that even though he
and Monica have entered their own minds, their entering into their own
minds drew them even closer together than before.

Second, the vision is not merely a change in the sense that the prior
ascent was done in isolation, while this ascent was done in companionship.
The visionary ascent at Ostia overturns the image of the desolate region of
sin that had shut down Augustine's earlier attempts to climb to God while
in Carthage. At Ostia, freed from that barren wasteland to which he was
handed over in his lusts, the visionary ascent brings him out of Carthage—
literally and spiritually—to a "region of inexhaustible abundance."[13] From
Carthage to Ostia, Augustine has moved from a place of physical and spiritual destitution to a place of physical and spiritual abundance. His cup over-
floweth not with his illicit loves but with the love of God and love of others.

Third, the truth he sought in Carthage as a Manichean is realized in
the truth and wisdom which is pure being—truth and wisdom—in the beatific vision at Ostia.

Fourth, Monica's dream and Augustine's visionary ascent in Milan
were received in isolation; now they share a vision together rather than
apart from each other. Where Monica's dream shared a spiritual presence
of Augustine, the vision at Ostia has him spiritually and physically by her
side—the two conjoined as one in multiples senses here.

Fifth, because Augustine's vision in Milan was by pure mind and
without company, it began in thought but couldn't sustain it, ending with
dialogue. The vision at Ostia, by contrast, both begins and ends in dialogue

10. Augustine, *Confessions*, 171.

11. Augustine, *Confessions*, 171.

12. Augustine, *Confessions*, 171.

13. Augustine, *Confessions*, 171.

with a loving mother. Rather than crashing down, Augustine returns to earth peacefully with his mother; and this return to earth Augustine captures so beautifully when he says, "we returned to the noise of our human speech where a sentence has both a beginning and an ending."[14]

Sixth, Augustine's earlier ascent ended in a vision where he reflected on how distant he was from the sublimity he encountered. In this vision, he not only beholds but touches. He can touch, along with Monica, not because of a concentrated mind but because of a concentrated heart. Love is intimate and something beyond that of the concentrated mind of Platonic love. By saying that it was the concentration of the heart that brought them to beholding and touching, Augustine shifts from the emphasis of intellect to the primacy of love: It is not by having a strong mind that one is capable of ascent and touching; it is by having a strong heart that one is capable of ascent and touching, because love is deeply intimate.

The vision at Ostia is a triumph in every possible sense of the word. It is a triumph of love through and through. It is a triumph of linguistic and literary skill. It is a triumph of dialogue. It is a triumph of chronological closure where the loose and incomplete visions and places of dwelling earlier in *Confessions* converge to a culminating point of abundance and completeness.

Augustine's *Confessions* is an odyssey of the soul. It is an odyssey of the human heart. It is an odyssey of the will. The odyssey of the *imago Dei* is completed in the threefold act of visions contained in *Confessions*.

The first act of vision(s) is merely hinted at and not given to the reader. Rather than concentrate on the visions, Augustine concentrates on the failures. The second act of vision occurs in Milan when Augustine has left behind the cesspool of Carthage for the more spiritual and godlier region of Milan. Not yet a Christian, this ascent is an act of the mind and done in isolated contemplation. He glimpses the blinding light of Christ but only at a very far distance before crashing back to earth. He wasn't saved, but he freed his mind from Manichean thinking. Now he needed to free his heart and will, which would come during his dramatic and unforgettable conversion in the gardens of Milan.

The final act of vision at Ostia is the culmination of the odyssey of the *imago Dei*. And the third vision is a vision of images. Augustine and Monica are together. Love flows freely between them and through them. The ascent begins in dialogue, like how God begins all things in dialogue. From a region of barren destitution, falsity, and slavery, the vision advances to a "region of inexhaustible abundance," where truth and wisdom are given

---

14. Augustine, *Confessions*, 171.

freely. The movement of the human images to the divine image is not one of intellectual prowess but of willful, that is loving, self-giving. The love that allows Monica and Augustine not only to behold but to touch is through the concentration of the heart rather than the concentration of the mind, which failed Augustine at Milan. Rather than burning out and falling back to earth, Monica and Augustine are gently carried back to the earth, as if on the wings of angels, and softly planted back together beside each other in a loving embrace.

This essay was originally published in *The Imaginative Conservative*, 9 March 2019.

9

The Song of Roland

The Triumph of Fealty, Truth, and Love

THE SONG OF ROLAND IS A STIRRING FRENCH MEDIEVAL POEM AND CLASSIC of medieval literature. It is the most well known *chanson de geste* (song of heroic deeds) and is an exhilarating and remarkable synthesis of the Frankish heroic and tribal tradition and Christianity. The poem manages to combine the Frankish virtues and values of honor, heroism, and fealty with a Christian theology of love, truth, and wisdom in a dazzling tale that truly represents the birth of the literary genus of medieval Christendom, the mixture of the heroic tradition of Frankish-Saxon tribalism and of the theological virtues of Christianity that eventually culminated in Torquato Tasso's *Jerusalem Delivered* in the sixteenth century.

Though the poem's author remains anonymous, the poet sets the tale in a historical context (though he certainly aggrandizes aspects of history, as all great poets do). The historical situatedness of the poem is the late eighth century in the immediate aftermath of the Battle of Tours and the Frankish defeat of Islamic forces that had conquered the Iberian Peninsula and invaded southern France. Charlemagne, not yet the emperor of Christendom (though stated to be emperor in the poem), had forged an alliance with the Abbasid Caliphate to afford him a campaign against the breakaway caliphate power in Iberia, the Umayyad Caliphate now centered in Cordoba. Having an alliance with the Baghdad caliphs, Charlemagne, with invitation from pro-Abbasid emirs in northern Spain, invaded the Pyrenees and began a long campaign against the Umayyads. The battle of which the poem sings is loosely based on the Battle of Roncevaux Pass, where Basque troops ambushed the rearguard of Charlemagne's forces and annihilated it.

The date of the poem's composition is still debated. Some favor an early date around the 1030s to 1040s, while others prefer a later date around the year 1100. The later date argument rests on the obvious theological drama of the poem. Christianity is represented by the Franks. "Paganism" is represented by the Saracens of King Marsile and the Islamic religion that they profess. Moreover, the twelfth-century dating also puts the poem at the birth of the *chanson de geste* genre, which included a trilogy of heroic poems dealing with the Crusades known as the "Crusade Cycle" (*Chanson d'Antioche, Chanson des Chétifs,* and *Chanson de Jérusalem*). The argument for the late date rests upon the assumption that the poem reflects the realities of the First Crusade and the battle between Christianity and Islam. This, however, is somewhat inconsequential to us, given the intensity of the poem and its values and symbolism, which don't depend on the early or later dating of the poem.

The poem is filled with grand characters given tremendous description. We are told of gallant knights and feudal lords with named swords and horses. We are told of their shiny armor, gold-platted shields, and glistening rings and necklaces. We are told of men with broad and noble physiques, long beards, and fierce eyes. The men of the poem come to life in a deeply picturesque way.

But it is in these characters that the poem communicates the values and virtues that the poet found important. The battle between Christianity and paganism that pervades the poem is not just a theological struggle; it is also a battle of fealty and truth against treachery and deceit. The characters who are lauded in the poem are depicted as being true vassals and honorable and heroic men, men who speak wisdom and truth and do not deceive those around them. The characters who are excoriated are depicted as conniving traitors and deceitful liars whose treachery and lies are the cause of their demise. As such, the feudal values of eleventh- and twelfth-century France are married to Christianity, while the negative values of eleventh- and twelfth-century France are associated with pagan Saracenism.

There are four principal characters in the poem: Roland, Charlemagne (Charles in English translations), Marsile, and Ganelon. Even though Roland's companions Oliver and Archbishop Turpin are also central characters, I have not included them among the four principal movers because Oliver and Turpin already exhibit and embody what Roland largely embodies—that is, fealty. The principal characters of the drama embody the values, positive or negative, that feudal France would have understood and known well.

Charlemagne is the simplest character to understand. He is the head of the feudal system and the emperor and king of the "fair land of France."[1] He is both general and missionary, king and servant. Charlemagne's first introduction is in the opening lines of the poem, "Charles the king, our great emperor."[2] Charlemagne's first speaking lines come after a successful campaign against King Marsile, the poet's invented king of Iberia. Charlemagne is contemplating returning home and enjoying the fruits of peace when the song begins.

There is a certain democratic atmosphere in the council. Democracy here is not the rule of the people as much as it is reflective of that older Anglo-Saxon and Frankish tradition of oligarchic and aristocratic self-rule that eventually morphed into civil self-rule in England and the United States. Though Charlemagne is recounted as emperor and king, by which he does have final authority, he nonetheless asks for advice from his noble lords. It is in this council of war and peace that Roland and Ganelon are introduced.

Roland suspects Marsile of treachery and makes this bluntly known to all around him. Marsile and his emissaries, as understood by Charlemagne, want peace. They are even going as far as to sacrifice their sons and convert to Christianity to save their power. But the Saracens are obviously deceitful in their intentions—at least, this is what Roland suspects. While Charlemagne is skeptical of Marsile's offer, the allure of the "fair land of France" and the possibility to enjoy peace are extremely enticing to the war-weary Franks. Though skeptical of Marsile's intentions, Charlemagne seeks peace and a return to home.

It is Roland therefore who acts as the only buttress against Saracen deception. When Roland speaks, he reminds the council that the Saracens have not been trustworthy since the war began. If they have never been trustworthy before, why should they be trusted now? As he reminds all, "King Marsile committed a most treacherous act; / He sent fifteen of his pagans, / each bearing an olive branch. / They addressed you with these very same words; / You sought advice from your Franks / And they counselled you in a somewhat reckless fashion. / You sent two of your counts . . . . / He took their heads on the hills beneath Haltile."[3]

Roland's speech reminds us of the deceit and treachery that Marsile has already committed and shown himself willing to commit to hold onto power. Through Roland's speech, we witness the manifestation of the struggle between truth and deceit, which is reflected and embodied in tribal

1. *Song of Roland*, 47.

2. *Song of Roland*, 29.

3. *Song of Roland*, 35.

fealty even unto death. Roland is trustworthy. He gives the wise advice during the council's deliberation, thus establishing Roland as a wise and heroic baron to Charlemagne. But he is overruled by his stepfather, Ganelon.

There is, on closer inspection, a longstanding rivalry and jealousy between Ganelon and Roland. The two dislike each other. One could go so far as to say they hate each other. In fact, Ganelon pronounces his hatred for Roland during and after the council in which he is selected by Charlemagne to meet with King Marsile. Ganelon believes that he will die on this mission, though Charlemagne's will, as lord and king, must be obeyed. Ganelon curses his compatriots as he leaves.

Ganelon is introduced in negative terms: "Ganelon came, who committed the act of treason."[4] The poet writes as if the audience or reader already knows of the treachery of Ganelon. Whenever Ganelon is around and speaks, the poet makes clear that he was the one who betrayed Roland and, more importantly, betrayed Charlemagne. As such, Ganelon betrayed all France and the very virtues and values that fair France and Christianity represent.

But the poet also describes Ganelon as a tempting figure; he is truly a prince of this world. In this respect, Ganelon is based on the greatest traitor and rebel of all time: Lucifer. Like Lucifer, Ganelon is well-spoken and a dashing and handsome figure. The poet describes Ganelon's earthly appearance in glowing terms: "His eyes flashed, his face was very fierce. / His body was noble, his torso broad; / So handsome was he that all his peers gaze at him."[5]

When Ganelon arrives at the court of King Marsile to make peace between the two kings, he hatches a plan to kill Roland under the pretext that if Roland lives, the two great kingdoms will be forever at war. Through his own deceit and treachery, Ganelon acts in a manner where he could defend himself as having complied with Charlemagne's will but also having rid himself of the thorn in his side (Roland). As Ganelon says, "If anyone killed [Roland], we should then all have peace."[6]

To underscore the depravity of Ganelon's actions, as Ganelon discusses with Blancandrin (King Marsile's advisor) the plan to kill Roland and secure peace, the poet again interjects his disapproval of treachery: "[Blancandrin] took Ganelon by the fingers of his right hand / And leads him to the king in the garden. / There they plan the wicked act of treason."[7] When Ganelon

4. *Song of Roland*, 34.
5. *Song of Roland*, 38.
6. *Song of Roland*, 41.
7. *Song of Roland*, 45.

convinces King Marsile to ambush Roland as Charlemagne and the army are returning to France, the poet again reiterates the depravity of Ganelon's actions when he seals his pact with the Saracens, saying, "[Ganelon] swore the treason and committed his crime."[8]

After devising the plan of battle, Ganelon is showered with praise by the Saracen nobles. They call him a "truly noble man,"[9] though the audience, thanks to the poet, knows otherwise. The various nobles also give Ganelon many gifts: swords, necklaces, jewels, and more. Ganelon wins the affections of this world, and his treasures are of this world. Ganelon wins earthly prizes for his treachery and is therefore barred from the gates of paradise, which, as we shall see, are open to those who uphold fealty even unto death.

In the poem, not only is Ganelon the devil in disguise but he also mirrors the other great biblical traitor found in the New Testament. As the battle rages, the poet alludes to Judas in conjunction with Ganelon's treachery. As Charlemagne weeps for Roland and his brave lords being killed in battle, the poet says, "[Charlemagne] was ill served that by Ganelon / Who went to Saragossa to sell his household; / He was later to lose his life and his limbs. / In the trial at Aix he was condemned to hang / And thirty of his relatives with him / Who did not expect to die."[10]

Here Ganelon morphs from Lucifer incarnate to Judas incarnate. Ganelon's betrayal of Charlemagne echoes the biblical testament of Judas's betrayal of Jesus for thirty pieces of silver by the "thirty of his relatives"[11] who died with him. Moreover, just as Judas hung himself and lost life and limb, so too will Ganelon be hung and lose life and limb in the process. Treachery is a most serious crime and sin. In fact, it is the worst crime and sin. The poet reinforces the depiction of Ganelon as a Judas during his trial scene near the conclusion of the work. Charlemagne declares: "[Ganelon] betrayed the twelve peers for money."

King Marsile, the pagan Saracen ruler of Spain in the poem, is the embodiment of deceitfulness and worldly power and is the contrast to Charlemagne's noble character. Interestingly enough, the poem opens in Marsile's court after the brief invocation of Charlemagne as lord and emperor. Marsile and Blancandrin (the king's wicked advisor) deliberate how best to maintain their rule despite the defeats they have suffered from Charlemagne and his forces. That is when they devise the plan to offer peace by

8. *Song of Roland*, 48.
9. *Song of Roland*, 43.
10. *Song of Roland*, 74.
11. *Song of Roland*, 74.

swearing fealty and conversion. The intent is to buy time to rebuild and strike later.

Unlike Ganelon, Marsile and the pagan Saracens are not traitors. They are, however, untrustworthy and deceitful people. They are interested only in power. As previously mentioned, Blancandrin is willing to go as far as offering his son as a sacrifice to temporarily gain peace and to recover their forces to do battle and defeat Charlemagne later. Though not traitors in the way Ganelon is, the pagan Saracens in the poem embody everything contrary to the virtues and values of Frankish fealty, loyalty, and loving servitude.

Through the contrasts of Marsile with Charlemagne and Roland, the poet presents Christianity as the religion in which trust and loving fealty reach their highest aspirations. Paganism, which is Saracenism in the poem, is cast as the dialectical opposite of Christianity. Those who seek power and are willing to lie and steal to obtain power (or hold power) cannot be good Christians or good vassals. Pagan Saracenism reveals itself as being incompatible with being a good lord; in short, pagan Saracenism as recounted in the poem forsakes fealty and leads to death (as we shall see). Therefore, Marsile embodies the antithetic ideals and values of Charlemagne, Roland, and Christianity.

The heart of the poem is the battle where Roland and his companions die. The battle is the instantiation of the values of tribal fealty that the poet is promoting. The Franks, under Roland, show themselves to be pious Christians and good vassals in their heroic stand against Marsile's army. They all, eventually, perish for their lord and land.

During the battle narrative, the thematic contrast between truth and deceit is also coursing through the lines as men have their limbs hacked off and entrails spilled out over the field. The first three pagans to die—Aelroth (nephew of King Marsile and therefore the blood opposite to Roland, who is Charlemagne's nephew), Duke Falsaron (brother of King Marsile), and King Corsablix (the Berber king and ally to King Marsile)—fall because they all utter a lie which demands that they be cut down. Lying is tied to death throughout the poem. Archbishop Turpin says it best when he kills Corsablix: "Vile pagan, you have told a lie; / [Charlemagne], my lord, will always guard us well."[12] Not only are the pagan warriors who speak lies during the battle struck down, so too is the greatest liar of them all (Ganelon) struck down by poem's end.

12. *Song of Roland*, 69.

To help underscore the negativity of treachery and bloodlust, the greatest of the pagan warriors, Abisme, is killed by Archbishop Turpin. Abisme is described as the greatest and most vile of villains in King Marsile's army:

> Out in the front rides a Saracen, Abisme;
> [King Marsile] had no greater villain in his company,
> A man of evil traits and mighty treachery.
> He does not believe in God, the son of the Virgin Mary;
> And is as black as molten pitch.
> He loves treachery and murder
> More than he would love all the gold in Galicia.
> No one has ever seen him play or laugh;
> He is a man of courage and great zeal
> And thereby a friend to Marsile, the treacherous king.[13]

But not all the pagan warriors are hewn down in battle. Margariz, "a very valiant knight, / Handsome, strong, swift and nimble," attacks Oliver early in the battle.[14] Margariz has spoken no lies about Charlemagne or the "fair land of France." Margariz is not killed when he attacks Oliver (who in turn is spared by a miraculous intervention by God during their duel). This, I think, is worth remembering when observing the contrast of values: the pagan antagonists who utter lies are all killed at some point in the poem.

The graphic and grotesque description of killing in the *Song of Roland* mirrors that of other great epic literature of antiquity. But by including commentary on the high virtues of fealty (honesty and loyalty), it differs dramatically from the language of antique heroic literature. Homer, Virgil, and Statius, in their respective poems, simply describe the horrific deaths of those men slain in combat. The men who die in antique heroic literature die because of the audacity of their opponents or the actions of the gods deflecting arrowheads and spear shafts. This is not the case in the *Song of Roland*. While the poem does describe in brutal and gory detail some of the killing blows, many of the pagan warriors who are slain die because of some preceding act of lying on their part, which the poet feels the need to include before killing them off.

The poet then could not make the association with lying and death any clearer than having men who have lied quickly slain on the battlefield in the most gruesome of ways. Their eyes are gouged out of their sockets. Their faces are split in half by sword strikes. Their brains spill out of their helmet. Listeners of the poem would have no illusion about the severity of lying. Lying is a betrayal of truth, but it is also a betrayal of one's duty to king

13. *Song of Roland*, 76.

14. *Song of Roland*, 71.

and land. Those who lie, thereby forsaking truth and betraying their oaths to king and land, must be struck down by the flaming sword of God who is also truth itself.

There is also much emotion permeating the poem. The death of Oliver breaks the heart of Roland; he clutches his friend in his arms as he passes from this world into the gates of paradise. The death of Roland, the death of Archbishop Turpin, and the weeping of Charlemagne all move the heart to pity and compassion; we are meant to weep alongside Charlemagne as he looks upon the mangled carcasses of his former friends and vassals.

But the heart of the poem communicates the values of fealty to lord and land that are combined with duty, heroism, and trustworthiness. The struggle that dominates the core of the poem, the battle between King Marsile and Roland, is not just a battle between Christianity and paganism; it is a battle for the soul of fealty and everything that eleventh- and twelfth-century France would have held so dear. Insofar as Christianity is the religion that demands fealty to king and country and is the religion of love that allows for one's love of king and country to be consummated, Christianity is the supreme religion for the Frankish people and their values.

The triumph of Roland is the triumph of fealty and all that is entailed and encompassed in the virtues and values of fealty. In his devotion to Charlemagne and the "fair land of France," Roland passed from this life into the next and was ushered into eternity. In fact, when Archbishop Turpin speaks to the men during the battle, he informs them to do their duty as lords and knights and to die as martyrs; this ensures life in paradise for them. The poet then marries tribal fealty to the highest reality offered in Christianity. Those who do their duty to lord and land reach the gates of paradise:

> And the archbishop told them what was on his mind:
> "Lord barons, do not indulge in base thoughts;
> In God's name I beg you not to flee,
> So that no man of worth can sing a shameful song.
> It is far better for us to die fighting.
> We are promised this: soon we shall meet our end;
> Beyond this day we shall cease to be alive.
> But in one thing I can act as guarantor:
> Holy paradise open to you;
> You will take your seat among the Innocents."
> At these words the Franks rejoice.[15]

The Song of Roland is a unique poem of the medieval world. The work blends Frankish-Gothic fealty and feudalism with the theological virtues of

---

15. *Song of Roland*, 77.

Christianity in a remarkable synthesis that provides for action, energy, and emotion. All the liars in play, including King Marsile (who is injured during the battle), die. The liars die because they betrayed the highest value of fealty, which is trustworthiness that is concretely manifested in duty to lord and land. There can be no mistaking the intent of this heroic song of valor. When Ganelon is hung, the poet says, "If he were *loyal,* he would seem the perfect baron."[16]

Fealty is the most important value communicated in the poem, and fealty is manifested by the love, duty, and loyalty to lord and land. The triumph and immortality of Roland is nothing short of the triumph and immortality of the fealty demanded by lord and land and consummated in the love of lord and land. Those who actualize their fealty—the highest reality of which is sacrificial love to lord and land—as Archbishop Turpin guaranteed, enter the realm of holy paradise, where loving fealty to the Supreme Lord and Land reigns forever and ever.

This essay was originally published in *The Imaginative Conservative,* 3 June 2020.

16. *Song of Roland,* 149.

10

The Pilgrimage of Love

Dante's *Divine Comedy*

Learning to Love Again: Dante's Descent in *The Inferno*

"Midway along the journey of our life / I woke to find myself in a dark wood / for I had wandered off from the straight path."[1] Thus opens Dante's grand epic of love. But why did the pilgrim poet have to descend into hell—of all places—before he could climb Mount Purgatory and take his seat in the blossoming bud of the white rose of heaven? The *Divine Comedy* is a love epic. It is the greatest love epic. It is the most ambitious love epic ever crafted by the hands of a mere mortal. Dante descends into hell to learn to love again by the most extreme examples of misdirected love and also through his relationship with Virgil.

That there is much depth to Dante is an understatement. There is much allegory, theology, political commentary, reflection on history, poetry, and economics, that give life to Dante's brilliant masterpiece. There are many ways to understand the multilayered world of hell, from its construction to why at the lowest circle, rather than a fiery pandemonium as imagined by John Milton, the lake of hell is cold, dark, and frozen. Yet the descent into the abyss that is the inferno is perplexing at first glance.

When Dante begins his epic, he states that he is having a sort of midlife existential crisis. The poem is about him. But it is about more than him. Dante says that midway along our life, he awoke to find himself in a dark

1. Dante, *Divine Comedy*, 3.

wood because he had wandered off the straight and true path. That straight and true path is the path of love.

It isn't surprising, given this reality, that the first proper circle of hell is the sphere of lust. Lust is the beginning of misdirecting love—as evidenced by the pilgrim's discussion with the wounded lusters Francesca da Rimini and Paolo Malatesta. The two had carried on an illicit affair for a decade. Francesca, in talking to Dante, subtly blames the poet. It was Dante's romance poetry that had captured the heart of Francesca and filled her heart with the erotic intent that ultimately was her own undoing. Dante takes pity on Francesca and faints.

In the beginning of all three parts of the *Divine Comedy*, Dante invokes poetry to guide him. "O muses! O high genius! Help me now!"[2] he frantically cries at the beginning of the second canto of the *Inferno*. Before ascending the slopes of Mount Purgatory, Dante invokes the muses again: "Here let death's poetry arise to life, / O muses sacrosanct whose liege I am! / And let Calliope rise up and play."[3] By the time he enters into heaven, Dante invokes Apollo (beyond being god of the sun, he was also god of poetry): "O great Apollo, for this final task, / make me a vessel worthy to receive / your genius and the longed-for laurel crown."[4]

Dante invokes the muses and gods of poetry in his journey because poetry, up through Dante's time, always had love as its great theme. The epic poetry of Homer, though surrounded by the maelstrom of war, chiefly concerns itself with love. The troubadours of Provence were love bards and poets who set the medieval world aflame—and Dante meets one such troubadour on his ascent up Mount Purgatory.

But in the Latin mind, no love poet stood out greater than Dante's own guide through hell and purgatory. Virgil was the chief poet of love in the Roman world. His epic is a grand tale of love in comparison to which Dante feels insignificant. "I am not Aeneas," he tells Virgil before journeying to the underworld.[5] Virgil's additional poetry, like the *Eclogues*, also chiefly concerns itself with love. *Omnia vincit amor*, as Virgil famously wrote in *Eclogue X*.

By invoking the muses of poetry and in being guided by Virgil, Dante tips his hand and reveals to the astute reader (or listener) that the journey into and through hell will require the flowering of love. Hell, after all, is a

---

2. Dante, *Divine Comedy*, 9.

3. Dante, *Divine Comedy*, 196.

4. Dante, *Divine Comedy*, 392.

5. Dante, *Divine Comedy*, 10.

loveless place. And Dante's journey is one in which the muses of love must nurture him.

The initial relationship between Dante and Virgil is standoffish and cold. While Virgil has been selected by Beatrice, Virgil treats Dante more as an insolent child than a son. Virgil is, at the poem's beginning, more of a reluctant guide. He regularly rebuffs Dante for his stupid questions and repeated mistakes journeying through hell. Dante repeatedly faints, much to Virgil's chagrin.

Two things are missing in their relationship when they enter into the gates which infamously reads: ABANDON EVERY HOPE, ALL YOU WHO ENTER.[6] There is a lack of trust between Dante and Virgil. As such, there is a lack of love between the two poets. In fact, these two missing ingredients are also the two missing values whose absence permeates hell itself. Moreover, the lack of trust and lack of love are also envisioned as being united together. Without trust, there can be no love; without love, there can be no trust.

While the two poets come closer through their trials and tribulations, the first major transformation in Dante and Virgil's relationship is when the poets are at the gates of the city of Dis. The famous Gorgon Medusa guards the entry. As she approaches the two, Virgil shields Dante's eyes.

This is significant for several reasons. First, Virgil had informed Dante not to look at Medusa's eyes after crossing over the River Styx. Virgil has come to care about Dante, as evidenced by the fact that he informed Dante not to look into the seductive eyes of the formerly beautiful Gorgon slayed by Perseus. Dante, we mustn't forget, is still alive, while everyone else is dead. If Dante had looked into the eyes of Medusa, he would have been killed. Virgil's reminding Dante not to look into the eyes of the Gorgon was done out of an act of concern for the pilgrim poet.

Second, the fact that Virgil shielded Dante's eyes ironically indicates his lack of trust. Despite informing Dante of the deadly powers of the Gorgon seductress, Virgil still places his arm and hand over Dante's face to prevent him from being turned to stone.

Third, the fact that Virgil shields Dante's eyes indicates his growing love for the poor pilgriming soul, even though the two still haven't reach that sacred bond of trust. (We should also remember that the ninth circle of hell is reserved for all the traitors who betrayed the trust of their benefactors, country, or family.)

The lack of trust between the two protagonists is soon remedied. Between cantos nineteen and twenty-one, there is a tremendous, grace-filled

---

6. Dante, *Divine Comedy*, 14.

metamorphosis between the two men. Dante makes the growing love exhibited between himself and Virgil the central image in a place of horrifying and pitiable images. This is, in my view, intentional. Because they are
in hell, and hell is a loveless place, love needs to grow into a burning fire
between Dante and Virgil in order for the two to further proceed down
the abyss, in order to exit hell and begin the long and arduous journey up
Mount Purgatory.

In the nineteenth canto, as the two are in the third bolgia of the
eighth circle of hell, Dante is tired on the slopes of the mountain. Yet
Dante wishes to have a conversation with one of the damned souls (soon
to be revealed as Pope Nicholas III). Exhausted, Dante appeals to his
master-becoming-father-figure:

> "Who is that one, Master, that angry wretch,
> who is writhing more than any of his comrades,"
> I asked, "the one licked by a redder flame?"
> And he to me, "If you want to be carried down
> along that lower bank to where he is,
> you can ask him who he is and why he's there."
> And I, "My pleasure is what pleases you:
> You are my lord, you know that from your will
> I will not swerve. You even know my thoughts."[7]

Here is the first great expression of self-giving and sacrificial love in
the whole of the *Inferno*. Moreover, trust between the two is growing, which
allows for the self-giving love that binds the two souls together. Virgil takes
Dante in his arms and whisks him down the slopes:

> Then he took hold of me with both his arms,
> And when he had me firm against his breast,
> He climbed back up the path he had come down.
> He did not tire of the weight clasped tight to him,
> But brought me to the top of the bridge's arch,
> The one that joins the fourth bank to the fifth.
> And here he gently set his burden down—
> Gently, for the ridge, so steep and rugged,
> Would have been hard even for goats to cross.
> From there another valley opened to me.[8]

There is no more fear or distrust in Dante reaching out and asking for
Virgil's help. Furthermore, Virgil is no longer incensed at Dante's questions

---

7. Dante, *Divine Comedy*, 101.
8. Dante, *Divine Comedy*, 105.

and pitiable condition. As the intermediary guide, a sort of *in persona Christi* in the journey through hell, Virgil is there to help carry Dante when he is exhausted and cannot continue any longer. Love, as we begin to see in flesh-and-blood imagery and activity, truly does conquer even the deepest levels of hell.

Despite the progress made in loving each other, wherein Virgil has become more of a father to Dante than a mere guide, there is a final barrier for the two to overcome. There is a hidden, invisible wall the two have yet to cross. That hidden barrier is forgiveness.

Though the two have learned to love each other in a self-giving and self-sacrificial way—with Virgil lifting up onto his being the burden that is Dante—the two have yet to learn the high value and virtue of forgiveness. Before they can proceed into the final circle of hell, this incredible literary construction on Dante's part must be realized: the two must learn to forgive each other as the highest expression of their learning to love.

In the thirtieth canto, that final barrier of learning to love is overcome. Dante, the typical childish pilgrim as he is at times in the *Inferno*, begins to dally and waste time absorbed in a debate between two narcissistic sinners (appropriately near a pond of water). Virgil is angered by Dante's dallying and accosts him. Dante tells us that in hearing Virgil's anger, he was filled with shame. Upon looking at the face of Dante, Virgil recognizes he has wronged Dante in his outburst of anger. Virgil tells Dante to forget about his outburst and forgive him. Dante pardons Virgil's outburst in the first and only act of loving forgiveness in *Inferno*:

> I was listening, all absorbed in this debate,
> when the master said to me: "Keep right on looking,
> a little more, and I shall lose my patience."
> I heard the note of anger in his voice
> and turned to him; I was so full of shame
> that it still haunts my memory today.
> Like one asleep who dreams himself in trouble
> and in his dream he wishes he were dreaming,
> longing for that which is, as if it were not,
> just so I found myself: unable to speak,
> longing to beg for pardon and already
> begging for pardon, not knowing that I did.
> "Less shame than yours would wash away a fault
> greater than yours has been," my master said,
> "and so forget about it, do not be sad.
> If ever again you should meet up with men
> engaging in this kind of futile wrangling,

remember I am always at your side;
to have a taste for talk like this vulgar!"[9]

This moment is important because, as mentioned, it is the only instance of forgiveness in the poem. Had the two not learned forgiveness, they would have been trapped in hell for all eternity. Without a moment of forgiveness, the journey to learn how to love again would have failed. Without forgiveness, Dante and Virgil would have been trapped in the eighth circle of hell. Without forgiveness, the reconciling reality of love which moves the stars would never have been revealed. In forgiveness, Dante realizes he has a fatherly figure "always at [his] side."[10]

In Dante's sojourn through hell, the great poet-pilgrim learned how to love again. It was his forgetting how to love that had caused him to wander from the straight and true and into a dark wood reminiscent of the cold darkness of hell. Hell is a cold, dark, and loveless place. The only light, warmth, and love that flickered through the nine circles was the love that Dante and Virgil learned in the presence of each other. Having learned love, they conquered hell together and began their ascent up Mount Purgatory with the beautiful stars as their guide: "I saw the lovely things the heavens hold, / and we came out to see once more the stars."[11]

Ascending the Mountain of Love: Purgatorio

"Here let death's poetry arise to life, / O Muses sacrosanct whose liege I am! / And let Calliope rise up and play / her sweet accompaniment in the same strain / that pierced the wretched magpies with the truth / of unforgivable presumptuousness."[12] Thus was Dante's opening prayer as he entered Purgatory and prepared to climb the seven-story mountain of love. Dante's *Divine Comedy* is more than just a Florentine's fantasy of revenge and poetic allegory of the Christian faith. In many ways it was an epic paying homage to the Book, interweaving, however, the history of love from the pen of mortals to be concurrent with the drama of salvation revealed in sacred Scripture.

Dante having "wandered off from the straight path" prefigures and foreshadows what the rest of the one hundred cantos of the poem will deal with: fleeing from that dark wilderness and returning to the straight and

9. Dante, *Divine Comedy*, 167.

10. Dante, *Divine Comedy*, 167.

11. Dante, *Divine Comedy*, 191.

12. Dante, *Divine Comedy*, 196.

true.[13] By wandering from the straight and true, Dante had strayed from love; and by finding himself in a dark wilderness, a dark forest, a blackened environ that blinded him, he had flung himself into hell by his aimless wandering. Sent by Beatrice, Dante's love, Virgil rescues him, and the two begin their famous journey to hell and back. It is noteworthy to recognize that a poet comes to guide him back to the straight and true.

There are many figures whom Dante meets and with whom he converses throughout the *Divine Comedy*. Why Virgil? Why Beatrice? Why Statius? Why Saint Bernard of Clairvaux? There is also much symbolism in the imagery of Dante's descent through hell and ascent into heaven. Why a hell that is cold and dark? Why is Purgatory a place that has light? Why is heaven the realm of the white rose? Here we shall briefly explore these questions.

There is a poetic genius to Dante's journey through hell and up Mount Purgatory. As to why Dante would choose Virgil to guide him through hell and most of Purgatory should be clear enough: Virgil was the great Roman poet of love. *Omnia vincit amor*; love conquers all. Additionally, the *Aeneid* is a grand tale of love where Aeneas embodies the love for family and fatherland through his arduous and painstaking journey to Lavinian shores. Aeneas's love for his father, his gods, and his countrymen drives him onward.

The relationship between Virgil and Dante is one of the most important developments for the reader to notice over the course of the epic. Virgil meets Dante under the direction of Beatrice. He serves as a functionary more than a friend and father figure in the opening cantos. When they begin their descent into hell, Virgil has a short temper with Dante and answers Dante's questions with a frank coldness reminiscent of the place into which they are descending. "Abandon every hope, all you who enter."[14]

Moving beyond the realm of the neutrals into Limbo, Dante is present with the great poets of antiquity. Hell begins with the poets, but the poets of love and of ancient lore have done enough to keep themselves from the punishment of what lay beyond Limbo. As Virgil and Dante descend through the remaining circles of hell, their relationship is tested, strained, but also transformed.

Hell is a loveless place. This is the primary reason why Dante constructs a cold and dark hell, and why it gets progressively colder and darker as they move into "a place where no light is."[15] Dante's facial complexion changes too to symbolize the reality of entering the inferno of death: he becomes

13. Dante, *Divine Comedy*, 3.

14. Dante, *Divine Comedy*, 14.

15. Dante, *Divine Comedy*, 125.

paler and paler. But as the two poets of love pilgrimage through hell and descend into the dark abyss which is Satan's domain, it is the love of Dante and Virgil that enables them to proceed in their journey; they become the only shining conduits of lights in a place "where no light is."[16]

Dante and Virgil bond with each other, and the two grow intimately connected to each other as they proceed down the circles of the abyss. In order to continue the journey through the loveless pit that is hell, they need to embody the love that is lacking in all the circles of hell. Virgil's concern for Dante is revealed when he shields Dante from the head of Medusa. His actions, though loving, do reflect a lack of trust between the two. That lack of trust is what must be overcome in the sixth through ninth circles of hell, where a definitive rejection of truth and trust is what permeates these lower circles of the cold and dark pit.

As they descend, the two grow in trust and love of each other. Descending into the third bolgia, Virgil helps to carry an exhausted Dante down the mountainside to converse with a damned soul (Pope Nicholas III), "If you want to be carried down / along that lower bank to where he is, / you can ask him who he is and why he's there."[17] This is a touching moment in the growing relationship between Virgil and Dante, because it represents a moment of self-giving by Virgil and receptivity to that self-giving love by Dante. "Then he took hold of me with both his arms, / And when he had me firm against his breast, / He climbed back up the path he had come down."[18]

Building on this transformation in their relationship, Virgil opens up to Dante about his home, revealing a sense of trust and friendship that eventually becomes a father-son relationship especially by their entry to and journey up Mount Purgatory. While love and trust grows between the two, which stands in stark contrast to the pits of hell where no love and trust exists, the final barrier for them to overcome—the need for forgiveness—is what they must manifest to journey into the final circle of hell. Virgil, fed up with Dante's dallying, barks at him. Realizing he has wronged Dante, Virgil asks Dante's forgiveness in the final symbolic act of their union together as companions and the necessary act of loving forgiveness to proceed into the ninth circle of hell.

Virgil's asking for forgiveness and Dante's granting of forgiveness is the only moment of forgiveness in *Inferno*. Love consummated itself in that act of forgiveness whereby the two pilgrim poets can venture into the loveless and unforgiving lair of Lucifer and all those human souls who malevolently

16. Dante, *Divine Comedy*, 125.
17. Dante, *Divine Comedy*, 101.
18. Dante, *Divine Comedy*, 105.

betrayed the trust and love of others. The genius of Dante is fully revealed in this brief but touching, indeed human, scene in the journey through hell. It is as if there was a moral, hidden, unseen barrier that the two needed to cross before descending into the final dark hole of the abyss. Without that consummated love through forgiveness, Virgil and Dante would have been stuck in the eighth circle of hell forever.

It was in hell and through hell that Dante learned love. He learned the bonding nature of love—that it is not good to be alone (as he was when we first met him wandering alone in the wilderness). He learned, through that bonding nature of love, that love requires relationships. He learned that love requires trust, which was exhibited with the trust built between Virgil and Dante. He also learned that love requires forgiveness, realized in that final and most touching—most human—episode in the thirtieth canto between Virgil and Dante that opened up the final circle of hell to them, where their love conquered death and allowed them to slip down the body of the beast and wind up at the base of Mount Purgatory, the mountain of love connecting the human world with the celestial realm of complete and total love.

Ascending Mount Purgatory is a grueling task for Dante. He is proud and therefore weighed down by his pride. Mount Purgatory has the most human of characteristics for it is the most human of the realms. Where hell saw the rejection of humanness through the corruption of love (in the circles of lust through wrath) and the formal rejection of truth and love (all the rungs of hell inside the city of Dis), Mount Purgatory is the place where love is nurtured, directed, and eventually realized at the top of the mountain. Through this realization of love, the opening up of the gates of heaven for all the pilgrims of love to enter commences.

Saint Thomas Aquinas argued that the soul is potentiality moving to actualization. In that actualization, which is found in agency, the understanding of the good, true, and beautiful to which all souls are directed realizes itself in the freedom to choose the good, true, and beautiful. Of course, what is that force, that reality, that moves the soul to actualization and the choosing of God's goodness and beauty? It is love. "Love is called the unitive force," the angelic doctor explains in the *Summa Theologiae*.[19] Love is that force that binds all things together in unitive harmony.

It is important to recognize that while hell was cold and dark, Mount Purgatory is a place where light and warmth is found. The sun appears, while it had no appearance in hell. Moreover, it is important to realize that the souls make their progress up the mountain of purifying love during sunlight. That sunlight is symbolic of love and wisdom, the light that

19. Aquinas, *Summa Theologiae*, 1.Q.20.

draws burning hearts after it. The author of Hebrews teaches that God is an all-consuming fire, and when the consuming fire of God is visible and beautifies the world of Purgatory, the souls—moved by that love—ascend closer to paradise before being able to pass from the earthly Jerusalem to the celestial Jerusalem.

The most important person Virgil and Dante meet in their pilgrimage up Mount Purgatory is the poet Statius. Statius was the author of the epic poem *Thebaid*, the second greatest Latin epic poem after Virgil's *Aeneid*. Statius serves many purposes in the poem. He is the heir of Virgil, and he was, according to Dante, a secret convert to Christianity. As such, not only is he the heir to Virgil (poetically and historically), he is the heir to Virgil as the poet instructor of love to Dante as they reach the top of Mount Purgatory. In that ascent, the poets all converse with one another about love, about the only thing that matters in life.

Statius is also the bridge connecting pagan Rome to Christian Rome. Statius represents the supersession of Virgil into the baptized waters of Christianity. Dante pays the great poet his homage by including him in the moving entourage of love poets—now numbering, symbolically, three—as they progress ever closer to the celestial realm of love about which they had all written in their own ways. The three poets of love in *Purgatorio* are burning and sojourning hearts of love who also engage in face-to-face conversation with one another (again, symbolically prefiguring the Trinity). They are then the poetic manifestation of the Trinity; for they are in a loving union with each other and engaged in acts of speech with one another.

Statius becomes the poet who symbolizes the passing of the torch of love poetry to Dante just as he took up the torch from Virgil and now, with Virgil and Statius having traveled with Dante, and Virgil returning to Limbo, that great flame passes to the immortal Florentine as they prepare to enter the realm of the white rose. Dante's inclusion of Statius in the pilgrimage is therefore theological and poetic. As mentioned, there are three poets journeying together up the mountain to enter the realm of the Trinity. Virgil may be relieved by Beatrice, thus keeping the pilgrim group at three, but the number three becomes a central guiding spirit in *Purgatorio*. Additionally, that all three are poets, and all three Romans, allows Dante to communicate the power and directionality of poetry.

Moreover, Dante's inclusion of many poets, some famous and others largely lost to history, is equally deep and essential to the movement of the *Divine Comedy*. If Dante's epic is the story of the drama of salvation—the greatest drama and story ever told—it is also a story of the history of love poetry from Hesiod and Homer (whom we met in Limbo) through Virgil and Statius, up to Arnaut Daniel, Guido Guinizelli, Bonagiunta Orbicciani, and Dante. "Here let death's poetry arise to life, / O Muses sacrosanct whose liege I am" as Dante poetically and magically began.[20]

Dante opened *Purgatorio* by brilliantly prefiguring what the journey up Mount Purgatory reveals (just as he had done in the opening lines of *Inferno*, where he cried out to muses for help: "O muses! O high genius! Help me now!"[21]). He is also informing his reader that poetry can lead to conversion and turn the human gaze up to heavenly things. In fact, without poetry—without love—we cannot ascend. That is the fundamental message of *Purgatorio*, just as it was in *Inferno*. Paradise, then, is the land to which all poetry directs the human heart and mind and, in another sense, is the land of poetic abundance where poetry (love) never ceases.

It is fitting that Dante's epic of love has the poets and the theologians of love (who are poets in their own right) guiding him into the land of the white rose (the very flower of love). Where the poets directed Dante to the celestial sphere, it is Beatrice who teaches Dante to always love God, and the great mystic theologian Saint Bernard of Clairvaux who explains to Dante the love of God that guides Dante through the heavenly spheres of love itself. Love literally carried Dante through hell. Love called Dante up Mount Purgatory. Love then instructs Dante in the cardinal and theological virtues.

Having ordered his love, and guided by poetry, Dante is ready to enter the realm of the white rose. The stars are once more the luminaries of beauty that capture his eyes while also reminding us of new growth. "From those holiest waters I returned / to her reborn, a tree renewed, in bloom / with newborn foliage, immaculate, / eager to rise, now ready for the stars."[22]

The Face of Love:
Beatrice as a Type of Christ in Paradiso

Dante's *Divine Comedy* is the greatest work of Christian literature, one of the greatest epic poems ever construed by human hands, and perhaps the greatest love song ever written by a mere mortal. T.S. Eliot famously said that the world is divided between Dante and Shakespeare and that there is no other in running contention. There are many facets and nuances to Dante's poetic splendor, but now I would like to examine Beatrice as a type of Christ—that *in persona Christi* who would have been well familiar to Dante's sacramental vision of the world and of others, wherein Beatrice acts like a prophet of

20. Dante, *Divine Comedy*, 196.
21. Dante, *Divine Comedy*, 9.
22. Dante, *Divine Comedy*, 387.

the Old Testament, pointing the way to Christ before being superseded by Christ himself.

Inferno opens with these famous lines: "Midway along the journey of our life / I woke to find myself in a dark wood / for I had wandered off from the straight path."[23] Dante's opening is remarkable in capturing everything about the human pilgrimage. He is having a quintessential midlife crisis, to speak, in recognizing his aimless wandering but not knowing how he sank to the abyss that he is in. He craves meaning and purpose; he craves understanding. In awakening to find himself in a dark wood, he is aware of his sin, his desolation, his utter emptiness for having wandered off the straight and true path of love. Indeed, the entire movement of the epic is a pilgrimage through love: Dante learns how to love in hell, learns how to order his love in purgatory, and learns the nature of divine love in heaven.

When Virgil informs Dante that he is to be his guide through hell, the old Roman poet informs the new Roman poet that a beautiful lady had summoned him and commanded him to help rescue the pilgrim poet from his aimless wandering. Beatrice's first invocation in the epic is as an angel of beauty and grace: "With eyes of light more bright than any star / in low, soft tones she started to address me / in her own language, with an angel's voice."[24] Though Beatrice is absent during Dante's sojourn through hell with Virgil, she is with him in spirit through his sacramental guide, Virgil, who has directly received the command from Beatrice's own voice. Here is part of Dante's brilliance: he needs others, not just God, to guide him back to the straight and true (and thus the pilgrim Dante is always with someone, instead of often being alone like Christian in John Bunyan's *Pilgrim's Progress*).

The awakening of Dante to new life then begins with hearing the call of Beatrice through another, much like how God spoke through the patriarchs, priests, and prophets in the Old Testament. When the prophets speak to the people of Israel in the Old Testament history, they often begin with "Thus saith the Lord" or "Hear the Lord thy God." The church's hermeneutical principle of typology led the official interpretation of the canon to mean that God, Christ, was literally speaking through the sages and prophets of old, though he himself was not yet revealed in the flesh. Dante is drawing upon this hermeneutical tradition when constructing his poem.

Beatrice doesn't appear to Dante until the thirtieth canto of *Purgatorio*. She is introduced as the embodiment of faith, hope, and love—the three theological virtues, according to Christianity. "Covering all the chariot," Dante says, "appeared a lady—over her white veil / an olive crown and,

23. Dante, *Divine Comedy*, 3.
24. Dante, *Divine Comedy*, 10.

under her green cloak, / her gown, the color of eternal flame."[25] The colors
that adorn her splendid gown each represent one of the virtues: white being
faith, green being hope, and red—the "eternal flame"—being love.

That Beatrice is dressed as she is, in the colors of the theological virtues, gives a prefiguration of the transfigured glory of heaven and all the
souls therein. Dante, as we know, had fallen madly in love with Beatrice
in earthly life. Her death, in part, caused Dante's downfall into darkness.
Now her beauty is so majestic that it whets his appetites for more; but, more
incredibly, her beauty orders his appetites to the proper order of things as
established by God (and with the help of Beatrice, who reminds Dante to
order his desires always to God).

Beatrice not only represents the supersession of pagan Rome, represented by Virgil, but she also bears the three virtues which remind us of the
Trinity—appropriate given that Dante is about to enter the abundant abode
of the Trinity. Her radiance is now that which will guide Dante into the
realm of love itself, and her guidance is that of teacher and comforter, like
the great teacher and comforter who walked the sands of Galilee. Beatrice
has become a literal vessel of light in the darkness. She brings illumination
to the world ruined in darkness.

As Beatrice begins to guide Dante through the spheres of heaven, she
reminds him, "Direct your mind and gratitude / to God, who raised us up
to His first star."[26] Like Christ, Beatrice's role here is to remind us of God
above all things. Like Christ, she leads the way for the wayward pilgrim to
be directed to all things good, true, and beautiful. She has become Dante's
teacher about the truths of the cosmos, of life, and of salvation:

> Among all things, however disparate,
> There reigns an order, and this gives the form
> That makes the universe resemble God.
> Therein God's higher creatures see
> The imprint of Eternal Excellence—
> That goal for which the system is created,
> And in this order all created things,
> According to their bent, maintain their place,
> Disposed in proper distance from their Source;
> Therefore, they move, all to a different port,
> Across the vast ocean of being, and each
> Endowed with its own instinct as guide.
> This is what carries fire toward the moon,
> This moving force of mortal heart,

25. Dante, *Divine Comedy*, 365.
26. Dante, *Divine Comedy*, 398.

This is what binds the earth and makes it one.[27]

Love, according to Beatrice, is the law of life, the law of the cosmos, and the law that makes all things whole. Love is also what orders our lives to derive the happiness that we seek. As she later tells Dante as they near the central sphere of heaven, "On that Point / depend all nature and all the heavens. / Observe the circle nearest it, and know / the reason for its spinning at such speed / is that Love's fire burns it into motion."[28]

As Dante grows with Beatrice in his understanding of love, the divine love that unaided human reason cannot know, the formerly overburdening beauty that shamed Virgil and Dante is transformed into a blessed and joyful smile that brings only happiness whenever Dante looks upon her face. Instead of fear, shame, or trembling, Dante is now enraptured by her beauty and wisdom. Moreover, after he meets the wise men of the fourth sphere of heaven, including King Solomon, Saint Albertus Magnus, and Saint Thomas Aquinas, Beatrice reminds Dante to still give thanks to God. "Then Beatrice said: 'And now give thanks, / thanks to the Sun of Angels by whose grace / you have ascended to this sun of sense.'" Dante tells us, "No mortal heart was ever more disposed to do devotion and to yield itself to God so fully and readily."[29] Beatrice's words are efficacious to the pilgrim, just as Christ's words are efficacious to those who hear and obey.

In paradise, Beatrice is a sort of high priest, conductor, and prophetess to the pilgrim Dante. She reveals to him the intricacies of the cosmos. She reveals to him how the divine love of heaven, that true love of God, is self-giving and freely receptive, and that all other types of love fall short in comparison to this freely giving and freely receiving love that binds together the Trinity and the whole cosmos. It is the self-giving and receiving love of the Trinity that flows forth to create and order all things to love.

Like the Mass, heaven is a place of constant worship, music, and harmony. Songs break out in perfect melody. Prayers are heard by the many congregants, so to speak, who are present in the cathedral that is heaven. For example, after Justinian's discourse, he ends with joyful prayer: "*Hosanna, sanctus Deus Sabaoth / superillustrans claritate tua / felices ignes horum malacoth* (Hosanna, holy God of hosts, you illuminate with your brightness the blessed flame of these realms)."[30]

This prayer by Justinian is apt because as Dante proceeds through the additional spheres of heaven, paradise grows brighter and more beautiful,

27. Dante, *Divine Comedy*, 395.
28. Dante, *Divine Comedy*, 554.
29. Dante, *Divine Comedy*, 448.
30. Dante, *Divine Comedy*, 428.

while he journeys closer and closer to the Trinity itself. All the while, with Beatrice as his companion, his light in the darkness, his first-fruits guide to divine love itself, Dante is transfigured and transformed in Beatrice's presence and through Beatrice's wisdom. In fact, Dante's purification, transfiguration, and transformation, are contingent on the light and wisdom of Beatrice (just as our purification, transfiguration, and transformation are contingent with the light and wisdom of Christ).

Through the course of the poem, God uses Beatrice to reach out to Dante to bring back this wayward son. Like the Old Testament prophets, whom God used to reach out to his wayward sons and daughters prior to the coming of Christ, Beatrice is the instantiated person from whom God's wisdom and grace flows to those who need it. And like the Old Testament prophets, through whom Christ spoke, divine Wisdom also speaks through Beatrice.

Beatrice was everything to Dante. This produced the double-edged sword that led Dante wayward after her death. Dante loved Beatrice to the point of forgetting God. Beatrice's arrival begins with a rebuke. She accosts Dante for having strayed after her death. Yet God knew the love that Dante had for Beatrice, so God sent Beatrice to resurrect him. In this way, Beatrice is acting in prefiguration of that which Christ does: resurrect us from death and usher us into the gates of paradise (which is precisely what Beatrice does for Dante). Beatrice is, at once, Dante's downfall and salvation.

And so Beatrice is again reminiscent of the prefigured Christ of the prophets. The prophets were the double-edged sword that caused carnal Israel so much trouble during their existence. The prophets accosted the people for forgetting God. The people, in turn, began to idolize some of the prophets instead of God, or, in the case of Jeremiah, loathe the prophet altogether and attempt to kill him. The prophets were sent by God to resurrect his people. The prophets were, at once, the downfall and salvation of Old Testament Israel. They came to announce judgment. They also came to announce repentance and wisdom, as does Beatrice to Dante. In her final words of instruction to the pilgrim-poet, she reminds him of the coming judgment and resurrection (like the prophet Isaiah to the Israelites long ago): "The greater goodness makes for greater bliss; / a greater bliss calls for a greater body, / if it is perfect in all of its parts; / therefore, this sphere which sweeps all of the world / along with it must correspond to this, / the inner ring, that loves and knows the most."[31]

The prophets, however, were not God in the flesh. They were, at most, a type of Christ who foreshadowed and prefigured the Messiah and God for

31. Dante, *Divine Comedy*, 554–55.

whom the Israelites waited. Likewise, Beatrice is not Christ. She is not the Son who bore the iniquities of the world and conquered Hades, leading captive souls from Limbo into heaven and whom we, as pilgrims on earth, need to follow in our ascent on high. This is why, repeatedly, Beatrice reminds Dante to always keep his mind and eyes set on the true prize, the true prize that is Christ. After being reminded of this truth, Dante repeatedly tells how Beatrice's words persuaded him to cleave to that which he had abandoned at the poem's beginning.

The Old Testament patriarchs and prophets pointed the way to Christ. They were individuals whom God used to reach out and instruct his sons and daughters. In every way, Beatrice mirrors this typological and sacramental reality. God sent Beatrice to reach out and instruct Dante, to bring him back to the flock. But in doing so, Beatrice speaks the eternal wisdom of love, just as the prophets did. Thus it is not Beatrice, per se, who is speaking to Dante. It is God speaking through Beatrice to reach the formerly obstinate and prideful poet. Dante sees Beatrice, but he hears love itself in her voice and in her teaching. It is his hearing love that allows for his transfiguration and ascent through the spheres of heaven.

As the two pilgrimage closer and closer to the final sphere, Beatrice is subsequently superseded by another gatekeeper, another type of Christ, the great theologian of love, Saint Bernard of Clairvaux. However, Beatrice as a type of Christ effected such great transformation in Dante that it is appropriate that she, like the Old Testament prophets, would leave him. Elijah was assumed up into heaven, and some Jewish apocalypticists waited for his return. Elijah was not the Messiah, though he was a prefiguration of the Messiah in many ways. The apocalypticists had set their eyes to the wrong thing, having forgotten what Elijah had taught them. The greatest of the prophets, John the Baptist, paved the way for Christ, before fading away and giving way to Christ. Beatrice follows this biblical and typological pattern in the poem.

God does not leave man, let alone his sons and daughters, without teaching and instruction from other humans. The Old Testament is filled with teaching and instruction. Christ's very ministry was grounded in teaching and instruction. Beatrice served as that agent of teaching and instruction to help perfect Dante's nature with the supernatural grace and love needed to transfigure broken and wounded man into a blossoming flower of life.

Thus as Dante nears that heavenly bud to behold Christ and the blessed Trinity, Beatrice fades away to take her place among the chorus of angels and saints to give praise to God. The tripartite journey to heaven is complete. We realize, at long last, that Dante learned love in hell, ordered his love in purgatory, then enjoyed the eternal fruit of love in paradise. As the Trinity takes center stage in Dante's heart and eyes, he takes his place in the eternal choir to sing of "the Love that moves the sun and the other stars."[32]

This essay was originally published in *The Imaginative Conservative* in three parts, under the titles "Learning to Love Again: Dante's Descent in the Inferno" (4 December 2019), "Ascending the Mountain of Love" (11 December 2019), and "The Face of Love: Beatrice as a Type of Christ" (19 December 2019). They have been compiled in this edition for a single continuous analysis of *The Divine Comedy*.

32. Dante, *Divine Comedy*, 585.

11

Shakespeare and the Tragedy of Politics

WILLIAM SHAKESPEARE, THAT IMMORTAL BARD FROM STRATFORD-UPON-Avon, is well-regarded as the English-speaking world's greatest dramatist and, arguably, the greatest dramatist in the history of drama. But Shakespeare is also a political thinker. In fact, political commentary pours through the lines of his many plays—especially his tragedies. Some of his most famous tragedies are also his most political works: *Hamlet*, *Julius Caesar*, and *Antony and Cleopatra* (notwithstanding *Othello*, *Macbeth*, and *King Lear*).

For the sake of brevity, I will limit this cursory exposition of politics as tragedy to *Hamlet*, *Julius Caesar*, and *Antony and Cleopatra*. The reason for this is because *Hamlet* is a stand-alone and deeply relevant to our world today, especially given the prevalence of spying and untrustworthiness in the play—themes that ought to be all the more important to us, considering our national security state and the continuing fraying of social and cultural trust through Western Europe and North America. *Julius Caesar* and *Antony and Cleopatra*, though stand-alone works, should be seen as companion pieces that continue to develop the mature themes of politics, power, and love begun in *Julius Caesar* and reaching fruition in *Antony and Cleopatra*; though questions of love and politics are also contained in *Hamlet,* they are not at the same level as in the Roman plays.

Hamlet

Reading *Hamlet* politically should immediately reveal the politics of para-noia that run through the play. The play opens with two inconsequential sentinels, Barnardo and Francisco, before giving way to more important characters—Horatio and Marcellus. Something strange has been occurring, and Horatio has arrived to investigate.

Horatio's entry into the play, which pushes the play forward, is brought forth by rumors, though, in this instance, the rumors turn out to be true. But the dramatic beginning of the play foreshadows the reality of the cold and dark whispers that carry the play forward. When the men encounter the ghost, Horatio demands it to speak. All to no avail. The ghost exits. The men immediately consider the worst possibility for interpreting this encounter. Horatio foreshadows the ominous nature of the play immediately after the ghost vanishes: "In what particular thought to work I know not, but in the gross and scope of mine opinion, this bodes some strange eruption to our state."[1] This is followed up by that most famous line "something is rotten in the state of Denmark."[2]

The "strange eruption to our state,"[3] and the rotting problem in the state, is what the rest of *Hamlet* deals with. King Hamlet, as we know, has recently died, and the ghost is his apparition. King Claudius, aptly named after the Roman emperor, has made his bid to the throne in murdering his brother and subsequently marrying Gertrude—thereby ascending to the throne. We are revealed through the ghost of King Hamlet that Claudius murdered him because of his lust for Gertrude and lust to wield crown and scepter. Claudius's marriage to Gertrude is not out of love but out of the pursuit of power and self-pleasure.

Lurking in the background is the feud between Denmark and Norway over land, which is boiling up to erupt in war. Compounded with these fears are the worries of Polonius that the young Prince Hamlet is madly in love with his daughter, Ophelia. Ophelia informs her father of Hamlet's sugges-tive behavior and love letters. Polonius offers to prove his loyalty to Claudius by spying on Hamlet (thus serving both Claudius and his own end to pre-vent Hamlet's love for Ophelia). But it is Claudius's fear, his paranoia that Hamlet will take revenge for his father's murder by killing him, that drives his antagonism toward the young prince, to rid himself of the perpetual threat at his side. Polonius is but a pawn in a larger and more sinister game.

1. Shakespeare, *Hamlet*, 13.
2. Shakespeare, *Hamlet*, 55.
3. Shakespeare, *Hamlet*, 13.

Shakespeare does a remarkable job in presenting politics as no pasture for saints. It is the domain of those sad and sorry humans inflicted with "the primal eldest curse" (a reference to Cain's murder of Abel).[4] Love is absent in the political scheming and skulduggery that consumes the state of Denmark.

So paranoid is Claudius that he effectively establishes a police and surveillance state to control every aspect of life in the palace. Polonius, through fidelity to Claudius and fear of Hamlet's love for Ophelia, is enlisted as a spy. Rosencrantz and Guildenstern, two childhood friends of Hamlet, are also conscripted in this game of spies, as they betray their friendship and memories with Hamlet in service to Claudius. Not even the sacredness of friendship and joyful memories can keep relationships from dissolving into utilitarian contracts. Claudius, for instance, doesn't care at all about Rosencrantz and Guildenstern. Claudius merely contracts them for his service; what happens to them is equally unimportant to Claudius, so long as Claudius's scheme to dispatch Hamlet succeeds. (I should also point out that as the second act comes to a close, Hamlet is counter-spying on Claudius and is very much bound up in this game of spies, as all the villains are.)

Hamlet, however, is not without suffering the degradation of the rotten sins of the Danish state and the brutal machinations of power politics inside the prison that is Denmark under Claudius. En route to England, Hamlet grows suspicious of his former friends; rewrites a letter, instructing the executioner to kill the two disposable spies; and, in battle against pirates, flees back to Denmark, leaving Rosencrantz and Guildenstern for dead. And die they do. But rather than offer any hand of forgiveness or redemption to his former friends, Hamlet abandons them to the fated contract for which they had signed up. We may feel Hamlet justified in his actions toward Rosencrantz and Guildenstern, but in his rather callous actions (though lesser in comparison to Claudius), we are revealed how truly changed Hamlet has become, in being enslaved to the politics of power and revenge.

Ironically, the security-surveillance state that has been erected to keep Claudius in power fails. The realm of the political, if it is to survive, must shed itself of the spying apparatus that constricts it. Thus Polonius is killed by Hamlet (though Hamlet thought he was killing Claudius in the heat of the moment). As hitherto mentioned, Rosencrantz and Guildenstern are also shed off and later die. In the end, the very elaborate system of security and spying that Claudius has built has done him no good. His crime is eventually revealed, and he pays the price.

4. Shakespeare, *Hamlet*, 165.

At the same time as Shakespearean irony reveals the limits of the se-curity-surveillance state, the tragic element of the play is seen in the deaths of Ophelia and Hamlet. Ophelia loved Hamlet; Hamlet loved Ophelia. Whatever possible love the two had for each other could not be consum-mated, because love is driven away by the madness of politics. Ophelia, in my opinion, committed suicide rather than being drowned in her own madness; that is neither here nor there, considering the bleaker portrait that Shakespeare is painting.

Hamlet, for his part, probably did love Ophelia, despite the debates over whether he did or did not. (At least this is more probable when analyz-ing the interactions between Hamlet and Ophelia, especially when Hamlet realizes Ophelia is the one being buried and he declares that he loved her, crying out, "I loved Ophelia. Forty thousand brothers could not with all their quantity of love make up my sum."[5]) In happier and more tranquil days, Ophelia would have been queen to Hamlet and the two would have gaily spent their days together. However, it is not Hamlet's destiny to be wed and live a happy life. He must deliver the state from the constrictive and enslaving machine that Claudius has built. As such, Hamlet is fated to a loveless life, too. For that is what Shakespeare is revealing about the empty and brutal nature of politics. Politics forsakes love, as it is about power.

But Shakespeare is no anarchist. The state must survive and be re-stored. While those who occupy its halls of power will be miserable crea-tures without love, the state plays an important role in facilitating the happy and loving lives of the rest of us, to bloom and flourish. As such, Hamlet is the tragic hero whose destiny it is to restore the state to its proper condition and sphere by destroying the intrusive security-surveillance state that has been constructed, which prohibits civil society and human-to-human rela-tionships from flourishing. (It has also been widely argued that Shakespeare was making esoteric commentary on the Elizabethan police state of his day.) So Hamlet does. So Hamlet dies.

Hamlet dies at the end of the play because he must. The political life, as we've said, chases away love and therefore cannot give life but can only serve to protect life. There is a difference between giving life and protecting life. Politics is a tragic enterprise, according to Shakespeare. It is, however, a necessary one—and that is why it is tragic.

5. Shakespeare, *Hamlet*, 255.

Politics and Love in Rome

Politics chasing away love and destroying love altogether is further mani-fested in Shakespeare's two great plays dealing with that most sublime im-perium in Western history: Rome. *Julius Caesar* and *Antony and Cleopatra* pick up, in many ways, where *Hamlet* left off. Like *Hamlet*, these two Roman plays are deeply political, and it is because of their political nature that they find themselves in the annals of Shakespeare's tragedies.

Where Hamlet was a sympathetic character, Julius Caesar, Antony, and Cleopatra are filled with an overabundant vanity, despite being the protagonists of their eponymous plays. Julius Caesar is clearly in love with himself, his grandiosity, and his power. Antony and Cleopatra, when they are introduced in the first scene of their play, enter as king and queen of the world. They enter the stage with servants, a golden train, and eunuchs fanning Cleopatra as if reminiscent of a Roman triumph. The pomp and circumstance of Julius Caesar, Antony, and Cleopatra are borne for all to see. Literally.

Part of the crisis of politics is its conflictual dimension of it. Brutus, Cassius, and the senatorial republicans who oppose Caesar are fighting a losing battle against the politics of monopoly represented by Caesar, who wields the unruly passion of the mob for his self-gain. Moreover, since Julius Caesar has now entered the domain of the political, his relationship with Brutus changes.

Prior to Julius Caesar's foray into politics, he counted Brutus as one of his best and most trustworthy friends. Brutus was able to be a true friend to Julius Caesar because he did not threaten the politics of power that the Senate held and embodied. With Julius Caesar now entering the domain of politics, the relationship between the two men must change—and change it does. Brutus is convinced by the conniving machinations of Cassius to slay his former friend—thus the great shock and sadness on Caesar's face when he is mercilessly cut down like Priam to see the one man whom he had trusted so dearly to deliver the killing blow.

The ghost of Caesar haunts Brutus, Cassius, and the rest of the con-spirators for the rest of the play. The moral law rears its horrifying and terrifying head against the men whom, in betraying trust, Dante placed in the ninth circle of hell. What was anticipated as their triumph becomes the whip of their flight. Brutus, Cassius, and the rest of the pro-republican forces thought that the murder of Caesar would stave off the rule of one and preserve the rule of many. It did not. The energy unleashed in the murder only speeds up the inevitable eradication of the politics of plurality into the politics of universal governance that will eventually be consummated by Octavius.

Antony and Cleopatra continues where *Julius Caesar* left off. "The triple pillar of the world"[6] (the triumvirate) still retains a vestige of the politics of plurality. Octavius, Antony, and Lepidus have split the Roman Republic among themselves. Sextus Pompeius, or just Pompey in the play, is a fourth leg in a three-legged race. Pompey controls the sea and therefore prevents Octavius, Antony, and Lepidus from getting at each other's throat. Ironically—and irony is a major feature of Shakespeare—this unintended fourth leg acts as the wall of peace between the triumviri.

Antony, however, is caught between a rock and a hard place. His erotic love for Cleopatra puts him outside of the domain of the political, despite being among the triumviri and a great Roman general. For a man of extreme pride and haughtiness, he speaks the only wisdom in the play: "Let Rome in Tiber melt, and the wide arch of the ranged empire fall! Here is my space, kingdoms are clay: our dungy earth alike feeds beast as man. The nobleness of life is to do thus; when such a mutual pair and such a twain can do't, in which I bind, on pain and punishment, the world to weet we stand up peerless."[7]

This most passionate and wise aside by Antony continues to develop Antony as a man of passion. After all, in *Julius Caesar*, Antony was the most passionate man after the death of Caesar. The one line that everyone knows from *Julius Caesar* was uttered by Antony: "Friends, Romans, countrymen, lend me your ears."[8] The passion exuded by Antony in *Julius Caesar* has now fully consumed him in *Antony and Cleopatra*. Love threatens the political: "Let Rome in Tiber melt, and the wide arch of the ranged empire fall." Love has its own domain: "Here is my space." Antony also reflects on the temporality of politics but the eternality of love: "Kingdoms are clay: our dungy earth alike feeds beast as man." Those who wish to build immortal houses and eternal arches are doomed to failure. Politicians are not lovers, thus lovers are not peers with politicians: "We stand up peerless."[9] Antony and Cleopatra are peerless because they are lovers.

Where Antony and Cleopatra are introduced as passionate and prideful individuals, Octavius Caesar is introduced as a cold and calculating man of bureaucratic management who talks only politics. In the fourth scene of the first act, as Octavius is introduced, he is described as having no grand

6. Shakespeare, *Antony and Cleopatra*, 4.
7. Shakespeare, *Antony and Cleopatra*, 5.
8. Shakespeare, *Julius Caesar*, 61.
9. Shakespeare, *Antony and Cleopatra*, 5.

entrance and gives no passionate and memorable speech. Instead, Octavius enters, along with the other Roman contenders for the prize of managerial power, in a dry and sterile room of banal politicking. Rome, as Shakespeare reveals in the scenes in Rome and among the Romans, is the center of the passionless world of cold and calculative politics.

Antony doesn't escape this reality when in the presence of his fellow Romans. His marriage to Octavia is purely political. There is nothing loving, erotic, or passionate about it. At first opportunity, with hostilities erupting, he sends Octavia back to Octavius to be rid of her.

The war for the world begins when Pompey is eliminated. Again, this unintentional fourth leg initially kept the peace, until Octavius and Lepidus allied together to destroy Pompey. Power, however, kept Pompey short-sighted. He despised Antony and cursed him in the opening of second act; he called Antony and Cleopatra "Epicurean cooks,"[10] a derogatory dig at their sensuality in each other's arms and bed. The politics of power blinded Pompey to his impending doom. (It did the same to Antony insofar that an alliance with Pompey would have proved beneficial in the coming struggle against Octavius.)

Lepidus may have been the third man in the triumvirate, but he too is of little concern. Octavius uses Lepidus to defeat Pompey, then has him imprisoned after his use. This is made tragic given that Lepidus, according to Enoborus, loved Caesar: "O, how he loves Caesar." Agrippa, a cold politico like his master, retorts, "Nay, but how he clearly adores Mark Antony."[11] Love, as we've mentioned, cannot survive in the realm of cutthroat politics. Loyal Lepidus was disposable, and disposed he was once his utility ran out.

The removal of Pompey and Lepidus cuts the world down into halves, one ruled by Octavius and the other by Antony and Cleopatra. The diarchy cannot survive the inevitable push to singular governance either. So at the mouth of Actium, the battle for the fate of the world commences. It is not a battle between Octavius and Antony; it is a battle of cold rationalism and bureaucratic managerialism (embodied and represented by Octavius) against the world of passion, love, and the erotic (embodied and represented by Antony and Cleopatra)—"Nature's infinite book of secrecy."[12] In this battle, the cold and calculative politics of Octavius wins when Antony,

---

10. Shakespeare, *Antony and Cleopatra*, 28.

11. Shakespeare, *Antony and Cleopatra*, 64.

12. Shakespeare, *Antony and Cleopatra*, 6.

lovestruck in seeing Cleopatra flee to the open seas, gives chase "like a dot-ing mallard"[13] after his beloved—abandoning men and material to be with Cleopatra.

The world of Antony and Cleopatra is one of sensual play and erotic catharsis. "Give me some music: music, moody food, of us that trade in love," Cleopatra famously says in the second act.[14] She follows this up by re-vealing the extent of her world of sport with Antony as she reminisces, "That time—O times!—I laughed him out of patience; and that night I laughed into patience; and next morn, ere the ninth hour, I drunk him to his bed; then put my tires and mantles on him whilst I wore his sword Philippan."[15]

With all lost, however, the only comfort that Antony and Cleopatra have is in retreating into that space of loving play. "Where hast thou been, my heart? Dost thou hear, lady? If from the field I shall return once more to kiss these lips, I will appear in blood; I and my sword will earn our chronicle. There's hope in't yet . . . . Come," Antony continues to say after his disastrous defeat at Actium, "let's have one other gaudy night: call to me all my sad captains; fill our bowls once more; let's mock the midnight bell."[16]

As Antony and Cleopatra retreat into her bedchambers for another night of gaudy sex, thereby mocking the midnight bell of death wrought by the inevitable ascent of politics, Shakespeare again shows us how politics chases away love. The crime of Antony and Cleopatra was that they were lovers in the world of politics. Being lovers in the cold world of politics, they had to die to make safe passage for the consummation of the universal bureaucratic imperium that rational politics demands, which had chosen Rome and Octavius as its vessel of realization.

Love cannot coexist with the political because love threatens the political. "Let Rome in Tiber melt," as Antony said.[17] To love is to forsake the political; to love is to "let Rome in Tiber melt" away in the fires that consumed Troy; to love is to allow the pettiness of politics slip away and dwell in the timelessness of love, just as Cleopatra did when waiting for Antony's return from Rome: "I might sleep out this great gap of time [while] my Antony is away."[18] When campaigning in Egypt to finish off Antony and Cleopatra, Octavius says, "The time of universal peace draws near."[19]

---

13. Shakespeare, *Antony and Cleopatra*, 83.

14. Shakespeare, *Antony and Cleopatra*, 43.

15. Shakespeare, *Antony and Cleopatra*, 44.

16. Shakespeare, *Antony and Cleopatra*, 96–7.

17. Shakespeare, *Antony and Cleopatra*, 5.

18. Shakespeare, *Antony and Cleopatra*, 23.

19. Shakespeare, *Antony and Cleopatra*, 106.

Universal peace can only be consummated with love destroyed; so it is that Eros (Antony's most trustworthy companion) dies, then Antony dies, then Cleopatra dies, in rapid succession.

Shakespeare is not, in my view, celebrating universal peace through universal order. Instead, he is revealing the tragic reality of the cold rationalism of politics: the inevitable law of politics is that it must destroy plurality to win universal peace. In doing so, "Nature's infinite book of secrecy"[20] must be destroyed, and all the personality that dwells in that world must also be eliminated. The triumph of Caesar and the bringing of universal peace entails the triumph of cold bureaucratic politics, the very bureaucratic politics embodied by Octavius in the play as he sits over desks, reads papers, and commands his lackeys to execute his will. Indeed, how very tragic.

Why We Read Shakespeare

Reading Shakespeare is a joy. He is, above all, a treasure of Anglodom and the English language. As great a dramatist as he was, he was also a first-rate political thinker. His tragedies, as demonstrated, are all political works. That they are tragedies also reveals Shakespeare's pessimistic outlook on politics. Politics is a tragic necessity. But it comes with a cost—namely, the forsaking of love.

Shakespeare's reflection on the need to dismantle the security-surveillance state is very much worth our consideration, especially in this brave new century in which we find ourselves. Likewise, Shakespeare's consistent presentation of the conflict between politics and love is something with which we must necessarily wrestle. Is it the case, as with Claudius and Octavius, that the consummation of the political is the dictation and control of the life of the masses? It surely seems that way, especially in rhetoric and reality. Does politics chase away love, and must love necessarily be fated to dissolution for those who become consumed by the coldness of politics?

Long before Max Weber insisted that politics is no realm for the saint, Shakespeare also reveals that politics is no realm for the saint, the lover, or the idealist. Politics beats us down. It spies. It schemes. It lies. It kills. It destroys friendships. Those who claim to enter politics because they are interested in love and helping others should be regarded with suspicion. That is the enduring political wisdom of Shakespeare.

Those who love and would dwell in the space of timeless play should remain out of the domain of politics. Otherwise your life will be a tragedy, as the coldness of politics consumes you. Or we can lay down the pursuit

20. Shakespeare, *Antony and Cleopatra*, 6.

of power as Prospero did and allow love to take its rightful place, protected and sanctified by the political. When we do that, like Prospero, we walk off into an uncertain future and ask the world—the audience—for forgiveness. Yet when we walk off into that uncertain future, we might just find something far more beautiful and meaningful when the fog clears and the breadth of "Nature's infinite book of secrecy" is open before us.

This essay was originally published in *Merion West* under the title "Shakespeare, a Political Theorist Too," 15 October 2019.

12

Shakespeare on Love and War

WHAT HATH SHAKESPEARE TO DO WITH THE POLITICS OF REGIME CHANGE? Given the long and unsuccessful history of what we call regime change, from the installment of the Shah over Persia, to the Bay of Pigs, to Libya, one questions the sanity of anyone who routinely calls for regime change. Yet long before our modern failures exposed the foibles of those who lust for power and the foolishness of political usurpation, the great bard of Anglodom provided wisdom enough for those who consider venturing into foreign lands.

Henry V

What we call regime change, the medieval and early moderns called usurpation. Like our forebears, we still hold to notions of political legitimacy. While we may find such political legitimacy rooted in the rule of law and how leaders treat their citizens instead of in lineages and lines of succession, the principle remains the same: there are those whom we deem illegitimate, and those we deem legitimate.

Shakespeare cannot be separated from the context and times in which he lived. In 1588, Spain, with papal sanction, attempted to conquer England through claims of inheritance and marriage tying the Habsburg dynasty to the crown and throne of Albion. The Spanish Armada was defeated, and a world historical shift occurred: the New World was no longer going to be the sole domain of the Spanish Habsburgs, but was now open to the

Anglo-Saxon and Anglo-Celtic peoples, who would bring Protestantism, common law, and the militia tradition of the right to bear arms to the Americas.

Henry V was written about a decade after the tumultuous events that preoccupied early modern English civilization. The play may have been about one of England's most beloved kings, but a very close inspection of the play reveals that it is not simply a memoriam of Henry V, but a drama concerning the politics of usurpation and war, in the throes of which England had just been. Elizabethan anxieties and fears over legitimacy, succession, and religious sanction for conquest are all present. The chorus might ask us to imagine the field of Agincourt, since they were incapable of reproducing such a spectacle on stage—"O for a Muse of fire, that would ascend / the brightest heaven of invention: / A kingdom for a stage, princes to act, / and monarchs to behold the swelling scene!"—but the movement of *Henry V* was certainly drawn from very recent memories and experiences, not distant ones.[1]

It is interesting to note, as have other Shakespeare scholars of the past, that there is much irony interwoven into a play about one of England's most celebrated monarchs. "Then should warlike Harry, like himself, / assume the port of Mars; and at his heels, / leash'd in like hounds, should famine, sword and fire / crouch for employment." In the choral introduction to *Henry V*, the chorus sings that Henry will bring not peace, prosperity, and fertility's blessings, but "famine, sword, and fire."[2] If the measure of a good ruler is presiding over hearth and home with a hearty fire and good stew, then Henry is no such king.

The play opens with the bishops of Canterbury and Ely fretting over a possible church tax. This reflects the angst and anxiety of the clergy in the turmoil of the Reformation. Fearing the loss of their established customs, the churchmen assume the role of conjuring up a justification for a war against France—which has long been on the mind of Henry.

When Henry gathers with the bishops and after they exchange the necessary pleasantries, Henry asks the archbishop of Canterbury to explain why he has claims to the throne of France: "Sure we thank you. / My learned lord, we pray you to proceed, / and justly and religiously unfold / why the Law Salique that they have in France / should or should not bar us in our claim."[3] The archbishop then gives a long, tedious, and banal speech about the technicalities of Salic law in what is one of the most boring and

---

1. Shakespeare, *Henry V*, 3.
2. Shakespeare, *Henry V*, 3.
3. Shakespeare, *Henry V*, 9.

snooze-worthy speeches in the great plays of Shakespeare. And that's the point. The archbishop conjures up the most technical, bordering on the absurd, pretexts for war. But perhaps the most important is when he tells Henry that Salic law forbids a woman from ever inheriting the throne: "No woman shall succeed in Salique land."[4]

The speech by the archbishop reveals the ambiguity and the blending of recent English history with that of medieval memory. The archbishop is analogous to the bishop of Rome, conjuring up the justification for war and regime change. "No woman shall succeed in Salique land" evokes the complexities and interweaving of women, Salic exceptionalism, and religious blessing that was the Spanish Armada and the Habsburg attempt to overthrow a certain queen of England. Accepting the Archbishop's justification, Henry prepares to "awake [the] sleeping sword of war"[5] that will disturb the tranquility of the vineyards and gardens of the world.

After mustering a small invasion force, Henry proceeds to venture deep into Frankish lands to establish his claim to the throne. There is only one image of fruitfulness in the play, at the very beginning, when the bishop of Ely says to the archbishop of Canterbury that "the strawberry grows underneath the nettle, and wholesome berries thrive and ripen best."[6] This tranquil image of serenity will soon be replaced by blood and mud. We must remember that "famine, sword, and fire" are what Henry unleashes.[7]

It is true that *Henry V* includes some of the most sublime of Shakespearean rhetoric. "Once more unto the breach, dear friends"[8] and "Cry God for Harry, England, and Saint George"[9] are among the most recognizable lines of all of Shakespeare. But we shouldn't let the beautiful and moving rhetoric Shakespeare inserts into Henry's persona distract us from the irony that lies in the same speeches. In the same "Once more" speech that opens the third act of the play, Henry says revealingly, "Let us swear / that you are worth your breeding; which I doubt not."[10] The value of man here is not in husbandry, but in war; only in war, in bludgeoning a fellow man to death, is a man's worth found.

The St. Crispin's Day speech continues to unveil this hypermasculine fraud. As Henry raises the spirit of the beleaguered and hungry English

4. Shakespeare, *Henry V*, 10.

5. Shakespeare, *Henry V*, 10.

6. Shakespeare, *Henry V*, 7.

7. Shakespeare, *Henry V*, 3.

8. Shakespeare, *Henry V*, 44.

9. Shakespeare, *Henry V*, 45.

10. Shakespeare, *Henry V*, 45.

troops, he extols the reality that they are few in number and therefore that a victory would mean more glory to the "happy few."[11] While the other men who remained home in England with wife and children will be forgotten, those who ventured with Henry into France for battle will be remembered for all eternity. The mark of his pride and immortality, won on "this St. Crispin's Day,"[12] will be the "scars" he shows to the younger generation and his age-old peers who sat out the battle.[13] This is, of course, the great masculine fraud unveiled by Homer as much as it is the fraud unveiled by Shakespeare. War, with its glory and honor to be won, is not the highest reality of life; love, as Shakespeare will show, is the true blessedness we seek.

When the French ambassador arrived earlier in the play to taunt Henry with tennis balls, during which Henry assured him that he would not kill the messenger, as it were, we are told that Henry is a pious and good Christian king: "We are no tyrant, but a Christian king, / unto whose grace our passion is as subject / as is our wretches fett'red in our prisons."[14] Here we again find more irony and the intrusion of the Anglo-Spanish War into the play. Henry declares himself a Christian king—in comparison to what? A non-Christian king? Of course, that is the argument that Philip II made against Elizabeth. Henry's declaration of being a just and graceful king, implying compassion, is subsequently juxtaposed with "wretches fett'red in our prisons."[15] An image of tyranny is placed side by side with the claim of not being a tyrant.

War unleashes the barbarism of Henry—as it does of man more generally—and this is fully manifested as Henry conquers town after town. "How yet resolves the Governor of the town?" he asks a besieged French garrison. "This is the latest parle we will admit: / Therefore to our best mercy give yourselves, / or like men proud of destruction, / defy us to our worst; for as I am a soldier, / a name that in my thoughts become me best, / if I begin the batt'ry once again, / I will not leave the half-achieved Harfleur / till in her ashes she lie buried. / The gates of mercy shall be all shut up, / and the fleshed soldier, rough and hard of heart, / in liberty of bloody hand shall range / with conscience wide as hell, mowing like grass / your fresh fair virgins and your flow'ring infants."[16] In this remarkable speech by Henry to the French townsmen, we see the nakedness of his warring pathos. Henry is willing to

11. Shakespeare, *Henry V*, 89.

12. Shakespeare, *Henry V*, 88–9.

13. Shakespeare, *Henry V*, 88.

14. Shakespeare, *Henry V*, 17.

15. Shakespeare, *Henry V*, 17.

16. Shakespeare, *Henry V*, 51.

slay virgin, woman, and child if the town does not capitulate. Likewise, we see once more the masculine fraud, that men can only be men in death and war: "Or, like men proud of destruction, / defy us to our worst."[17] So much for the merciful and graceful Christian king he claimed to be earlier.

Yet we see the other side of Harry, the human side, when he is with Katherine. War, Shakespeare is telling us—especially in the name of political conquest (regime change)—barbarizes us. Love, or at least the hope of love, humanizes us.

After winning the improbable victory at Agincourt, much like the English winning against the much larger Spanish fleet in the English Channel just a decade before the premier of *Henry V* on stage, we see a different Henry as he courts his bride. The war acts, the third and fourth, give closer inspection to the person of Henry than the first and second acts. His psychology is revealed as we learn his anxieties over his tenuous and fragile rule inherited from his father and from his stark brutalism in threatening to wipe out entire villages and their non-combatant populations. In the final act with Princess Kate, however, Henry is metamorphosized into a more tender, compassionate, and wholesome individual. No longer beset by the lust to seize the French crown and intent instead on winning the heart and affection of Kate, Henry lets go of his imperial ambitions to rise into the flower of the white rose instead.

The meeting of Henry and Kate face to face as subject creatures of affectivity brings the peace for which the chorus was hoping in the prologue to Act Three. The bravado of Henry is humbled by Kate; he is brought low by falling in love her, as she reminds us when she speaks to him in French with ironic closure: "*Laissez, mon seigneur, laissez, laissez! Ma foi, je ne veux / point que vous abaissiez votre grandeur en baisant la main d'une de / votre seigneurie indigne serviteur.*"[18]

The Henry of the sword, whom we see nakedly revealed in Acts Three and Four, is transfigured by his encounter with love in Act Five. "O fair Katherine, if you will love me soundly with / your French heart, I will be glad to hear you confess it / brokenly with your English tongue.... An angel is like you Kate, and you are like an / angel."[19] While Kate is confused and blushing (manifesting signs of life), Henry doesn't mince words about his affection for her. Henry offers no great speech. No "unto the breach," "cry God for Harry," or "band of brothers" can be conjured out of the lovestruck

17. Shakespeare, *Henry V*, 51.

18. Shakespeare, *Henry V*, 122.

19. Shakespeare, *Henry V*, 117–18.

heart and tongue of the king. "I know no way to mince it in love, but / directly to say, 'I love you,'" he exclaims to Kate.[20]

There are, then, two Henrys in the play. There is the Henry of the sword and the Henry of love. The more endearing, indeed, transfigured ruler is the Henry of love. Given that we have just seen the bloody mess of Agincourt, the ending of *Henry V* is hopeful in its closure in marriage. The prospects of prosperity, as Henry himself confides, are tied entirely to the blissful and blessed marriage between himself and Kate, "Prepare we for our marriage; on which day, / my Lord of Burgundy, we'll take your oath, / and all the peers', for surety of our leagues. / Then shall I swear to Kate, and you to me, / and may our oaths well kept and prosp'rous be!"[21] As the chorus closes the play, we are reminded that Henry lost France and caused England to bleed, but that he also found salvation in Kate.

Richard III

The other great drama of Shakespeare that deals with regime change is *Richard III*. One of the earlier historical plays, *Richard III* is nonetheless a masterpiece of the Shakespearean canon. If *Henry V* reveals the outcome of the attempt of international regime change, wherein trust is frayed, hangings commence, and men die on fields afar, depriving their wives and children of husbands and fathers back home, then *Richard III* reveals the disastrous effects of regime change in the country itself—the evil of civil war.

What makes *Richard III* such a shocking play is how it showcases the extent to which a person will go to usurp power. Richard III wishes to "prove [himself] a villain"[22] and so has his brother murdered to seal his fate as one of the immortal villains of English literature. Like the good black operation it has to be, Richard hires expendable third-party executioners instead of getting his own hands dirty. He must appear clean, like modern presidents and secretaries of state.

Furthermore, Richard has totally and entirely forsaken love. His courting and marrying of Lady Anne expose the hollowness of his affection, as the marriage is for purely political ends. Richard nonetheless feigns repentance and forgiveness like any good two-faced politico. But his marriage with Lady Anne is just for show. It serves only a political purpose.

Murder ascends Richard to the throne, and murder is how Richard attempts to maintain his power. Like Cain, Richard is a fugitive of the law he

20. Shakespeare, *Henry V*, 118.
21. Shakespeare, *Henry V*, 127.
22. Shakespeare, *Richard III*, 4.

is meant to uphold for others but bends and distorts for his own purposes. Richard's descent into paranoid madness ends with more murder. Buckingham, an erstwhile champion of Richard, sees himself on the way out, like Soviet lieutenants during the Great Purge. No amount of loyal service can protect one from the vain insanity of a man who sold everything to usurp power.

Richard's regime change ends in civil war. During the Battle of Bosworth Field, when Richard cries that famous line "A horse, a horse, my kingdom for a horse!,"[23] we realize just how fragile political power is. For all the power and state infrastructure Richard had at his disposal, from his ascent to his fall, a simple horse was all for which he cried out when all else was vanishing away in blood and fire.

Richard III is also the scourge over England for having deposed Richard II in another regime change prior to his murdering his way to power. A long train of abuses and tragedies befalls England for having committed the first act of regime change prior to Richard's life, which leads to the culmination of Richard's brutal politics in the backstabbing, murder, and civil war dramatized in the play. What was born in blood must end in blood.

Lastly, we see just how isolated and lonely Richard becomes over the course of the play. True, he was always isolated in a certain manner to begin with, but he was only a scheming man with grandiose intentions at the beginning of the play and spoke to the audience as if having a conversation. Moreover, the veil was not yet torn, so he still had the favor of his mother and friends. They are by his side even as Richard descends into madness. However, as the play develops and Richard seizes power and falls into madness, all his former confidants and supporters desert him or die (sometimes even killed by Richard.) The endearing but cunning asides inserted into the play also begin to fade out. Richard is now an empty shell of a man, alone, deprived of family and friends and even the audience.

Civil war is associated, first and foremost, with political usurpation in the play. Richard's usurpation culminates not in dark dungeons and chained cell rooms, but in a war that rips England apart. Neighbor fights neighbor; brother fights brother. The sacred bonds of family and land evaporate as the sword of war rears its ugly head.

Richard's death is met by that recurring image of Shakespeare, love in marriage. Richmond's marriage to Lady Elizabeth signifies the rebirth of war-torn England. How fitting it is that the rebirth of a shattered nation is in holy matrimony, with the prospects of a fertile womb giving birth to new life.

---

23. Shakespeare, *Richard III*, 143.

The Subversive Brilliance of Shakespeare

What Shakespeare so brilliantly reveals in *Henry V* and *Richard III* is the horror of war wrought by political usurpation—or, as we call it today, regime change. Shakespeare lived through the turmoil of attempted regime change and civil war. Shakespeare's adolescence and youthful maturation were during the final days and aftermath of the saga of Mary, Queen of Scots. The prime of his life intertwined with the Habsburg attempt to overthrow Elizabeth I and claim England for the Habsburg Empire (not to mention the Elizabethan police state critiqued in *Hamlet*, which revealed how black politics and paranoia also chase away love). We see in a close inspection of Shakespearean themes and ironies the very concerns of the Elizabethan age brought to life on stage and in the movement of the dramas. Indeed, the drama of the Elizabethan age dominates Shakespeare's historical dramas. Civil war, political usurpation, and political legitimacy are not distant memories of the medieval past, as the choral introductions seem to suggest, but very recent memories and ongoing concerns during Shakespeare's own lifetime.

The drama of war that was so near to Shakespeare and the farce of bloody manhood and political scheming come to the fore in his English historical plays. War brings distrust, deceit, murder, hangings, scars, and famine. The sword of war unleashed in the lust for power, manifesting itself in political usurpation, makes villains of us all and awakens the hounds of "famine, sword, and fire" to sweep over the fair and plentiful world we inhabit.

The wisdom of Shakespeare is in his exposing the naked horror of war wrought by regime change, and how it is countered not by more political calculation but by the encounter and flourishing of love. Like all great poets, whose theme is love, and unlike the political theorists, whose theme is power, Shakespeare reminds us of what truly matters in life. The Henry of the sword is not much better than Richard III upon a very close inspection of the barbarous Henry in the opening acts of his eponymous play. But the Henry of love is still open for those sorry souls who have dwelled in blood and mud; but they will have to "los[e] France" if they are to gain angels. Shakespeare heals the world destroyed by politics not with a political solution, but a far more human and interior solution: love.

This essay was originally published in *The Imaginative Conservative*, 5 February 2020.

13

The Quality of Mercy

THE MERCHANT OF VENICE IS ONE OF SHAKESPEARE'S GRANDEST COM-
edies, standing alongside the *Taming of the Shrew* and *A Midsummer Night's
Dream*, notwithstanding *As You Like It* and *Twelfth Night*. While it is much
easier now to transform the *Merchant of Venice* into a tragedy (where the
crude comedy of modernity appears in implicit ridicule and hypocriti-
cal exposé of the now truncated Christian characters), to do so strips the
play of its power and insight in contrasting legalistic justice and merciful
forgiveness—the two themes that reveal to us two polar opposite worlds
and Shakespeare's passionate plea for the world of forgiveness instead of
the world of strict justice, which reminds us of the Greek understanding of
retributive punishment. Just as it was in Shakespeare's time, the questions of
justice, mercy, and society remain as relevant as ever, and we have much to
learn from the great bard of Anglodom.

Like the poets of antiquity, the troubadours of France, and the poets
of the late Renaissance, Shakespeare is preoccupied with the theme of love
(and how it is often contrasted to politics). While the poets of old often
found love in the form of struggle, especially in the context of war, where
love becomes the single refuge and respite from the chaotic storm of bloodshed, part of the Shakespearean revolution was to find the struggle for love
in the adventure and misfortune of life itself (however mundane or exciting). Here the *Merchant of Venice* undeniably shines as the struggle for love,
specifically between Portia and Bassanio, is threatened by the turbulence
of misfortune, revenge, and the legalities of justice. But love, in this play,
is secondary to the thematic deconstruction of the strict legality of justice.

Shakespeare thus is exploring the question of whether love can flourish in a world of dog-eat-dog justice.

It is important to remember that traditional comedy was a dramatic form that began in unhappiness and ended in happiness. Comedy wasn't about cheap laughs (to distract us from the daily grind of modern industrial life) at the expense of the target of ridicule, like most contemporary insult comedy is today, but was principally concerned with the struggle for happiness to manifest itself in a cruel, cold, and often dark world. *The Merchant of Venice* sets the somber tone of sadness with the weariness of Antonio (likely over losing his camaraderie with Bassanio): "In sooth I know not why I am so sad. / It wearies me, you say it wearies you."[1]

The restlessness of Antonio, whose "mind is tossing on the ocean,"[2] is subsequently contrasted with the hopeful love of Bassanio and Portia—prefigured for us when Bassanio exults, "In Belmont is a lady richly left; / And she is fair and, fairer than that word, / Of wondrous virtues. Sometimes from her eyes / I did receive fair speechless messages. / Her name is Porta."[3] From the onset of the play Shakespeare tips his hat to us; he begins the play in an atmosphere of unease and restlessness but also prefigures the hopeful end in marriage—an image with which Shakespeare often deals and that can be found in *Henry V*, *Richard III*, and *The Tempest*, among other plays.

While Shakespeare introduces us to the lead characters and prefigures others, the sudden emergence of Shylock is not previously hinted at, and his appearance and subsequent development in the play help pry the worlds of justice and mercy apart. As we know, Shylock is a Jew and a usurer. He has lent Bassanio three thousand ducats for him to help court Portia (as we later learn, Bassanio has lost his estate and lives in relative poverty compared to other high lords and merchantmen in Venice). Shylock is a merciless exploiter of his customers, seeing them not as soulful persons but as mere bonds and pieces of paper with which he has contracted. After we are introduced to Shylock, he quickly makes an aside when learning that Bassanio's benefactor is Antonio, "How like a fawning publican he looks. / I hate him for he is a Christian; / But more, for that in low simplicity he lends out money gratis, and brings down / The rate of usance here with us in Venice . . . . / Cursed by my tribe if I forgive him."[4]

We learn that Antonio and Shylock have a long and tangled history together. Antonio treats Shylock poorly, even cruelly, but also rescues

1. Shakespeare, *Merchant of Venice*, 3.

2. Shakespeare, *Merchant of Venice*, 3.

3. Shakespeare, *Merchant of Venice*, 9.

4. Shakespeare, *Merchant of Venice*, 16.

Shylock's hapless victims from his gripping legalism, which adds to Shylock's venom against Antonio. Shylock's animosity toward Antonio is, as the
famous "Hath not a Jew eyes?" speech reveals, all too natural.[5] We all share
this fallible human condition with a dark tendency for resentment and want
for revenge.

Whenever Shakespeare inserts an aside into his plays, most visibly
manifested in plays like *Richard III* and *Hamlet*, we learn the true mo-
tives and thoughts of the characters. When Shylock says he hates Antonio
and that he will be cursed if he forgives the Christian Venetian merchant,
Shylock really means it. He has no veil to hide his innermost thoughts and
desires. Shylock's aside reveals the totality of his psychology.

Yet in his aside, Shakespeare also begins to foreshadow the need for
forgiveness and how forgiveness heals the ruptured world of legalistic justice, hate, and revenge. Indeed, forgiveness and mercy—which are themes
tied together throughout the play, just as love and joy are—are the most
commonly recurring themes throughout the play. Earlier, Portia had spoken of the value of forgiveness when speaking of the Monsieur Le Bon,
one of her many potential suitors. Thus the stage is set, as it were, for the
conflict between the natural desires for (vengeful) justice and the mercy of
forgiveness.

The Merchant of Venice explores the worlds of strict justice and merciful forgiveness. Justice, in the play, carries an overtone of hypermasculinity
with its insistence on the legality of technicality and desire for harm. Mercy,
by contrast, carries an overtone of the feminine and the need to set aside
one's desires in a spirit of sacrificial giving as revealed by Portia (and, interestingly enough, also by Bassanio).

In fact, the test of the suitors to win Portia also reflects this masculine-
feminine division. The prince of Morocco chooses the gold casket because
it promises all that "men desire," and the prideful prince of Aragon chooses
the silver casket because he believes himself meritoriously deserving Portia's
heart in marriage: "Who chooseth me shall get as much as he deserves."[6] In
both cases, the prince of Morocco and prince of Aragon see marriage as a
contractual rite for their desires; as such, both fail to see the need for sacrifice in marriage: "Who chooseth me must give and hazard all he hath."[7] It
is only Bassanio, who has an aura of the feminine through his compassion,
friendliness, and willingness to sacrifice (perhaps most pertinently because
of his courtship of Portia) who chooses correctly. Portia gives Bassanio her

5. Shakespeare, *Merchant of Venice*, 49.
6. Shakespeare, *Merchant of Venice*, 38.
7. Shakespeare, *Merchant of Venice*, 38.

ring as the visible sign of their love and marriage; Portia also advises Bassanio to aid Antonio in his time of need.

With Antonio's ships having been struck with misfortune overseas, Shylock pounces on both with his strict insistence on the justice owed to him and a desire to now harm Antonio over his past grievances and affairs. Antonio begs for mercy. Shylock scoffs and brushes aside Antonio's pleas. The movement to the dramatic court scene is nigh.

Shakespeare's great parody of justice, and his criticism of the legality of justice and the dark hole that it digs, comes into view during the infamous court scene. Shylock insists that he secure his bonds and oaths made with Antonio. Antonio insists on mercy. The duke of Venice also pleads for some mercy: "But touched with human gentleness and love, / Forgive a moiety of the principal, / Glancing an eye of pity on his losses, / That have of late so huddled his back,"[8] but ultimately abdicates his responsibility to the doctor of laws who, it turns out, is none other than Portia.

That Portia enters the public world of men disguised as a man reveals the hypermasculine legalism of the justice system and offers Shakespeare's subtle critique of it. Punishment and the letter of the law hold sway. The masculine desire for harm is, Shakespeare is saying, cruel. Thus Portia, a woman, offers a heartfelt plea for mercy in one of the most universally celebrated Shakespearean speeches:

> The quality of mercy is not strained.
> It droppeth as the gentle rain from heaven
> Upon the place beneath. It is twice blest:
> It blesseth him that gives and him that takes.
> 'Tis mightiest in the mightiest; it becomes
> The thronèd monarch better than his crown.
> His scepter shows the force of temporal power,
> The attribute to awe and majesty
> Wherein doth sit the dread and fear of kings;
> But mercy is above this sceptered sway.
> It is enthronèd in the hearts of kings;
> It is an attribute to God Himself;
> And earthly power doth then show likest God's
> When mercy seasons justice. Therefore, Jew,
> Though justice be thy plea, consider this:
> That in the course of justice none of us
> Should see salvation. We do pray for mercy,
> And that same prayer doth teach us all to render
> The deeds of mercy. I have spoke thus much

---

8. Shakespeare, *Merchant of Venice*, 72.

To mitigate the justice of thy plea,
Which, if thou follow, this strict court of Venice
Must needs give sentence 'gainst the merchant there.[9]

Moreover, Portia's plea for mercy evokes Deuteronomy 32, a subtle nod to the qualities of mercy deep within the Jewish religion: "My doctrine shall drop as the rain, my speech shall distil as the dew, as the small rain upon the tender herb, and as the showers upon the grass."[10] Portia's plea therefore also calls forth the best in Shylock's committed Judaism to overcome the mere letter of the law and see the spirit that the law itself is meant to foster and promote.

However, Portia's plea for mercy doesn't crack the hardened heart of Shylock. Consequently, Portia becomes a man, so to speak, in resorting to the technicalities of legalism to break Shylock and make him beg for mercy, just as he made Antonio and so many others beg for mercy. When Bassanio arrives and offers to pay off, thrice over, the debt owed the Shylock, an ensuing quibble breaks out over "the pound of flesh"[11] that was stipulated in the bond. Portia reads the bond literally through the letter of the law; Shylock may take his "pound of flesh" but not a drop of blood, because blood was not stipulated. With that, Shylock is cornered. Portia further enters this manly world of strict legalistic justice to bring forth an old law in Venice wherein a foreigner intending to kill a Venetian forfeits one half of his belongings to the intended victim and one half to the state.

Portia's delving deeper into legalistic justice, what the Greeks called *tisis* (retributive justice), reveals for us the absurdities and darkness of obsessive justice. The justice of the law only sinks us deeper in the abyss. There can be no reconciliation through the strict following of the law. Justice has all condemned (as Portia reminded everyone in her speech).

In a brilliant sequence, Shakespeare lays bare for us the limits of justice and the futility of justice in providing for the so-called just society. Justice leaves us blinded; the insistence on justice, as reflected by Shylock and as parodied by Portia, turns us all into ravenous animals in a fight against each other that ends in destruction. Indeed, this is what was implied by Gratiano when he spoke to Shylock how Shylock's insistence on the letter of the law would lead him to "waver in [his] faith"[12] and "hold opinion with Pythagoras / That souls of animals infuse themselves / Into the trunks of men. Thy currish spirit / Governed a wolf who, hanged for human slaughter, / Even from

9. Shakespeare, *Merchant of Venice*, 78.

10. Deut 32:2 KJV.

11. Shakespeare, *Merchant of Venice*, 74.

12. Shakespeare, *Merchant of Venice*, 75.

the gallows did his fell soul fleet, / And whilst thou layest in thy unhallowed dam, / Infused itself in thee; for thy desires / Are wolvish, bloody, starved, and ravenous."[13]

It is the court scene where Shakespeare mocks and deconstructs the hollowness of justice. The justice demanded by Shylock is merciless. "I crave the law!" as Shylock says.[14] But the reflection on legalistic justice making us "wolvish, bloody, starved, and ravenous"[15] applies to the Christians as much as it does to Shylock; here, Shakespeare deconstructs the constant failures of Christians (as he also does through Shylock's eloquent speech "Hath not a Jew eyes") to live up to their high ideals of mercy and forgiveness. What shall win in this great contest? Merciful forgiveness or the retributive justice demanded by the letter of the law, before which we all stand guilty? Portia's speech reminds us we are all guilty: "Though justice be thy plea, consider this: / That in the course of justice none of us / Should see salvation."[16]

In the midst of this storm, we must remember that the beautiful marriages of Lorenzo and Jessica and Portia and Bassanio have been disturbed by the misfortunes now plaguing Antonio, Shylock, and Bassanio. Their misfortunes extend beyond themselves and impact many others. The world of retributive justice disturbs the harmony of marriage, love, and joy. With that world interrupted, how can love be restored and reconciled to the "naughty world"?[17] The answer, of course, is through mercy.

The reality of merciful forgiveness restoring the world to right relationships is how the play concludes. True, Shylock now begs for mercy as he made Antonio and others beg for mercy; but mercy is granted, and he is reborn through his conversion to Christianity (admittedly implying, here, that Judaism is the religion of strict justice, whilst Christianity is the religion of mercy.) Though sensitive to modern audiences, we must remember the power of this scene and the deconstruction of justice that Shakespeare had in mind when he composed his work. Having just laid bare the insufficiencies of justice and the need for mercy to win the hearts of all, it would have been natural for the Christian audience to want revenge against Shylock for his malevolence toward Antonio. But this would have pulled us right back into the abyss out of which we were climbing. The return to the abyss through the demands of *tisis* is not what Shakespeare gives us.

13. Shakespeare, *Merchant of Venice*, 76.

14. Shakespeare, *Merchant of Venice*, 78.

15. Shakespeare, *Merchant of Venice*, 76.

16. Shakespeare, *Merchant of Venice*, 78.

17. Shakespeare, *Merchant of Venice*, 93.

The mercy extended to Shylock and his conversion are meant to be scandalous. The conversion of Shylock breaks the normative expectations of the audience and the audience's desire for retribution; it also exposes the venomous shortcoming of the audience in how it would have wanted to deal with Shylock due to their own bigotry and prejudices. Mercy wins out, as the duke somewhat calculatedly states, "That thou shalt see the difference of our spirit, / I pardon thee thy life before thou ask it."[18] Furthermore, the fact that such merciful forgiveness is extended to a minority and malcontent like Shylock also tells us much about Shakespeare. Shakespeare is literally calling for mercy to be extended to minorities and malcontents, who often suffer the full force of legalistic justice from an unempathetic society. This appeal for mercy to the minority and malcontent, dare we remember, is an appeal found in the late sixteenth century.

In a lighter and more comedic vein, the ending of the *Merchant of Venice* reinforces the need for merciful forgiveness that we just witnessed in dramatic fashion in the fourth act. While Lorenzo and Jessica flirtatiously play with each other in Belmont near a garden (witness, here, the imagery and language of fertility, love, and serenity), Bassanio returns to make good his life with Portia. However, Bassanio has given away the ring that Portia had given him as the sign of their marriage. Bassanio now pleads for forgiveness before Portia. In order for marriage—for love—to endure, forgiveness (as Portia now long ago said in the first act of the play) must triumph. And triumph it does.

When Portia forgives Bassanio and reveals herself to have been the judge all along, the "little candle" and its shining "light" is manifested for all to see. This dim light shines forth brightly and triumphantly in the dark "naughty world" that is tarnished by retribution and the demands of justice.[19] Song, joy, and party now abound in the world healed by merciful forgiveness. The world absent of merciful forgiveness is a "naughty," "bloody," and "ravenous" world. The world filled with merciful forgiveness heals and brings life, with light and love illuminating it.

Not only does Shakespeare deconstruct the limits of justice for us, he also shows us how a world strictly concerned with justice cannot be a world where love and life itself can flourish. Mercy is the necessary antidote to the world of justice. Moreover, the feminine quality of mercy and the feminine insistence on compassion balance the masculine quality of justice and the masculine insistence on retributive right. Shakespeare does more to advance the compassionate and softer side of life through his comedy than

18. Shakespeare, *Merchant of Venice*, 84.
19. Shakespeare, *Merchant of Venice*, 93.

those who transform the play into a tragedy where the difficult struggle for compassionate mercy is brushed aside and unmeaningful.

May we follow Shakespeare and pardon the crimes of others and bring forth reconciliation, rather than demand the strict letter of justice, which only divides and deepens the chasm between aggrieved and vengeful parties. *The Merchant of Venice* still stands as one of the greatest of Shakespeare's plays, because it does deconstruct and lay bare the shortcomings of society and expose the emptiness of those who demand strict justice. The struggle for mercy is not an easy one, as the play attests. But the manifestation of mercy brings us healing and closure; the fruits of mercy are the end of retributive revenge and the realization of the joyous serenity of love, marriage, and song, as witnessed at the play's conclusion.

This essay was originally published in *Merion West* under the title "What *The Merchant of Venice* Has to Say about Justice," 19 July 2020.

14

Milton's Erotic Cosmos

IS JOHN MILTON A MAN FOR OUR TIME OR ALL TIME? THE BLIND AND PUG-nacious, indeed radical, English poet arguably wrote the greatest epic in the English language. While claiming to "justify the ways of God to men,"[1] Milton's remarkable poem is not only a window into the battles of early modern English civilization, but also a gateway into the mind of a prescient man who served as a precursor to the English Augustan age—an age that confronted the sterile mechanicalism and materialism of the emergent Enlightenment philosophy, an era duly remembered as the Age of Passion.

The Erotic Cosmos

Eros, in Greek, does not singularly mean sexual passion, as it does through our deracinated English inheritance. While *eros* does mean love, in ancient Greece, from Homer down through Thucydides and Plato, *eros* could better be understood as the intensity of the passions which produce ecstasy—both sexual and non-sexual. At various points in the *Iliad*, Homer employs *eros* in non-sexual and sexual settings, and Thucydides incorporates *eros* in purely non-sexual ecstatic political contexts (especially in the *Funeral Oration* and Alcibiades's speech advocating the Sicilian expedition). We might better understand *eros* then as the passionate life force that moves affective creatures into "madness" or ecstasy—from which the intensity of the passions manifest themselves in sexual or non-sexual ways.

1. Milton, *Paradise Lost*, 3.

One might ask then, why not consider Milton's cosmos as passionate instead of erotic? To be sure, "passion" and "passionate" are more neutral terms that are not loaded with the potential negativity of "*eros*" and the "erotic." However, passion and passionate fail to capture that august *Lebens kraft* that *eros* and the erotic do. Moreover, at the end of *Paradise Lost,* the love that the archangel Michael explains to Adam is more in line with the classical tradition concerning the connectivity of *eros* and *theoria*, to which I shall return at the end of this essay. So while I will use the terms somewhat interchangeably, know that the *eros* of which I speak of is an ecstatic intensity of passion that the word *eros* more fully embodies and implies than does the word passion.

Milton's grand epic is an intense poem, a passionate poem, an erotic poem. From the visual imagery to the very descriptive language Milton uses to portray his lively scenes, there is no escaping the reality of the life force that moves his poem. Why, however, does Milton choose to write such a poem, and to whom or what is he writing and responding?

By the time Milton was composing *Paradise Lost,* the Caroline era had come to a violent end in the English Civil War, and the Restoration under Charles II was under way. Milton was a devoted nonconformist, an enemy of the "popish" aspects of the Anglican Church but also a heterodox nonconformist rejecting the deterministic supralapsarianism of Cambridge Calvinism, exemplified by men like William Perkins and William Ames. This is all reflected in his poem, which presents a theodicy of free will. The intellectual currents in philosophy are also important—if not over-riding—for us. Francis Bacon had just published his *Novum Organum* and *New Atlantis,* which charted out the modern scientific-materialistic outlook that would give birth to mechanical philosophy and utilitarianism. Thomas Hobbes had also recently published his *Leviathan,* which, among other things, continued the materialization of philosophy and denied transcendent morality altogether, strongly promoting (especially in the first part) a mechanical philosophy of causality. The emergent materialism of English philosophy was stripping the world of love, of passion, of *eros,* and turning it into a bland world of causality and motion without any zest. This intellectual reality must never be lost to the reader of *Paradise Lost,* alongside Milton's own political and theological radicalism.

In the Land of Eden

The focus on the individual and the individual's genius to understand the reality of the world through private revelation and the poet's reinvention of genres was, for Max Weber, the great creative cultural enterprise of Protestantism. Freed from the constraints of the priesthood, intermediaries, and defined forms and traditions to which one needed to belong, the shattering of old norms and established hierarchies gave the Protestant poet—even if, perhaps, still a practicing Catholic, like Alexander Pope—a new power to embark on his own adventure. In all respects, Milton is then the quintessential Protestant poet of individual genius and reinvention, who reverberates down to the present day, even with postmodern criticism.

Milton's poem is a truly passionate poem. Passion bleeds through its pages from start to finish. The visuality of the poem, its ability to conjure up images in our mind, is intense. The poem begins with a sort of preface (re)stating the standard Christian theodicy of the fall of man and speaks of the promised coming of Christ: "Of man's first disobedience, and the fruit / Of that forbidden tree, whose mortal taste / Brought death into the world, and all our woe, / With loss of Eden, till one great man / Restore us, and regain the blissful seat."[2] The poem then shifts into its true epic narration, beginning with the defeated rebellious angels having been expelled from heaven for their rebellion, the construction of Pandaemonium, and the parliamentary-like debates over their next course of action.

The debate in Pandaemonium begins to reveal Milton's cosmos as being governed by *eros*, intense passion, through the speakers involved. Belial, one of the speaking demons whose advocacy mirrors that of the defeated Latitudinarians, gives an uninspired speech calling for submission and peace before God who has expelled them. Belial's name, in Hebrew, means "worthless." He gives a truly worthless speech because it is not a passionate speech. The counterweight to Belial's speech is the intemperate Moloch, who gives an impassioned plea, more than a speech, about trying once more to storm heaven with greater vigor and resolve than before. Beelzebub also speaks, advocating an "easier enterprise" by seducing the heart of the new race of man created on earth. Beelzebub's speech is passionate but also seductive; Satan decides that Beelzebub's course of action should be followed, but he is the only fallen angel capable of making the ascent out of hell onto earth to see, with his own eyes, this new race created by God.

Satan's "heroic" journey to Eden draws on many classical parallels. It is a journey of trial, visions, and encounters much like Odysseus or Aeneas. Milton was well read in the classics and had a knowledge of not only the canonical classics like Homer and Virgil, but had also recently rediscovered poems of antiquity like Silius Italicus's *Punica*. All of this influenced his rather scandalous re-imagination of the heroic journey/descent/ascent

2. Milton, *Paradise Lost*, 3.

trope with Satan's laborious struggle through the chaotic watery void of the earth and entry into Eden. Satan swims through primordial chaos and overcomes the dangers to eventually spot Adam and Eve perched in each other's arms in paradise, but not without first meeting Sin and Death, who ominously foreshadow the malevolent intentions of Satan. Satan is no hero; his journey is an inversion and cruel parody of the classical heroic journey.

The encounter with Adam and Eve sparks a sort of jealous love triangle. The real reason Satan is so filled with resolve to destroy God's new creation is because he beholds all the good things that the new world holds, of which he is deprived. We witness then a passionate Satan, rather than some banal villain with plans of vainglory and egoism. The Satan who looks over Eden, Adam and Eve, and the beautiful world just created is a jealous figure, a figure filled with emotion and passion just like the rest of creation—but passions that are manifested through deprivation rather than fulfillment. And this is one of the remarkable achievements of Milton, for Milton informs us that evil and sin are the byproducts of the deprivations of our passions, rather than mere attempts to fulfill them.

Satan's spotting of Adam and Eve strikes us as peculiar, perhaps thanks to our puritanical sentiment, but the image is very moving, because it is scandalously erotic:

> From this Assyrian garden, where the Fiend
> Saw undelighted all delight, all kind
> Of living creatures new to sight and strange:
> Two of far nobler shape erect and tall,
> Godlike erect, with native honour clad
> In naked majesty seemed lords of all.[3]

The second image of our earthly parents is an equally sensual one:

> So spake our general mother, and with eyes
> Of conjugal attraction unreproved,
> And meek surrender, half-embracing leaned
> On our first father; half her swelling breast
> Naked met his under the flowing gold
> Of her loose tresses hid; he in delight
> Both of her beauty and submissive charms
> Smiled with superior love, as Jupiter
> On Juno smiles when he impregns the clouds
> That shed May flowers; and pressed her matron lip
> With kisses pure: aside the Devil turned
> For envy, yet with jealous leer malign

3. Milton, *Paradise Lost*, 81.

Eyed them askance, and to himself thus plained.[4]

What we witness, with Satan, is an Eden—a world, a whole cosmos—that is teeming with radiance and life. The cosmos which Milton has just described, from the storms of primordial chaos to the wondrous and sex-filled garden of Eden, is a world antithetical to the mechanical philosophers and scientists who see only material objects moving and bouncing off each other as predetermined laws of physics demand. The cosmos through which Satan journeys and which he sees, the cosmos that fills him with intense jealousy and envy, is an erotic cosmos moved by love, passion, and intimacy. The world in its ecstasy and radiance is Milton's poeticized *fruitio Dei*. Milton's material world is not dry or sterile but governed by the passions that bring life to the dirt, trees, and leaves, and, most of all, our human father and mother.

Milton is confronting the sterile materialistic cosmos emerging from the proto-scientific intelligentsia that is stripping the universe of its mystery and beauty, just as much as he is offering theological criticism. The world we witness is a steamy world of life, spirit, and zest. It is a world of grandeur and beauty, pleasure and erotica, intensity and intimacy.

Not only is the newly created world filled with great passion, Satan himself is filled with newfound passions—envy, jealousy—in being deprived of the good things the world holds. As such, his new resolve is what propels him onward to destroy this truly beautiful and loving world. Yet in this juxtaposition, we see a passionate villain tied to the passionate world he seeks to upend. Satan, again, is no cold, mechanical, or lifeless supervillain but a villain of flesh and blood emotion; Satan is a villain filled with the emotions of jealousy and envy that stem from the deprivation of his passions.

The Fall of Man and Hope in Love

The fall of man, as Milton poetically describes, is the product of relational deprivation. When Adam and Eve were first created, Eve is nearly enslaved by her own voluptuous beauty when she sees herself in a puddle (reminding us of Narcissus): "As I bent down to look, just opposite / A shape within the wat'ry gleam appeared / Bending to look on me: I started back, / It started back, but pleased I soon returned, / Pleased it returned as soon with answering looks / Of sympathy and love; there I had fixed / Mine eyes till now, and pined with vain desire, / Had not a voice thus warned me."[5] Adam saves Eve

---

4. Milton, *Paradise Lost*, 86.
5. Milton, *Paradise Lost*, 85.

from herself. This brief moment is important for the reader to remember
going forward because it establishes the precedence of loneliness and the
impossibility of passionate embrace, which would be tragic. In the intimacy
of embrace, however, we find love and the fulfillment of the passions. Alone,
we lack intimacy and can only embrace unreal distortions of ourselves that
can never fulfill our passions.

Satan, if we recall, is in Eden—alone. Satan's loneliness deprives him of
the intimacy and passionate ecstasy of life and sensuality that he sees, which
drives him to jealousy and envy. He ventured alone into the world and is
therefore deprived of the intimacy that comes with others. Alone, he tries
to wreak havoc.

The passions that Satan exudes in his loneliness are really passions
governed by deprivation. Here Milton is very Augustinian. Satan is not
without passion in *Paradise Lost*. But the passions which govern Satan are
negative ones, because they are the result of a privation. Satan cannot love,
because he has no partner to love. Satan cannot make love, as he sees Adam
and Eve doing, because he has no partner with whom to make love. Satan
cannot rescue others, as we just saw Adam do for Eve, because he has no one
to rescue. Because he is alone, the passions that govern Satan are necessarily
reductive and destructive; hence he is gripped by envy, jealousy, and hatred,
the ultimate passions born from lack. Adam and Eve initially share a relational mutuality; thus they are completed in the presence of each other, and
to destroy this relational mutuality—thereby depriving Adam and Eve of the
good passions they enjoy in each other's arms and presence—is now the task
of Satan. (The sympathy toward Satan among Romantics in the nineteenth
century and onward is due to these readers and critics having been deprived
of many things in their own lives, thus causing them to passionately yearn
for love, restoration, intimacy, and naturally to have sympathy for Satan,
because they lacked the same things Satan lacked; in their own lack, they
haphazardly sympathized with the one character of the poem who is most
like them.)

God, however, has seen the serpent and dispatched Raphael to warn
Adam of the danger that faces them. This leads to a lengthy discourse on the
War in Heaven and the intensity of that conflict, with great battles, duels,
and heroes in arms reminiscent of the great classical war poetry of antiquity.
Even these sections of *Paradise Lost* continue the theme of passionate gover-
nance over the poem—whether in heaven, hell, or Eden.

Nevertheless, the fall of man occurs when Eve separates herself from
Adam. "Refreshment, whether food, or talk between, / Food of the mind,
or this sweet intercourse / Of looks and smiles, for smiles from reason flow,
/ To brute denied, and are of love the food, / Love not the lowest end of

human life"[6] is precisely what will be lost in the fall. Here, however, Milton explicitly states that love is "not the lowest end of human life." On the contrary, love is the highest end of human life. Eve's request to divide their labor apart from each other, to separate and go alone just as Satan had attempted to achieve in planting the first false dream in Eve earlier in the poem, is the catalyst of our demise. Our fall is predicated on separation, on loneliness.

What Milton suggests through the separation of Adam and Eve, whom we have seen together throughout the poem, is that love, pleasure, and enjoyment—all those good things we have in relationship—are lost without intimate mutuality. In other words, loneliness is the cause of evil because loneliness is the ultimate form of deprivation from the interconnected world that we have beheld throughout *Paradise Lost*. The paradise lost is nothing less than the intimately connected world of relational mutuality, from which love truly flows and in which smiles are manifested.

This is revealed to us in Eve's eating of the fruit. "Greedily she engorged without restraint," Milton writes.[7] She eats without control and with no relationship to the world: life is just about her. The images of passion that tickled our fancies and made us fawn so lovingly over the splendid world of Eden in the earlier books are now images causing revulsion and disgust. Lastly, Eve falls into idolatry by praising the tree rather than God as Adam and Eve had been doing earlier. (Note here that when Adam and Eve were together, they praised God; but now alone, Eve falls into idolatry). As Eve realizes her death in disobedience, jealousy—an emotion previously tied only to Satan—enslaves her. As she says to herself, "I shall be no more, / And Adam wedded to another Eve, / Shall live with her enjoying, I extinct; / A death to think. Confirmed then I resolve, / Adam shall share with me in bliss or woe."[8] The loss of mutuality and relationship is what caused the fall in Milton's poetic rendering.

With this as our understanding, we can now fully realize the gravity and romance of Adam's decision to die with Eve. As our mother and father reunite and have sex, they are overcome with guilt, shame, and humiliation. The negative passions, the emotions wrought from deprivation, are now enslaving them both. This too, however, is a grand achievement by Milton. Given the reality of his erotic cosmos—a cosmos governed by passion—the cosmos, even after the fall, is still governed by passion and remains an erotic cosmos. But the cosmos after the fall is a cosmos where passion no longer

---

6. Milton, *Paradise Lost*, 192.

7. Milton, *Paradise Lost*, 206.

8. Milton, *Paradise Lost*, 207.

leads to enjoyment but to hatred, jealousy, and envy. The passions of deprivation now rule the world.

Why, then, given the chance for reconciliation, does Adam choose
instead to die with Eve? On the one hand, Milton's hand is forced by the
biblical narrative to include the fall of both sexes. Adam and Eve must die
together. On the other hand, we realize that Adam's decision to die with
Eve rather than live alone is what must transpire in a cosmos of mutuality.
Alone, Adam would be miserable. With Eve, however, he still has a partner,
a wife, and a lover. To choose loneliness would be to choose damnation. To
choose togetherness, even in the fall, paradoxically brings salvation—and
this is what must transpire for our own salvation and the coming of Christ.
Adam's choice to die with Eve rather than live alone in paradise is the ultimate act of love (something a handful of church fathers saw in Adam's
decision to die for his beloved as prefiguring Christ and the church).

The archangel Michael then appears and informs Adam of the future
of the human race as he presents the grandest *theoria* (vision) in the poem.
In yet another great achievement by England's greatest poet, we receive a
spectacular retelling of the biblical story from Cain and Abel to the incarnation, death, and resurrection of Christ. When Michael informs Adam of
the terrible stories of sin, Adam grows despondent and is governed by fear
and sadness. When Michael informs Adam of the goodness of God, the
triumph of love, and the coming of Christ, Adam rejoices and is governed
by happiness.

With these revelations now complete, in faith (and in love) Adam rejoices and, together with Eve, leaves Eden on "their solitary way."[9] The end
of *Paradise Lost* contains the greatest erotic image—*eros*, again, in that classical understanding linked to ecstatic visuality. The revelation parted unto
Adam of the future of the world and human race fills him with joy; he is
overwhelmed by the great love of God before departing the garden and is
thus governed by happiness instead of despair.

The end of *Paradise Lost* also foreshadows salvation and love in its
fullness. Adam and Eve are reunited, "hand in hand," and embark on their
pilgrimage beside each other. The intimate and passionate world that Milton
created and defended against its critics is also the bridge to our own journey in life. Solitary, he writes, their journey may be—but they are not truly
alone. Upon closer inspection, they are together, and "Providence with their
guide" is also beside them:

> They looking back, all th' eastern side beheld
> Of Paradise, so late their happy seat,

9. Milton, *Paradise Lost*, 288.

Waved over by that flaming brand, the gate
With dreadful faces thronged and fiery arms:
Some natural tears they dropped, but wiped them soon;
The world was all before them, where to choose
Their place of happy rest, and Providence with their guide:
They hand in hand with wand'ring steps and slow,
Through Eden took their solitary way.[10]

Love, intimacy, and togetherness remain the final image of Milton's splendid poem. We just need to know where to look. And when we do see that reality, we shall understand how love binds all things together and keeps us from separating dissolution, the separating dissolution that causes us to be governed by the deprived passions bringing misery, jealousy, and envy in their wake. The beauty and paradox of Milton's ending is that while Adam and Eve are said to begin their pilgrimage in solitude, they are together just as they were before the fall, and they have "Providence [as] their guide," which they previously did not have in the garden. God was always at a distance and working through angels; but now, in the final sentence of *Paradise Lost*, we are told that Providence is with them as their guide. The journey Adam and Eve now begin, having been expelled from Eden, is a journey guided by the very intimacy of love that we had glimpsed all along: "hand in hand, with wand'ring steps and slow," they begin their pilgrimage with "Providence [as] their guide."[11]

This essay was originally published in *The Imaginative Conservative*, 1 February 2020.

10. Milton, *Paradise Lost*, 287–88.

11. Milton, *Paradise Lost*, 288.

15

The Fall and Degeneration
of Man in *Gulliver's Travels*

On October 28, 1726, the book known today as *Gulliver's Travels* was published as *Travels into Several Remote Nations of the World*. A mock work of travel literature, Jonathan Swift's famous novel is a far deeper work than one of just Juvenalian and Horatian satire. It is an indictment against the prevailing spirit of Enlightenment philosophy and utopianism, an esoteric defense of Christianity against its Enlightenment critics, and a prophetic vision into the future degeneration of humanity in following the dictates of the natural philosophers of modernity.

Swiftian irony is one of the great joys of the work. And irony runs replete through Lemuel Gulliver's fall and degeneration—not to mention the shifting narrative voice of Swift and Gulliver leaving the gentle reader to detect if they are reading Gulliver's voice or Swift's authorial wit. But where traditional literary narrative has the travelling protagonist return home to comfort and love, Swift's Gulliver returns home deranged and a hater of humanity. This is a far cry from being one of the greatest "lovers of mankind" when he initially arrived in the Houyhnhnm country.[1]

Gulliver's journey to hell and bringing hell back with him can be broken down into two parts. There is the voyage to Lilliput and Brobdingnag. Then there is the voyage to Laputa and the Houyhnhnm country. While all four journeys are inexorably interlinked in a journey of decline, Lilliput is in dialectical contrast more to Brobdingnag, as Laputa is to the Houyhnhnm

---

1. Swift, *Gulliver's Travels*, 215.

country. When Gulliver arrives shipwrecked on Lilliput, he is tied down by the six-inch men and women of the island, who view him as a threat. The other, the stranger, the foreigner, is always met with suspicion. While the Lilliputians have a certain vigor and ingenuity, they are ultimately contemptible creatures. Their smallness is meant to represent their lack of virtue and finer qualities. After all, despite what Gulliver had done for them, they come to condemn him as a traitor out of vindictive jealousy, so as to punish him by cutting out his eyes.

For putting out the fire at the royal palace in the most humorous of ways, and therefore saving the emperor's palace, he is condemned by an ancient law that prohibits the discharge of any liquid in the palace. For saving Lilliput from invasion and advocating peace between Blefuscu and Lilliput, where the people may flourish in the peace, the Lilliputians condemn Gulliver as a traitor—especially since Gulliver didn't let the Lilliputians indulge their fantasy of imperial conquest and domination at Blefuscu's expense. The condemnation for treachery is magnified in Gulliver's flight to Blefuscu simply on account of his want to have his liberty restored to him. The Lilliputians, in Gulliver's flight from them, are cast as ungrateful people. Gulliver's bigness really comes out here; he was the bigger man physically and spiritually.

Where the tininess of the Lilliputians shows their shortcomings, the largeness of Brobdingnagians magnifies their imperfections. No Brobdingnagian is without flaws, all perfectly on display for Gulliver to see, much as no human is without the stain of original sin. But Swift's genius is in the dialectical role reversal of Gulliver between Lilliput and Brobdingnag.

Gulliver is now the equivalent size of the Lilliputians from earlier and is placed in their shoes in his journey to Brobdingnag. But where the Lilliputians—for all their shortcomings—saw Gulliver with certain awe and majesty, Gulliver sees the Brobdingnagians as ugly, disproportionate, and marred. This is because the Brobdingnagians are the incarnate Europeans of Swift's time. The Brobdingnagians are also experiencing a technological revolution. This is made clear by the fact that Gulliver is nearly killed by multiple machines, feels alienated and isolated at every turn in the farmer's home despite their generous care of him, and by the fact that the Brobdingnagians examine Gulliver under intense scientific scrutiny.

In fact, when the Brobdingnagian wisemen inspect Gulliver, they conclude—by the dictates of natural philosophy, divorced from divinity—that Gulliver is a freak of nature. While Swift's satire of Brobdingnagian society is the beginning of his longwinded criticism of materialist philosophy and what we now call scientism, there is also an ironic symbiotic understanding between Gulliver and the Brobdingnagians. Both see each other as freaks of nature. Gulliver, due to the largeness of the Brobdingnagians, is attuned to their flaws, scars, and diseases. The Brobdingnagians, due to the intense examination of matter with only themselves against which to judge, conclude Gulliver to be a freak accident, despite his form and rationality matching him with them.

This is a defining moment in the work. Through Gulliver, Swift states that the Brobdingnagian assertion that he is a freak of nature is "exactly agreeable to the modern philosophy of Europe."[2] In other words, the emerging materialist philosophy of the Enlightenment will eventually do away with the incarnate humanism of Christian anthropology and conclude humans to be freaks of nature and no different from other animals. How prescient, all things considered.

The lack of beauty and proportionality in Brobdingnag is equally reflective of the emerging scientific outlook of the new science. In putting nature on the rack of interrogation, as Francis Bacon advocated, the interrogation of nature reveals all her flaws. Beauty cannot survive the withering scrutiny of a purely mechanistic and reductionist disposition. Hence where the Lilliputians looked up to Gulliver with some sense of awe and wonder, the Brobdingnagians look down at Gulliver as a freak, and Gulliver the same at the Brobdingnagians. The directionality of vision is a subtle importance in shifting consciousness from seeing awe and wonder in nature to condemning nature as freakish and ugly. The Brobdingnagians may share a sense of classical natural right—duty and obligation to Gulliver symbolized by their care of him, despite his being a freak of nature—but that is not the discovery of modernity but the inheritance of the classical tradition, which is quickly being lost in the modern project. The downward plunge of history and the degeneration of man is now just beginning.

Despite returning home for a brief respite, Gulliver accepts pay and advancement to go on yet another journey—leaving behind his wife and children. The advancement of commerce, exploration, and industry is too alluring for Gulliver, and life with his family is what must be sacrificed for the sake of progress. While the Lilliputians and Brobdingnagians are dialectically paired with each other for reasons hitherto explained, there is also a connection with the Brobdingnagians and the Laputans insofar as the Laputans are the apex of the scientistic and mechanical-mathematical outlook of man, which began with the Brobdingnagians. But the journeys to Laputa and the Houyhnhnm country are better dialectical contrasts because of the hyperrationalism exuded by both societies and the detriment that such a worldview is to humans.

2. Swift, *Gulliver's Travels*, 94.

There is even greater irony in Gulliver's journey to Laputa. Though a city that is high in the air, as if in the heavens, its inhabitants are deformed and fallen in a far more grotesque way than even the Brobdingnagians. Gulliver's journey may have taken him upward in a physical sense, but it has also taken him downward in a spiritual and interior sense. The distorted eyes of the Laputans represent the distortion of man's vision clouded by the arrogance and pretense of scientific rationalism. They can no longer see the straight and true and will quickly get lost like the pilgrim Dante, who wandered from the straight and true in the opening of the *Divine Comedy*.

Moreover, the distinctiveness of the Lilliputians and Brobdingnagians—despite their flaws—is now reduced to homogenized sameness in Gulliver's entry into Laputa. As Gulliver recounts, he had never "seen a race of mortals so singular in their shapes, habits, and countenances."[3] It is in Laputa that Swift begins his blistering satirical criticism of the Royal Society and their mathematical obsession, because Swift perfectly sees the exhaustive end of this outlook: atheism. And the Royal Society today is a bastion of anti-Christian hatred, embodying the very arrogance and pretensions of the scientific Laputans.

In terms of knowledge, the Laputans consider only mathematics and natural science discoveries as counting toward knowledge. The wealth of knowledge that comes with arts, culture, and tradition is meaningless to them—except for music, but that's only because of the mathematical symmetry that music can produce. Furthermore, through their mastery of nature, the Laputans have turned nature into the plaything of man. Again, Swift is far ahead of his time in seeing where the utilitarian-mathematical mindset leads. From discovery just for the sake of knowledge, the Laputans turn their knowledge of nature and its movements into tools for their own lusts, often terrorizing other people with their mastery and manipulation of nature.

Despite the scientific prowess of the Laputans, they lack common sense and civility. The Flappers that attend them and do all the now-mundane tasks of daily living represent common sense in a world that has drifted away from common sense. Swift fires all the cannons in ironically showing how a materialistically obsessed civilization loses common sense and cannot function without a subservient race of dispossessed toilers. Additionally, family life is entirely lacking in Laputa. The men are concerned only with their work. They leave their wives feeling alienated and estranged, which causes them to engage in adultery; but the men, unable to see clearly,

---

3. Swift, *Gulliver's Travels*, 146.

either don't know or don't care about the cries and depression of their wives. Laputa then is a highly atomized society—which is to say, no society at all.

The Laputans also live extremely hollow lives. They are empty people. The Laputans then can be seen as an early prefiguration of T.S. Eliot's "hollow men" or C.S. Lewis's "men without chests."[4]

It is this hollowness and sterile rationalism that the Laputans exude that dialectically pairs them with the Houyhnhnm rather than the Brobdingnagians—though there remains that general linkage between all, as Gulliver descends further down the mountain of insanity when he reaches the Houyhnhnm country. The Houyhnhnm are a satirical parody of the hyper-stoic rationalism of Baruch Spinoza and deductive-only reasoning that shuns ratiocinative reasoning (the Houyhnhmn cannot a priori conceive that Gulliver came from another land, because they have no evidence of any other lands besides their isle, which already exposes the limits of their rationality to the gentle reader, as the reader knows Gulliver is from England). At the same time, Swift's portrayal of the Houyhnhnm as naturalistically rational animals in a seemingly harmonious relationship with the world in which they live is a prophetic foreshadowing of the movement of naturalistic primitivism that culminated in Jean-Jacques Rousseau's noble savage.

The Houyhnhnm are singularly rational animals divorced from all passion. They are the final descent into this brave new life of dead bodies to which the modern project is leading man: hyperrationalist, body only, eros denying, hunks of thinking meat and matter. Swift's brilliance in this respect is captured by the fact that one of the most passionate animals filled with *thymos*, the horse, is now depicted without passion. The Houyhnhnm have the form of horses but lack the spirit, the essence, of horses. There is another creature that is filled with passion: the human. The loss of passion in the Houyhnhnm represents the loss of passion in humans in the neo-stoic push for hyperrationality as the highest good in and of itself (rather than love).

Swift's Christianity cannot be divorced from *Gulliver's Travels*, though the work, at the surface, seemingly has little to do with religion. The fourth book, however, has almost everything to do with religion and theological anthropology between the lines. The modern project of anthropology is, as Swift knew, a wholesale rejection of the Christian understanding of man. It is a rejection of his fallenness, a rejection of his uniqueness, and a rejection of his lovingness, simultaneously. The rejection of fallenness leading to wild ideas of perfectibility is soundly satirized at the end of the third book, when Swift lampoons the supposedly rational want for immortality and through the Houyhnhnm, who think reason alone is capable of

4. Lewis, *Abolition of Man*, 1.

human empowerment and salvation. The rejection of man's uniqueness and particularity is shown in Gulliver's time spent in Laputa, where they are singular masses of bland sameness. While the Laputans lack the ability to love but are still seeking love, the Houyhnhnm are entirely divorced from passion, seeing passion as something that is wholly incompatible with reason, so love is entirely eviscerated from Houyhnhnm consciousness. Thus, the Houyhnhnm language has no word for compulsion, since compulsion is unbefitting to a rational animal.

Gulliver entered the Houyhnhnm country as a lover of his native country and a self-professed great "lover of mankind."[5] In his dealings with the Houyhnhnm, he comes to hold his native country in nothing but contempt and likewise comes to view humanity with scorn. Ashamed that the Houyhnhnm consider him a Yahoo—the degenerate hominid species analogous to humans in the Houyhnhnm country—Gulliver falls for prideful supremacism in thinking himself above the herd: "I expressed my uneasiness at his giving me so often the appellation of Yahoo, an odious animal, for which I had so utter an hatred and contempt. I begged he would forbear applying that word to me."[6]

The allusions to Saint Augustine's *Confessions* and *City of God* in the fourth book are even more apparent as Gulliver slips into the sin of pride, like the Stoics and Porphyry whom Augustine critiqued in his works. Gulliver is like Porphyry, a man who claims to be dedicated to the pursuit of truth as the Houyhnhnm are, but who rejects that which is self-evident because of his egoistic pride. So too has the same fate befallen Gulliver, who becomes the primary target of Swift's satire, more so than the Houyhnhnm.

While Gulliver may have been taken over by the false rationalism of the Houyhnhnm, the gentle reader should be able to see through the veil of the Houyhnhnm disposition. There are no marriages of love in Houyhnhnmland, only marriages of convenient breeding. Life is advanced through eugenics as the dictates of pure reason, so-called, demand. Future generations of Houyhnhnm are specially bred with the intermixing of the best male and female Houyhnhnm. Most egregiously, the Houyhnhnm are shown to be genocidal when they take up the question of exterminating the Yahoos from the earth.

Swift's subtle deconstruction of the Houyhnhnm exposes the amorality, or immorality, of the hyperrationalist and anti-humanist position that must come about from the disintegration of the true and only humanism contained in the Christian anthropological position. If man is nothing but

---

5. Swift, *Gulliver's Travels*, 215.
6. Swift, *Gulliver's Travels*, 221.

a bodily, greedy, and destructive animal who has no harmony with nature (and no soul)—as represented by the Yahoos—what is to stop the self-proclaimed arbiters of reason and naturalistic nobility (represented by the Houyhnhnm) from culling undesirables, for the sake of the earth?

As the Houyhnhnm contemplate killing all the Yahoos for the sake of the earth, Swift incorporates many direct allusions to the fall of man from John Milton's *Paradise Lost*. The educated and cultured gentle reader, who would have been familiar with these references, is now caught between Swiftian or Gulliverian voices. Who is really the fallen and degenerate race? The supposedly hyperrational Houyhnhnm fro whom Gulliver has fallen hand over feet, or the Yahoos whom the Houyhnhnm despise out of prejudice for being irrational creatures? The Houyhnhnm account of the expulsion of the first two Yahoos from the mountain—an allusion to the fall and expulsion of man in *Paradise Lost*—is not tied to the Yahoos but to the Houyhnhnm, who are considering wiping the Yahoos off the face of the earth. Swift ties the fall of man not to the Yahoos but to the Houyhnhnm.

The reduction of man to just rational animal is the degeneration of man to insanity. When Gulliver finally leaves Houyhnhnmland, teary-eyed and overwrought with grief from having to part company with such noble animals, Gulliver returns home disgusted at the sight of his wife and children, who thought him dead and greet his arrival with tears of joy as passionate and loving animals. There is no special homecoming for Gulliver. Gulliver shuns his wife's affection for him and cannot stand being around Yahoos—which he has now taken to calling all humans he encounters, despite the gentle nobility, compassion, and kindness shown to him from Don Pedro and his joyful wife and children.

Gulliver's sin of pride reaches the point of blasphemy where he makes a mockery of the Eucharist in his separation from his family at dinner: "To this hour they dare not presume to touch my bread, or drink out of the same cup; neither was I ever able to let one of them take me by the hand."[7] Not only is this a blasphemous mock of the Lord's Supper, it also highlights the misanthropic and atomistic attitude of Gulliver. Gulliver shuns his family and human relations for two horses he buys and with which he spends all his time—preferring their company, imagining them as Houyhnhnm, and neighing with them, thinking he is communicating with them. Gulliver has literally become an animal upon his return to England. This is not an isolated reality contained to Gulliver. Swift is warning that England will become a den of blasphemy and animalization if she continues her degenerative direction, epitomized by the direction her intellectuals and leaders

7. Swift, *Gulliver's Travels*, 271.

in politics and the Royal Society are taking the country. (This is made even more incredible, given Swift saw this emerging future in 1726.)

The degeneration of man is completed by the modern project that bore its weight down on Gulliver, who succumbed to the unbearable weight he initially was able to fend off in his earlier travels. The animalization of man culminated in Gulliver's transformation into an imitator of the Houyhnhnm—which is no imitation of nature at all, because nature is hollow and vacuous, as the Enlightenment physiologists, scientists, and philosophers asserted. Gulliver's estranged relationship with his wife and children ends on the pessimistic note that love and joy are not possible in this brave new world where beauty, passion, and the sacred have been stripped away. Thus *Gulliver's Travels* is—in its Swiftian genius—a work that defends beauty, passion, and the sacred, which becomes eminently clear by the book's conclusion, through its relentless exposure of the absurdity of the modern project, which has destroyed beauty, passion, and the sacred.

This essay was originally published in *The Imaginative Conservative*, 3 January 2019 and again 23 January 2019.

16

In the Ruins of Babylon
The Poetic "Genius" of John Keats

THE BEST THINGS WE HAVE COME FROM MADNESS, SO SOCRATES SAID IN the *Phaedrus*. John Keats died at only twenty-five of age after contracting tuberculosis. During his lifetime, he was a remarkably unsuccessful poet, despite being propped up by Leigh Hunt and his band of radical writers and poets around the *Examiner*. Despite his premature death and relative obscurity in those years, Keats grew in immortal fame afterward—becoming a sort of priest and prophet for the more radical Romantics of the nineteenth century who dreamt of abolition, emancipation, and revolution.

Keats grew up in the shadow of the French Revolution, Napoleonic War, and Metternichian settlement, which reacted harshly against the radical politics of emancipatory Jacobinism. Keats also grew up in the bosom of materialism and an emerging utilitarianism in his native England, the same hollow materialism against which earlier forebears like Swift rebelled. It goes without saying that Keats's two great intellectual fantasies and interests, love and radical politics, were suffocated by the general currents of his day.

"Give me women, wine, and snuff . . . . My beloved Trinity."[1] Keats's sensual and dramatic poetry, in its eroticism and veiled social commentary, earned him the scorn of Tory reviewers in the English press, which effectively killed his poetic career. While Keats saw a vulgar superstition in the "melancholy . . . church bells" and "gloominess" of "horrid" sermons in his day[2]—seeing Christian puritanism as a soul-crushing and love-suppress-

---

1. Keats, *Selected Poems*, 5.
2. Keats, *Selected Poems*, 32.

ing religion that contributed to the eradication of romantic love and the consummation of "men of cruel clay"[3]—there is a tragic irony in Keats's flight from Jerusalem and indulgence in the ruins of Babylon, while still carrying with him unconsciously inherited prejudices from Jerusalem. The "Love [that] never dies, but lives, [as] immortal Lord"[4] is not the paganism of Cronus overthrowing Uranus, or Jupiter assaulting Ganymede, but a paganized window dressing of the God of love.

William Wordsworth rightly described Keats's poetry as "very pretty paganism."[5] But the romanticized and mythologized paganism of Keats, while vulgar in its sexual yearnings and fantasies, was a paganism that was as much de-mythologized from its actual roots as it was re-mythologized from an unconscious theology and divinization of love from the very Christianity from which Keats was fleeing in favor of Sodom and Gomorrah. This paganized Christianity in which Keats and other second-generation Romantics indulged would fit nicely into some neo-pagan circles today, which would earn Keats the title of political radical, but not the radicalism sanctioned by contemporary elites.

The disordered passions that Keats eulogized were the exhaustive end of a world that had the baptized heart of sacramentality and the demands of a life of sacrifice stripped away from it. The edifice of Christianity that remained, which was a bulwark against the political radicalism that equally seduced Keats, subsequently became the entombing coffin of the dead body that Keats wanted desperately to resurrect. Keats didn't want to wait for the day of resurrection for love to be fully consummated and present: "Give me women, wine, and snuff / Until I cry out, 'Hold, enough!' / You may do sans objection / Till the day of resurrection; / For, bless my beard, they aye shall be / My beloved Trinity."[6]

The impulsive passion and fantasized love of which Keats wrote could have emerged only from a theological culture that prized beauty and love. But the romanticizing of the fairness and sensuality of Babylon as something noble, and indeed salvific, was only possible from a pen that had inherited the theological culture that affirmed beauty and love as giving life to the world. "A thing of beauty is a joy for ever" is very true,[7] but not from the city of frenzied confusion and sizzling lusts in which Keats danced.

3. Keats, *Selected Poems*, 115.

4. Keats, *Selected Poems*, 123.

5. Keats, *Selected Poems*, xx.

6. Keats, *Selected Poems*, 5.

7. Keats, *Selected Poems*, 38.

Part of the project of Keats's poetry was to reenchant a dead world. This effort was needed in his day and remains needed in our day. However, in this ambition to help reenchant and re-mystify the world, Keats overlooked Christianity and that religion whose God is love.

"The Eve of St. Agnes," one of Keats's later poems and rich—if not overly sensual—masterpieces, tells the tale of two virginal lovers erotically embracing each other and fleeing outward into a storm. This poem, more than others, so concisely captures the madness of Keats's poetry. The educated reader is torn between shock and sympathy as Keats writes soteriological poetry in the cold and dark confines of Christianity, while the spirit of Christianity looms over Keats's entire project to the knowledgeable reader.

At the beginning of the poem, we are introduced to a beadsman in a cold and frozen environment. The cold and frozen environment, like Dante's hell, is symbolic of the coldness of a place without love at its heart. Very quickly, however, we learn the beadsman is praying the rosary, and Keats's condemnation becomes clear for all readers: Christianity is responsible for the coldness of the world now occupied, which forbids romantic love. The beadsman is too busy praying and engaging in dark ritualistic piety than he is living a life of warming love; Keats's social commentary is at once as esoteric as it is exoteric. As the beadsman retires inside a house, which is reminiscent of a monastery or Christian structure or chapel, "his deathbell [had] rung."[8]

Inside this cold and moonlit place are two impassioned virgins, Porphyro and Madeline. Keats's imagery and descriptions of their fantasizing and bodily actions can only be described as the descriptive language of boyhood fantasies. But Madeline's sensual dancing and undressing and Porphyro's lusts tell another story. Madeline is a modern girl repressed by the structures and world around her. Porphyro is an old god, like Cupid, needing to rescue his Psyche, Madeline, in order for light and warmth to reenter the world.

Keats was a philhellene, not altogether dissimilar from other Romantic poets from England like Lord Byron or Percy Bysshe Shelley. That the two lovers have two radically different names, one harkening back to antiquity and another common to nineteenth-century England, is very much part of the story of erotic revival that Keats wishes to tell. Moreover, Madeline's transfiguration is reminiscent of Aphrodite's birth, and Porphyro's gaze like any pubescent boy longing to be in the place of Paris at the judgment of Athena, Aphrodite, and Hera.

8. Keats, *Selected Poems*, 165.

Porphyro and Madeline are both resurrected in their longings for love. Porphyro "played an ancient ditty, long since mute." Madeline awoke: "Her blue affrayed eyes wide open shone" as "she uttered a soft moan." In this moment, perhaps the mad climax of Keats's fantastical imagination, the first contrast to the coldness and frozenness of the dead world with which the poem began is revealed; Porphyro's whispering and pleasant playing is described as "warm."[9] Furthermore, the flight of Porphyro and Madeline from their imprisoning castle begins at dawn, in contrast to the cold and dark night that dominated much of the poem. The burning hearts of Porphyro and Madeline burn for the illicit loves of the body, crackling away in the frying pan of sensualism instead of finding the love offered by the author of love.

Keats's love poetry is a remarkable achievement, all things considered. Yet it pales in comparison to the substance of George Herbert and the religious poets who predated him. In contrast to that great English poet, Keats's eulogies of love border on mad parody of the Love that Herbert more truthfully and powerfully captured:

> Love bade me welcome. Yet my soul drew back
> Guilty of dust and sin.
> But quick-eyed Love, observing me grow slack
> From my first entrance in,
> Drew nearer to me, sweetly questioning,
> If I lacked any thing.
>
> A guest, I answered, worthy to be here:
> Love said, You shall be he.
> I the unkind, ungrateful? Ah my dear,
> I cannot look on thee.
> Love took my hand, and smiling did reply,
> Who made the eyes but I?
>
> Truth Lord, but I have marred them: let my shame
> Go where it doth deserve.
> And know you not, says Love, who bore the blame?
> My dear, then I will serve.
> You must sit down, says Love, and taste my meat:
> So I did sit and eat.[10]

9. Keats, *Selected Poems*, 175.
10. Herbert, "Love (III)."

Keats also desired the nourishment and fulfillment of love, even the love of "one moment's pleasure."[11] "Hither, hither, love— / 'Tis a shady mead— / Hither, hither, love, / Let us feed and feed!"[12] Where Herbert's Love informed by Christianity is satiating and redeeming, Keats's love is fleeting and ends only with death. "Hither, hither, hither, / Love this boon has sent— / If I die and wither / I shall die content."[13] Herbert's nourishment of the soul from the plate of true meat shows the emptiness of the carnal meat that enslaved Keats's heart and imagination. The "bright torch ... [and] warm Love"[14] to which Keats sings his songs of praise is a different Love than the Love of Christianity. Keats fell for the same conception of love that flung Francesca and Paolo into the torrential storm of lust in hell.

Between Aristophanes and Glaucon, Keats falls into the tradition begotten by Aristophanes. The poetry of Keats is a window into the mad genius of the Romantics: their lusts and hopes, their ambitions and ignorance, their radicalism and fantasies. In reading Keats, one is simultaneously scandalized and sympathetic to the longing of the Romantic heart like the burning hearts of Porphyro and Madeline who awoke, only to run into a storm akin to Dante's abode of the lustful. "Fanatics have their dreams,"[15] and Keats was undeniably a fanatic who dreamed dreams. It is truly a poetic irony that the prophet who sang and danced for love died in the city conquered by the author of love. Genius is often a form of madness, and a mad genius Keats certainly was. If Christians were able to baptize Plato, Aristotle, and Virgil, so too should Christians be able to baptize the poetic splendor of John Keats as a road to George Herbert, instead of ending with Porphyro and Madeline running into the eternal storm of lust to join Francesca and Paolo.

This essay was originally published in *The Imaginative Conservative*, 29 May 2019.

---

11. Keats, *Selected Poems*, 36.

12. Keats, *Selected Poems*, 35.

13. Keats, *Selected Poems*, 36.

14. Keats, *Selected Poems*, 189.

15. Keats, *Selected Poems*, 221.

17

A Tale of Two Resurrections

"WITH A ROAR THAT SOUNDED AS IF ALL THE BREATH IN FRANCE HAD BEEN shaped into the detested word, the living sea rose, wave on wave, depth on depth, and overflowed the city to that point. Alarm-bells ringing, drums beating, the sea raging and thundering on its new beach, the attack began."[1] Charles Dickens crafted an unforgettable image of the sea in its tumult and turbulence, rising over the barriers that contained it, wreaking chaos, destruction, and hazard all around. Dickens's image of the sea rising builds on two ancient traditions concerning the sea: the more traditional and universal depiction of the sea as the center of chaos and storm and the traditional Christian depiction of the sea as an element of chaos, confusion, and sin.

When Mr. Jarvis Lorry visits the Manettes, his dear friends, he is greeted by the exhausted but loving Ms. Pross who remarks that "crowds and multitudes of people"[2] have begun to seek Miss Lucie Manette. This unsettles Mr. Lorry. He expected to be overwhelmed in a tidal wave of rushing incomers. It is in this scene, and others like it, that Dickens's literary genius slowly emerges as he crafts the story. Mr. Lorry is at the Manettes with only two gentlemen present alongside him: Charles Darnay and Sydney Carton. Outside, a chaotic commotion is heard, which causes Carton to reflect on the swirling and chaotic multitude that is bearing down on them. Protected in their castle of a home and with the multitude simply fleeing a natural storm, the rising multitude and the sea don't rear their ugly heads against

1. Dickens, *Tale of Two Cities*, 223–4.
2. Dickens, *Tale of Two Cities*, 99.

them at that moment, but the barrier of their house and England won't be there to protect them in the final part of the book.

The prefigured foreshadowing by Dickens is a stroke of literary genius. Carton looks out and says, "There is a great crowd coming one day into our lives."[3] Everyone present in that house would be greeted by a great crowd and a dangerous storm, but the storm of human passions is far more dangerous than the thunderclap of lightning and downpouring of rain encountered in that ominous moment.

A Tale of Two Cities is a triumph of the Christian literary imagination. Original sin, bloodguilt, sacrifice, intertangling covenants, love, and resurrection are all embedded in the novel. Indeed, these themes are integral to understanding Dickens's great work—not to mention the craftily inserted references to messianic and eschatological passages from the Old and New Testaments, which become apparent for all to see, like the incarnation, toward the end of the novel, when the guillotine supersedes the cross as the instrument of rebirth and salvation, and this blasphemy of the French revolutionaries is counteracted by Sydney Carton's dwelling on one of the memorable lines of Saint John's gospel: "I am the resurrection and the life, saith the Lord."[4]

A Tale begins with the promise of being recalled to life. Though it is easy, but sloppy, to identify Dr. Manette as the individual being recalled to life, the more obvious candidates who are being recalled to life—but for different reasons—are Charles Darnay and Sydney Carton. Darnay suffers from the bloodstain of original sin in the novel. He has inherited the sin of being an aristocrat—and a dastardly aristocrat at that. Though not his father, the Marquis St. Evrémonde is the blood relation to Darnay, and Darnay inherits the bloodguilt of his uncle, which makes him a wanted man back in France during the climax of the work. Conversely, Carton does not suffer from the bloodstain of inherited original sin like Darnay. Instead, he is just a sinful wretch who has squandered away his talents and has become a reprobate man, and he knows it. He indulges his sins and is unable to get out of the desolate hole he has dug himself. Despite abundance around him, Carton is stuck in a cesspool of desolation because of his own actions. Carton is drowning in his own sins.

Dickens does an incredible thing in intertwining two men heading to their Calvary for different reasons. Of course, the genius of Dickens is in how this intertwining of two men being recalled to life plays itself out. Dickens's novel is a picturesque story, a picturesque story that deliberately

3. Dickens, Tale of Two Cities, 107.

4. Dickens, Tale of Two Cities, 389.

mirrors the most famous picturesque story of all time: the biblical story that culminates in Christ's death and resurrection, which brings life back to a lifeless world.

The resurrection of Charles Darnay is not as memorable as the resurrection of Sydney Carton, in part because Carton is clearly the more Christlike figure of the two insofar as he undergoes the penal swap; and, in that swap, gives life to Darnay; and who is resurrected in the second child of Lucie and Charles, who bears his name. Nevertheless, Darnay does undergo a resurrection in the story, too. More to the point, Darnay's death to the law, need for replacement, and restored life only through an act of sacrifice, are a resurrection with which all should be familiar. It is easy to get wrapped up in the replacement Christ-figure that is Sydney Carton, but to do so misses a greater part of the wholeness of *A Tale,* which mirrors the story of man's salvation by having two men made in the image of each other undergoing sacrifice and resurrection.

As already mentioned, Darnay is tainted by the original sin of bloodguilt through being a relative of the Marquis St. Evrémonde. This blood guilt is something from which Darnay is trying to escape. He emigrates to England to find a new life. He tries to reject his bloodguilt inheritance by forsaking the aristocratic title passed on to him by his uncle's death. He has assumed, in England, a new identity. Darnay is attempting to be a new man, but he cannot outrun who he is. He cannot outrun or ignore the fact that he is of aristocratic blood—which is Dickens's literary equivalent for imputed Adamic sin in the story.

Though the circumstances in France change for the worst with the onset of the Revolution, Darnay is called back to France and—in being called to return to the land of his ancestral blood—must come face to face with the reality of his bloodguilt. Upon his return, he is greeted by the depersonalized forces of the totalitarian revolutionary state. He is not referred to by name but by "emigrant," in contrast to "citizen." In being arrested, the Jacobin citizens tell him he is cursed and to be judged on account of his blood inheritance. "You are a cursed emigrant," a farrier tells Darnay, "you are a cursed aristocrat." This is subsequently met by the statement "He will be judged in Paris."[5] All the sins of his uncle, the Marquis St. Evrémonde, are transferred onto Darnay. Covenants of blood abound in *A Tale.* And Darnay has entered the storm of the multitude that eluded him back in England.

What follows in the third book is the great Dickensian triumph of the work. Interweaving Scripture, Christian symbolism, and imagery, and mixing it with the faux substitute of state salvation offered up by the new

5. Dickens, *Tale of Two Cities,* 257.

republic being born in blood, Dickens manages to make explicit that which he had ingeniously prefigured in the earlier books. The third book reveals the Christian meaning and symbolism of the story. There can be no mistaking the Christian implications of the story anymore. What was hinted at earlier is now fully revealed like the incarnation itself. Indeed, Darnay as the sinner in need of a sacrificial atonement to be recalled to life is made manifest by his tribulations and trials before the law. The law is not enough. After his first arrest and acquittal, Darnay returns with his family with the prospects of life and liberty. But rather than entering an abode of abundance, he is arrested again and sentenced to a new trial. Darnay is brought before "that unjust Tribunal"[6] where he is said to be "Dead in Law." In the false courtroom, it is read aloud, "Charles Evrémonde, called Darnay, in right of such proscription, absolutely Dead in Law."[7] The law cannot save Darnay. The law demands his death. Only an act of loving sacrificial replacement can save him. Echoes of Saint Paul abound in Dickens's masterful construction.

While Darnay is dead in law, Sydney Carton is dead to himself through his own sin. Where Darnay is the embodiment of the reality of original sin, Carton is the embodiment of the reality of the consequences of personal sin. The once promising and intelligent Carton, like Adam in the garden, has been brought low in his sin. A drunkard and general lowlife, Carton describes himself as a degraded profligate to Lucie in their touching scene that prefigures what is to come at the closure of the story. "For you, and for any dear to you, I would do anything," Carton informs her. "If my career were of that better kind that there was any opportunity or capacity of sacrifice in it, I would embrace any sacrifice for you and for those dear to you."[8]

The contrasts between the two men who are, in their own ways, dead to sin, couldn't be starker. Darnay is under the taint of bloodguilt and the covenant of blood. Carton establishes, in that earlier moment with Lucie, a covenant by word and a covenant of sacrifice; Carton's covenant will fully unveil itself in Darnay's hour of need. Through Carton, Dickens reveals what true love is all about—sacrifice and self-giving. Through sacrifice, the love of life is manifested. It is a thoroughly and completely Christian outlook on life and the world. "Greater love hath no man than this, that a man lay down his life for his friends."[9]

The covenant of blood and original sin, as well as the covenant of the promise and sacrificial self-giving, are now running their course through

6. Dickens, *Tale of Two Cities*, 327.
7. Dickens, *Tale of Two Cities*, 328.
8. Dickens, *Tale of Two Cities*, 159.
9. John 15:13 KJV.

the story, and they will soon be intertwined with each other. When Darnay is imprisoned and sentenced for execution, the dripping blood of the blade of Madame Guillotine—the false and Satanic imitation of the cross—begins to stare Darnay in the face. He is, after all, "Dead in Law."[10]

The callous hypocrisy of the Dafarges, like all religious hypocrites, has been revealed to the reader also. From helping the Manettes to condemning the Manettes; from feigning religiosity and hope that Darnay would not return to France, aware of the danger in which the aristocrats are, to becoming the active players in Darnay's second arrest and trial, the emptiness of the Dafarges is fully manifested, just like the crowds who demanded Christ's death after having welcomed him in with palm branches and shouts of jubilee. But even the emptiness of the Dafarges was prefigured in the earlier parts of the novel.

Madame Dafarge, the most barbaric and cruel woman and revolutionary of them all, was always seen knitting. Knitting was a symbolic activity for lack of compassion and pity during the French Revolution. Thus, what was prefigured in the beginning is revealed in totality at the end. The seeming compassion of the Dafarges is revealed as an utter nothingness.

To this end, Dickens also created a remarkable literary construction that mirrored traditional Christian hermeneutics. What was prefigured in the Old Testament was revealed in the New Testament. In fact, this is the only proper way to interpret Scripture. Dickens, aware of this, replicated this hermeneutic as integral to the unfolding of *A Tale*.

Throughout the first two books, we find prefigurations of what is to come: a recalling to life; the lack of compassion and pity of the Dafarges (especially Madame Dafarge); bloodguilt and the demand for so-called justice; a great crowd like a raucous sea crashing into the lives of the protagonists; Jarvis Lorry as a guardian angel; and a covenant of sacrifice made by a promise. These prefigurations are all revealed in the third and final act of the story. The third and final act of the story allows us to make sense of everything that was previously veiled and alluded to.

The emptiness of the shallow utopian politics of the French Revolution is contrasted to the substantive life offered by self-sacrifice (in the person of Carton, who becomes the novel's *in persona Christi*). "Liberty, equality, fraternity, or death;—the last, much the easiest to bestow, O Guillotine!"[11] But the guillotine, the instrument of France's supposed deliverance and rebirth from the sins of the *Ancien Régime*, can bestow only death instead of life. The bloodthirsty Jacobins even callously joke about how many she has

10. Dickens, *Tale of Two Cities*, 328.
11. Dickens, *Tale of Two Cities*, 285.

decapitated, with no concern given to the victims. But Carton, like Christ with the cross, will redeem this horrible instrument of brutality by following through on his covenant promise with Lucie.

A Tale's climax is the recalling to life of two men and how their recalling to life intersects each with the other. Darnay is recalled to life when he is drugged and swapped by Sydney Carton, who takes his place on the execution block. Darnay, who was dead in the law, is recalled to life by this act of sacrificial replacement, and he can now live his life with Lucie and his daughter without fear of imprisonment or death. Carton is recalled to life by his action of self-sacrifice and fulfillment of the covenant promise he made to Lucie—his spiritual bride, who could never be his actual bride. There is no greater love than to lay down one's life for one's friend or beloved, and this Carton does with great dignity and nobility. Through Carton's act of sacrificial self-giving, he is recalled to life alongside Darnay.

Rebirth, Dickens informs us, is not through the instrumentalizing and depersonalizing arm of politics, as virtually all moderns have been falsely indoctrinated to believe. Rebirth is only possible through spirituality. Specifically, through sacrifice. More specifically, through the imitation of Christ and Christ's sacrifice.

Through Carton's sacrificial atonement, the Manette family, who were shattered by original sin and the demands of legal punishment, are restored and made whole. The first man is resurrected to life by the actions of the second man, and lest we forget, the two men are made in the image of one another. The harmony of the family which should have been is now realized through the sacrifice of the second man.

Additionally, Carton is resurrected by his very act of self-giving sacrifice. He finally showed his great magnanimity of which Lucie told Charles he was capable: "I am sure that he is capable of good things, gentle things, even magnanimous things."[12] And there was no greater magnanimous action than his sacrificing his own life so that Darnay could live and Lucie be happy with her husband. "I am the resurrection and the life, saith the Lord."[13]

When Sydney Carton imagines his statement to the crowd, he foreshadows the beatific vision that calls us to abundant love and life. Carton ends by prefiguring that last joyful rest and nourishing abundance that waits for all who imitate Christ. "It is a far, far better thing that I do, than I have

12. Dickens, Tale of Two Cities, 217.
13. Dickens, Tale of Two Cities, 389.

ever done; it is a far, far better rest that I go to, than I have ever known."[14] Amen.

This essay was originally published in *The Imaginative Conservative*, 20 April 2019.

---

14. Dickens, *Tale of Two Cities*, 390.

18

Pip's Confessions

"My father's family name being Pirrip, and my Christian name Philip, my infant tongue could make of both names nothing longer or more explicit than Pip. So I called myself Pip, and came to be called Pip."[1] *Great Expectations* is not an autobiography. Yet in many ways the fictional novel reads as an autobiography. As Pip narrates the tale of his great expectations, the seeds of a spiritual confession are laid bare for those with the eyes to see and the ears to hear.

Charles Dickens was, arguably, the greatest of the Victorian writers. Though he personally struggled with many things, the moralist that Dickens was is reflected throughout his works. Whether serious and technical like *A Tale of Two Cities*, endearing and charming like *David Copperfield* and *Great Expectations*, or shocking and powerful like *A Christmas Carol*, the moralism and Christian allegory and symbolism in Dickens's many works led Leo Tolstoy to consider him the greatest of Christian authors. *Great Expectations* certainly reflects that reality.

Great Expectations is a novel of self-introspection—especially as the story relates to our narrator and protagonist, Pip. The question of who Pip is and what he shall become is the fundamental theme that drives the story forward. Through Pip we have recapitulated the great Augustinian question: *mihi quaestio factus sum?* Pip is an ignorant but honest and kind simpleton with a deep moral fire burning within when we meet him. As he grows older, more educated, and sophisticated, he struggles with his moral conscience—though this was already prefigured for us in his youth. Pip is torn

1. Dickens, *Great Expectations*, 3.

between two selves and two worlds: his simple, moral, and honest self, which is represented by his working-class roots; and his sophisticated, cunning, and lustful self, which is represented by his desire to be transformed and accepted into the higher echelons of English high society. Janus-faced Pip wrestles with himself throughout the novel until one face reigns supreme.

There are, as such, two Pips in the novel—just as there are two sides to human nature. There is the good, honest, and loving side to human nature. Then there is, in the words of young Pip to Biddy, "the bad side of human nature."[2] That bad side of human nature is lust, ingratitude, and irresponsibility. These two forces inside Pip wrestle for control of his soul and are archetypally embodied in Orlick and Herbert Pocket, who represent, in their own ways, the expectations of Pip. The brute Orlick, like the brutish Drummle, is the dark shadow of Pip's "bad side of human nature." The gentle and kind Herbert, by stark contrast, is Pip's better angel: an educated and kind gentleman instead of an educated but hollow dead body (which characterizes Mr. Jaggers). Orlick is what Pip may devolve to in his pursuit of vanity. Herbert is what Pip may pass into through a higher divinization.

The two Pips at war for his soul are entangled in the darkness of Satis House, a place that is closer to Dante's hell than it is to the vengeful caldron of Pandaemonium. Dante's construction of hell was a place where love has been so eviscerated that only cold darkness remains. In much the same way, Satis House, with Miss Havisham and Estella, exists in that cold and dark, loveless abode. Dante's hell is also a place where truth does not exist, and in Pip's return to Joe's forge after his first visit, he begins to lie about his time spent with the wounded Havisham and the icy Estella. Pip's nature is contorted by visiting Satis House, and his nature remains corrupted by the specter of Satis House calling his soul to enslavement.

But the two sides of Pip were visible before his entry into the conniving claws of Miss Havisham. Pip's moral guilt is a recurring theme throughout the book. He fears, after helping the escaped convict from the marshes, that the law will catch up to him and bring him to justice. When the soldiers, as instruments of the law and justice, unexpectedly arrive at Joe's forge to ask assistance, Pip is frightened into thinking they've come for him. The moral conscience of Pip, even as revealed in the opening chapters of *Great Expectations*, reveals a deep interiority and consciousness to him with which he will struggle as the novel develops and his character grows simultaneously more complex and compromised.

The young Pip before his Satis House encounter is comedic and cute. We laugh with Pip in his innocent reflections, like when he shrieked in terror

---

2. Dickens, *Great Expectations*, 149.

at a Christmas dinner, staggered around the house "like a little drunkard,"[3] and confessed that his catechetical instruction to walk the way of the Lord "laid [him] under an obligation always to go through the village from [his] house in one particular direction."[4] But this comedic and innocent Pip with whom who we laughed becomes an ungrateful and stuffy shell of his former boyhood self whom we come to detest. As Pip ascends into his great expectations, he falls to become more like Orlick and Drummle than Herbert in a brilliant reversal of the image and notion of ascending. Pip may outwardly look like a gentleman, but interiorly he has dissolved into a pale shadow of his former self, who is cold and, at times, heartless to those who love him.

Herbert looms over Pip throughout the novel too. They memorably meet in the courtyard, where Herbert challenges Pip to a sporty fight. Though Herbert is weak and "did not look very healthy—having pimples on his face, and a breaking out at his mouth,"[5] Herbert is soon revealed to be a beautiful and tender-hearted individual precisely because of his interior soul rather than exterior presentation. This is equally prefigured when Pip and Herbert meet again at Bernard's Inn and Herbert wears his raggedy suit in a dignified manner, his unhandsome face and ungainly figure radiating amiable cheerfulness. Herbert's openness, honesty, and gentle kindness—as they grow older and nearer their inheritance—remind us of the Pip who sat beside Joe at the marshes as "ever the best of friends"[6] and who poured his heart out to Biddy about his desire to be a gentleman and win Estella's nonexistent heart. Herbert is what the better side of Pip could be.

Orlick and Drummle—who "reminded [Pip] of Orlick"[7]—also begin to hang over the specter of Satis House and tug at Pip to become that bumbling, empty, and disheveled fraud like them. As with Dante's sinners in hell, they are fallen copies of each other, with all threads of individuality destroyed by a common darkness.

In various ways, the moral guilt that Pip always exuded is what keeps him from sinking entirely into the abyss of darkness. Though he acts in a proud and ungrateful manner to Joe and Biddy, he cannot escape his true self; he cannot escape the young, cheery, and good-natured lad to whom we were introduced in the church graveyard and who poured himself out to Joe and Biddy before he left to live in the corrupt city of London and the corrupt shadow of Satis House. His ill treatment, especially of Joe, haunts him. But

3. Dickens, *Great Expectations*, 42.

4. Dickens, *Great Expectations*, 43.

5. Dickens, *Great Expectations*, 92.

6. Dickens, *Great Expectations*, 48.

7. Dickens, *Great Expectations*, 358.

the more he thinks of growing into his great expectations, which are tied to Satis House, the more he tries to push aside his nature as Pip the gentle, loving, and cute boy to whom we were introduced at the forge.

Indeed, this wrestling with himself is even poetically embodied in his christened name when he enters high society. He is to keep his name Pip. His movement into high society doubly reinforces his blacksmith self. So too is this true when Herbert christens him "Handel." The reason Herbert names Pip Handel is because of the song "Harmonious Blacksmith." Thus, even the formal renaming he receives by Herbert keeps him attached to his graceful and innocent old self that made such an impression on Abel Magwitch.

The interiority of Pip, as recounted, is matched only by Dickens's spiritual master—Saint Augustine. Indeed, even secular scholars and readers of Augustine have remained enamored by the bishop's genius and discovery of psychological interiority. And the psychological interiority of Pip is regularly revealed with both an endearing and repugnant character, depending on the circumstance and situation in which it is revealed. Pip's narration is not just about the world that lay before him but very much about the interior world inside of himself and the complexity of emotions, feeling, and guilt with which he wrestles. If anything, that interior world is the real world with which he struggles throughout the story.

As the novel climaxes, it is no surprise that Pip is trapped by his bad shadow, Orlick. It also is no surprise that his salvation comes from Herbert, his dearest and loving friend who constantly serves to lift Pip to a higher plane of existence. It is then fitting that Pip hang suspended between the muck and mud of Orlick and the heavenly face of Herbert in his moment of new birth, compelled by the spirit of Abel instead of the spirit of Compeyson.

Having been freed from his dark shadow and looking upward as if to the heavens to see his savior, Pip "saw [his] supporter to be—Herbert!"[8] The same Herbert who brought out the good side of Pip when he needed it most; the same Herbert whom Pip helped, which reflected the vestiges of his good nature during his time of tumultuous struggle; the same Herbert who invites Pip to take responsibility for his life instead of living a fantasy. Joe may have paid the debt at the story's end, freeing Pip from the bondage of servitude, but Pip had already gone through his metempsychosis.

Pip's rebirth is subsequently followed by his redemption through forgiveness. He stays beside Magwitch to the bitter end, despite his earlier wanting to abandon him. When he cries out "O Lord, be merciful to him, a sinner!" he may well have been praying his own prayer—and Pip has been

---

8. Dickens, *Great Expectations*, 430.

absent of prayers since leaving Joe and Biddy.[9] He reconciles with Joe and Biddy and pours out his heart to them again, just as he did as a young boy. He prays their forgiveness and cries in his repentance of the ill he has done to them. It is at the end of this wrestling with his dark shadow and being freed from the corrupting influence of Satis House that Pip steps into a church to be the best man and witness to Mr. Wemmick's marriage. In sum, the good-natured Pip has returned, and we find, in the final pages, the Pip to whom we were introduced in the beginning, which is the summary of salvation history. That original image is restored from its corruption.

When Providence brings Pip and Estella back to the remains of Satis House, we find that they have changed tremendously. The ruins of Satis House, hell, have freed them into a new world of love and possibility. There the two reconcile, as the haunting image of Satis House disappears forever. If Estella was "bent and broken . . . into a better shape," so too was Pip.[10] Looking out over the horizon of the world now revealed with the disappearance of the morning mist, Dickens inverts the image of Milton's expulsion of Adam and Eve from Paradise not as an image of tragedy but an image of new beginnings, as they hold hands that have been brought together rather than remain apart.

The trajectory of *Great Expectations* is, with the important concluding words of Estella, the bending and breaking of Pip into a better shape. Estella is not alone in this regard; in fact, the whole story is the bending and breaking of Pip into a better shape. Pip's bending and breaking—literally in wrestling against Orlick and the shadow of Satis House—culminates in rebirth, his reshaping after being bent and broken. Pip sheds the shadow of Orlick and his past ingratitude and coldness and fully embraces the flashes of his earlier goodness as he becomes selfless, forgiving, and, most of all, seeking forgiveness from others. It is as if he ends his confession asking the reader to forgive him. And forgive him we do, as we welcome Pip back into the family of saints.

This essay was originally published in *The Imaginative Conservative* under the title "Dickens' *Great Expectations*: Pip's Confessions," 2 July 2019.

---

9. Dickens, *Great Expectations*, 460.
10. Dickens, *Great Expectations*, 484.

19

Memory, Love, and Eternity in Tennyson's "In Memoriam"

ALFRED LORD TENNYSON'S 1850 POETIC MASTERPIECE "IN MEMORIAM" IS rightly considered one of the greatest poems of the nineteenth century and one of the great poems of the English language. Written as a eulogy to his friend Arthur Hallam, the poem captures the torrent and pilgrimage of a soul in flux as the poem moves from imprisoned grief to joyful memory to incarnate memorialism governed by love. The poem's three-part construction, well known among critics, reveals the place and role of memory in the movement of salvation and the triumph of love in and over death.

Hell

The first twenty-seven cantos of the poem, including the most famous line, "'Tis better to have loved and lost / Than never to have loved at all,"[1] constitute the "hell" of the poem. "In Memoriam" begins, depending on whether you start with the prologue or the first canto proper (and here I take it to begin with the first canto), with grief and sorrow and the desire to ascend to a plane of divinization. "I held it truth, with him who sings," Tennyson begins, "To one clear harp in divers tones / That men may rise on stepping-stones / Of their dead selves to higher things. / . . . / O Sorrow, cruel fellowship, /

---

1. Tennyson, *Major Works*, 220.

O Priestess in the vaults of Death, / O sweet and bitter in a breath, / What whispers from thy lying lips?"[2]

It goes without saying that the death of Arthur pushed Tennyson into a bout of depression and an immense sorrow. The friendship and possible love they shared is now seen as an extensive burden from having had such a close and intimate relationship. "Cruel fellowship,"[3] Tennyson reflects, as he curses the "lying lip"[4] of the priestess of death and her false sweetness that had earlier soothed Tennyson into believing friendship was such an important thing.

Early in the poem we move from cries of sorrow to images of death and descending. Darkness covers the mind and heart of the grieving Tennyson as he is locked in an imprisoned torrent of his former fellowship. The "her" of whom he speaks in the third canto is the spirit of sorrow. Thanatos, in a certain unseen way, is the divinity that dominates Tennyson's plunge into the abyss.

> For now her father's chimney glows
> In expectation of a guest;
> And thinking "this will please him best,"
> She takes a riband or a rose;
> For he will see them on to-night;
> And with the thought her colour burns;
> And, having left the glass, she turns
> Once more to set a ringlet right;
> And, even when she turn'd, the curse
> Had fallen, and her future Lord
> Was drown'd in passing thro' the ford,
> Or kill'd in falling from his horse.[5]

Tennyson here inverts the imagery of a bridal marriage to be. Love, seen in a fiery glow; the expectation of a guest; ribands and roses; and a burning color (that is, the burning heart of love) are soon quenched by the curse of death. The imagery of fallenness, as mentioned, comes to the fore. Rather than ascend in love, love has caused a descent into the dark pit of grief. Sorrow reigns supreme.

The climax of Tennyson's hell comes when he "sing[s] to him that rests below, / And, since the grasses round me wave, / I take the grasses of the

---

2. Tennyson, *Major Works*, 204.

3. Tennyson, *Major Works*, 205.

4. Tennyson, *Major Works*, 204.

5. Tennyson, *Major Works*, 207.

grave, / And make them pipes whereon to blow."[6] Tennyson is singing to death, not even to Arthur, but to Thanatos. In singing to death rather than the author of love and life—a stark contrast with how the poem will conclude—Tennyson sinks into the pit of loneliness, deprived of the "murmur of happy Pan."[7] The poet, lover, and pilgrim, Tennyson, is so overcome with the news of Arthur's death that he is incapable of good memories and only laments in despair.

By the twenty-fifth canto, however, after having reached the pit of loneliness, love starts to become more prominent as Tennyson is, in a symbolic way, resurrected by the memory of love. It is the revelation of love that leads Tennyson to recognize the unity between loving and losing—much as how Plato understood love—leading to his famous declaration at the conclusion of the twenty-seventh canto: "I hold it true, whate'er befall; / I feel it, when I sorrow most; / 'Tis better to have loved and lost / Than never to have loved at all." In sorrow, Tennyson realizes his love for Arthur was real. Love is only possible if one has lived. And if one has lived, one needs to love to have lived a meaningful life. Thus, "'Tis better to have loved and lost / Than never to have loved at all."[8]

Purgatory

Immediately after the twenty-seventh canto, time and Christ appear in the poem. In this revelation we can surmise, I think, that the first twenty-seven cantos were timeless; just as hell is without time—causing one to abandon all hope once in it, unless resurrected by love. As such, there was no way out except for the divine intervention of love. And love did appear in the twenty-fifth canto to help Tennyson and lift him up, "As light as carrier-birds in air."[9] Love has taken Tennyson up into the realm of time and space, the realm governed by Christ, in which an ongoing and remarkable transformation in the poem (through the poet-pilgrim Tennyson) begins.

After invoking Christ, time, and Christmas—that season of sumptuous and joyful feasts and memories—a remarkable metamorphosis begins even with the language used by Tennyson. From despairing in the misery and sorrow of the self, where he constantly used *I* to grieve over Arthur (which is ironic, because while grieving for Arthur, Tennyson is more concerned with his own sorrow and misery than with Arthur Hallam's), he now speaks in

6. Tennyson, *Major Works*, 216.
7. Tennyson, *Major Works*, 218.
8. Tennyson, *Major Works*, 220.
9. Tennyson, *Major Works*, 219.

the plural *we*. Self has been united with another. Moreover, Tennyson begins to speak of his joyful memories with Arthur in the thirtieth canto, which began with a memory of time spent together during Christmas: "With trembling fingers did we weave / The holly round the Christmas hearth."[10] From dark clouds and tears of sadness to a new day, a new dawn, and a new life has occurred, "Rise, happy morn, rise, holy morn, / Draw forth the cheerful day from night: / O Father, touch the east, and light / The light that shone when Hope was born."[11]

Not only does Tennyson shift the focus from the *incurvatus in se* to a relationality of togetherness, he also changes the imagery and the perspective of the reader from the perspectival imagery of fallenness to raising. From being "fallen," "drown'd," and "falling from [a] horse"[12] to "Rise, happy morn, rise"[13] is the language that now guides the poem. Light and hope appear as well, as they should, given that time is now present in this new purgatorial reality in which Tennyson as poet-pilgrim is now. To further reveal his hand of this new lease on life, Tennyson begins the thirty-first canto by referencing the raising of Lazarus from the dead and consummates the canto by celebrating the resurrection of a man from the dead: "Behold a man raised up by Christ! / The rest remaineth unreveal'd; / He told it not; or something seal'd / The lips of that Evengelist."[14]

Faith, hope, and love, the three great theological virtues that provide for a person the most fulfilling of lives on earth are now everywhere present and accompany the relational and memorial tone of the poetic shift. This resurrection of Tennyson, and, in some respects, Arthur, is due to the newfound appreciation of the memories they shared together. Though Arthur has physically perished, the memories that Tennyson has of him ensure his immortality in the very seat of the *imago Dei* in man: the mind.

Additionally, Tennyson continues to progress in this new life by making biblical allusions. He speaks of "A life that bears immortal fruit"[15] and "The baby new to earth and sky."[16] There can be no mistaking the newfound reality and life that Tennyson is trying to communicate. Opening or reopening that wellspring of memory has lifted Tennyson out of the grave and, in doing so, has brought Arthur up from the earth too.

10. Tennyson, *Major Works*, 221.
11. Tennyson, *Major Works*, 222.
12. Tennyson, *Major Works*, 207.
13. Tennyson, *Major Works*, 222.
14. Tennyson, *Major Works*, 223.
15. Tennyson, *Major Works*, 228.
16. Tennyson, *Major Works*, 230.

At the fiftieth canto, through to the end of this second section identified by scholars, there seems to me a split in this "purgatory" for Tennyson. From the twenty-eighth to forty-ninth cantos, the living memories of Tennyson and Arthur bring newness of life into a dark and dreary world formerly dedicated to Thanatos. Afterward, however, the poem shifts again from happy memories to serious questions about life and love. It is as if Tennyson must now begin to unlock the secrets of life and love to continue his climb up the mountain.

Tennyson begins to struggle and wrestle with the concept of love. "I cannot," he says, "love thee as I ought; / For love reflects the thing beloved; / My words are only words, and moved / Upon the topmost froth of thought."[17] Love is indeed more than just words. Love requires an incarnate relationship between incarnate persons. As that immortal saying goes, actions speak louder than words.

From memory to reflection, Tennyson is advancing through wrestling with the questions of life and love. This culminates in the fifty-ninth canto when Tennyson reconciles sorrow and love, thereby linking love with sorrow instead of perceiving mere sorrow and misery. To have loved and then to have lost the beloved is to be sorrowful for what one has lost. But rather than melt away in his miseries, Tennyson reaches the conclusion that love transcends space and time and that the sorrow one has is a true reflection of one's love. As he says, as if an invocation: "O Sorrow, wilt thou live with me . . . / O Sorrow, wilt thou rule my blood."[18]

Following this revelation, if you will, Tennyson returns to happy memories and how such joyful memories can never die. The memories we hold are in our mind, and our minds exist forever in the mind of God (as per George Berkeley). As Tennyson begins to "move up from high to higher,"[19] again reflective of this progression through wrestling with love, the return to memory is beautiful, peaceful, and quaint. "He plays with threads, he beats his chair / For pastime, dreaming of the sky; / His inner day can never die, / His night of loss is always there."[20] In the seventy-first canto we also see, through Tennyson's image-based language, the idyllic image of friendship:

> While now we talk as once we talk'd
> Of men and minds, the dust of change,
> The days that grow to something strange,
> In walking as of old we walk'd

17. Tennyson, *Major Works*, 234.
18. Tennyson, *Major Works*, 238.
19. Tennyson, *Major Works*, 240.
20. Tennyson, *Major Works*, 241.

Beside the river's wooded reach,
The fortress, and the mountain ridge,
The cataract flashing from the bridge,
The breaker breaking on the beach.[21]

In the "purgatory" of "In Memoriam," the resurrection of Tennyson and Arthur is through the restoration of blissful memories that foreshadow the joy of heaven. Following the return of happy memories in daylight and within the Christmas season, Tennyson begins to wrestle with the nature of life and love in his climb upward. This wrestling with love brings forth the reconciliation of sorrow and love, leading to that new reality that permits Tennyson to understand that sorrow and love are not mutually exclusive but often accompany each other. Following this breakthrough, Tennyson moves ever higher up the mountain, and we have the return of joyful memories.

It is also fitting that this grand reunion of Arthur and Tennyson, walking intimately in a green pasture and coming to a bridge, signals the third shift of the poem as we prepare to enter the "paradise" of the poem. They made the journey together, as Tennyson's language indicates, for love is never an isolative reality. The pathway into paradise begins with the joyful memory of friendship in green pastures and land of life. How very fitting then that the bridge to paradise is opened by the reality of friendship.

Entering Paradise

The paradise of Tennyson's masterpiece is the longest section of the poem. Perhaps it is Tennyson's way of delineating the eternity that is paradise by making it longer than the previous two sub-divisions of the poem. The seventy-second canto begins, fittingly, with "Risest thou thus."[22] For to enter paradise entails ascending, rising, on the ladder of ascents.

Paradise, in the poem, is associated with songs of praise and relief. Drawing on the Bible, especially Genesis and the Psalms, as well as from the poetry of Dante, Tennyson says, "I care not in these fading days / To raise a cry that lasts not long, / And round thee with the breeze of song / To stir a little dust to praise."[23] Much like Dante's paradise, Tennyson's paradise is dominated by singing and is permeated with loving praise instead of disordered outbursts of grief, rage, and sorrow—the very things that had dominated the prose at the beginning of the poem. "My darken'd ways," Tennyson

21. Tennyson, *Major Works*, 244.

22. Tennyson, *Major Works*, 244.

23. Tennyson, *Major Works*, 246.

sings, "Shall ring with music all the same; / To breathe my loss is more than fame, / To utter love more sweet than praise."[24]

The first memory that Tennyson has while in paradise returns us to Christmas, that season of caroling and joyous warmth: "Again at Christmas did we weave / The holly round the Christmas hearth; / The silent snow possess'd the earth, / And calmly fell our Christmas-eve."[25] It is fitting that the first memory Tennyson has in the poem's equivalent of heaven evokes Christ, salvation, and song through the direct references to Christmas.

Beneath the songs of praise, one realizes that love swims across the lines of paradise. Love attempts to burst out of the frozen cold and warm the world to life, "That longs to burst a frozen bud / And flood a fresher throat with song."[26] Beauty also makes her triumphant entrance into the poem in paradise when the poet-pilgrim announces, "For us the same cold stream-let curl'd / Thro' all his eddying coves; the same / All winds that roam the twilight came / In whispers of the beauteous world."[27] Tennyson's heaven is a place of images and memories that evoke warmth, friendship, and beauty.

Furthermore, the I-You dynamic of human relations reaches its fruition in paradise. "My spirit is at peace with all," Tennyson says. He just as quickly returns to relationality and speaks in the relational "we" as serene memories with Arthur come to the fore. "By night we linger'd on the lawn / . . . / While now we sang old songs that peal'd / From knoll to knoll, where, couch'd at ease / The white kine glimmered."[28]

In a spectacular moment of resurrection, Tennyson turns winter into summer, symbolic of transformation from death to life. "These two—they dwelt with eye on eye / Their hearts of old have beat in tune, / Their meetings made December June, / Their every parting was to die. / Their love has never past away; / The days she never can forget / Are earnest that he loves her yet, / Whate'er the faithless people say."[29] Love is life, and love can never die; thus life is eternal through love.

It is interesting to highlight that while love is life and love can never die, it is "faithless people" who are blind to this reality and therefore never see the light. Those who are of faith know of the transformative power of love, how love turns the cold and bleak midwinter into the high noon of summer with the sun at its peak and the green pastures teeming with life.

24. Tennyson, *Major Works*, 247.

25. Tennyson, *Major Works*, 248.

26. Tennyson, *Major Works*, 251.

27. Tennyson, *Major Works*, 248.

28. Tennyson, *Major Works*, 262.

29. Tennyson, *Major Works*, 265.

Love brings life. Love transcends death. As Tennyson says, "I cannot understand: I love."[30] Love really does flow across the ethereal air of paradise.

Additionally, Tennyson evokes the pilgrim's climbing progress in the one-hundredth canto: "I climb the hill: from end to end / Of all the landscape underneath, / I find no place that does not breathe / Some gracious memory of my friend."[31] Again Tennyson recourses to spectacular imagery in paradise. The hill he climbs belongs to a wondrous landscape. There is not a flower, a tree, or blade of grass that does not "breathe" with the memory of life that makes Tennyson's heart flutter. Moreover, joyful memory is all that dwells in Tennyson's mind.

We rapidly enter the magical realm of the Christian and Anglo-Saxon synthesis, common to Romantic poetry, in which Christian themes and symbols are infused with Anglo-Saxon mythology. Tennyson describes paradise further, as a type of new Eden, a lush garden flowing with rivers of life with a mead hall reminiscent of England's Anglo-Saxon heritage:

> On that last night before we went
> From out the doors where I was bred,
> I dream'd a vision of the dead,
> Which left my after-morn content.
> Methought I dwelt within a hall,
> And maidens with me: distant hills
> From hidden summits fed with rills
> A river sliding by the wall.
> The hall with harp and carol rang.
> They sang of what is wise and good
> And graceful. In the centre stood
> A statue veil'd, to which they sang;
> And which, tho' veil'd, was known to me,
> The shape of him I loved, and love
> For ever: then flew in a dove
> And brought a summons from the sea.[32]

There is, in Tennyson's construction, a divine hill and river of life. The maidens, like muses, arise to sing of love and poetry. The dove, a symbol of the Holy Spirit (who embodies the flame of divine love), is brought forth from the sea of eternity in this most picturesque image. After this remarkable vision in paradise, Tennyson again recourses to Christ and his salvific

---

30. Tennyson, *Major Works*, 266.

31. Tennyson, *Major Works*, 267.

32. Tennyson, *Major Works*, 270.

incarnation: "The time draws near the birth of Christ."[33] How fitting, all things considered. By the poem's end we have the soulful (re)union of Tennyson and Arthur "With faith that comes of self-control, / The truths that never can be proved / Until we close with all we loved, / And all we flow from, soul in soul."[34]

The epilogue is the consummation of Tennyson's journey to blessedness and blissfulness. Instead of weeping forever because of the loss of Arthur, Tennyson ends in hope and thanksgiving to God for the time and friendship that they had—however brief—on earth. And so the poem concludes with those famous lines that rival Dante: "That friend of mine who lives in God, / That God, which ever lives and loves, / One God, one law, one element, / And one far-off divine event, / To which the whole creation moves."[35]

This essay was originally published in *The Imaginative Conservative*, 15 November 2019.

---

33. Tennyson, *Major Works*, 271.
34. Tennyson, *Major Works*, 288.
35. Tennyson, *Major Works*, 292.

20

An Annunciation on the Battlefield

On December 2, 1805, the French Emperor Napoleon Bonaparte achieved his most spectacular victory at the Battle of Austerlitz against an allied army of Russians and Austrians. The battle is remembered for its brilliance and savagery and was immortalized in Leo Tolstoy's *War and Peace*. On the blood-stained slopes of the Pratzen Heights, Prince Andrei Bolkonsky—wounded and looking up at the skies—gazes upon its immense beauty before he passes out. For the first time in the story, Andrei puts aside his empty personal ambitions and allows the serenity around him to lift him up to the heavens, despite the chaos of a battle surrounding him.

Prince Andrei is one of the many and memorable characters in Tolstoy's epic, which is rightly considered one of the greatest works of literature and the seminal Russian odyssey. Andrei stands in for Tolstoy, you, and me. The young prince seemingly has everything going for him. He is handsome. He comes from a wealthy and important family. He has a successful career as the aide-de-camp to Mikhail Kutuzov, the greatest of the Russian generals. Yet Andrei has also abandoned his pregnant wife to seek glory in war. Leading up to Austerlitz, he constantly fantasizes of having his "Toulon" moment.[1] He idolizes Napoleon to the point of erasing his own identity. Andrei is the tragic man of Saint Augustine's insight, a man turned entirely inward to himself, who can think only of himself and his desires, to the exclusion of others.

During the Battle of Schöngrabern, Andrei experiences the encounter as a relatively detached observer. He heaps praise upon Captain Tushin's

---

1. Tolstoy, *War and Peace*, 281.

isolated battery as the heroic unit that stymied the French advance and allowed the Russians under Prince Bagration to withdraw in good order and
link up with Kutuzov before the disaster at Austerlitz. In his report, he is like
a giddy child, a reproductive image of the artillerists who were described as
having a childlike joy at watching the town catch fire and blasting grapeshot
at the French soldiers advancing on their position. He is—like his hero,
Napoleon—unable to see the human faces of war; the enemy are dehuman-
ized or entirely invisible to him. He has lost his own humanity, too, in the
process.

Andrei embodies the discontented and alienated lives that many live.
He is away from home and therefore away from his family. He does not seek
the true masculine value of fatherhood; rather, he passes off his responsibility to his father and mother, leaving them to look after his wife and coming
child. He indulges in vanity and self-centered individualism that borders on
narcissism, as he dreams of being the lone hero who will lead the Russians
to a glorious victory against Napoleon—his hero—and win the laurels of
all Russia. He is a man with his face centered on the muck and mud of the
earth rather than the sky above that illuminates man and calls him to higher
things.

War and Peace is a profoundly Christian novel. It is a story of the
struggle to find joy and meaning in life. What is joy? How is it found? Andrei, like the rest of the characters at the beginning of the novel, is either
unsure or seeking to find life's fulfillment in things that cannot ultimately
bring contentment to life. While the story develops and it becomes clear
that love is the answer, especially the love found in marriage—family—the
many characters are still unable to properly ascertain why marriage is that
which will bring joy. Pierre, the other great hero, is the first to intuitively
gather that love has something to do with it, despite all his flaws and waffling
agnosticism during his conflicted torment on whether to marry Hélène,
whom he acknowledges he doesn't really love, though proceeds to marry
her. Although this exhausts itself in disaster for all persons involved, he later
becomes a sort of missionary to others, as the story develops.

The transformation of Andrei begins as he lies wounded at Austerlitz.
Filled with an impetuous nihilistic streak when he grabs a fallen standard
and charges the French, knowing that he will die, his peering up at the sky
after being wounded is one of the most majestic scenes in the novel. His
wounding and solemn reflection upon the sky above leads to his admittedly
slow transformation away from himself to others. "How quiet, peaceful,
solemn, not at all as I ran. . . . How was it I did not see that lofty sky before?
And how happy I am to have found it at last! Yes! All is vanity, all falsehood,

except the infinite sky."[2] Instead of forcibly changing the world—as was the dream of his hero Napoleon—Andrei finally accepts the world as it is and dwells in the marvelous beauty of it all for the first time.

Andrei's first transformative moment is from the encounter with beauty amid chaos and individual wants. That he is looking up at the sky, the stars, is not something to overlook either. His slow march to embodying forgiveness and love of others begins with the clouds and fog of the battlefield giving way and his finding, for all intents and purposes, that true star which directs one to the incarnate God who preached love on earth and goodwill to men. Andrei's conversion moment, his reorientation, ought to remind one of the annunciation to the shepherds in the gospel of Saint Luke. It is not until Andrei has been brought low, humbled, that he glimpses eternity. Andrei's slow journey to love of God, culminating in forgiveness and love of others (which is agape, or brotherly love), begins with his looking up to the heavens and finding a wonderous sight before his eyes. At long last, he has the eyes to behold and receive. He is visited by the divine as he lies wounded, looking up at the sky in all its wonder and majesty rather than the clay to remold into a shallow parody of politicized and utilitarian life.

In fact, the Austerlitz transformation of Andrei continues when Pierre visits him for the first time in two years. While Andrei has become something of a reclusive contemplative monk who seeks to shun the world, Andrei is brought to life in this crypto-annunciation where Pierre serves as the angelic figure who snaps Andrei out of his contemplative slumber. As they journey in the carriage and discuss the great chain of being, Pierre ends his conversation by pointing to the sky—the sky that Andrei experienced in all its glory and majesty as he lay wounded. It is a slow journey with many trials, but Andrei's transformation began as he crossed the threshold at the Battle of Austerlitz. In their conversation, it becomes clear that Andrei, though confused and still disoriented in reorganizing his life, is on the path of service to others, though he remains adamant that he has forsaken that in service to himself.

The orientation of the eyes, which are also the windows of the soul, to the skies is an important inclusion that is not to be missed. Imagination is that which is directed to the infinite, and the skies above are the window to the soul of God, much as human eyes are the windows to human souls. It is the encounter with beauty, all-consuming beauty, the infinite, that directs the human soul back to God. The sky calls us up; the earth drags us down.

From Austerlitz to Borodino, Andrei's pilgrimage to God is completed as he lies beside Anatole Kuragin. Anatole, the man who carried on an affair

---

2. Tolstoy, *War and Peace*, 299.

with Natasha while married and destroyed Andrei and Natasha's relationship, is moaning and whimpering like a child, having lost his leg in battle. In that moment, feeling great pity for Anatole, Andrei utters unforgettable words: "Compassion, love of our brothers, for those who love us and for those who hate us, love of our enemies; yes, that love which God preached on earth."[3] A lesser man, a vengeful and spiteful man, could have found sadistic pleasure in the sufferings of such a man who has wounded one over the course of the years. Andrei takes the higher road. Dying, he asks for the gospels, and, in meeting Natasha again, who begs him to forgive her, Andrei's self-giving love is consummated when he tells Natasha that he already has forgiven her. Andrei's heroic journey is complete, from embodying the image of Achilles to becoming an image-bearer of Christ.

Part of Tolstoy's realism is how one must go through chaotic struggle to find peace—love—in life. While not everyone will have to go through an Austerlitz and Borodino to reach that place, all need to reach the same place to which Andrei arrives by novel's end. He is at peace with the world, himself, and others. This peace he finds, as Tolstoy indicates by many subtle and not-so-subtle clues, is through God. The removal of the centrality of God, however invisible, in readings of *War and Peace* cannot therefore help one understand the real heart of the work. Austerlitz and the other great battles are the battles with which all struggle against sin; the reward of running that race is the bliss found in God, which permits a true dwelling in and appreciation of the world. Rather than conquering and remaking the world, one finds peace in the world and is lifted up to the infinite expanse that is the heavens, which transforms the soul to a love of the majesty (rather than the blandness) of the world, including love of others.

Advent, for Christians, signifies God's love for humanity. It marks the first step of God's desire to dwell with men—through the incarnation and birth of Christ. Amid chaos, internal and external struggles, one could look to the sky to see the light pointing to the ultimate beauty and majesty of God's indwelling with man. The incarnation and birth of Christ is meant to be a beautiful and majestic moment—the time when God broke into the world of men for all to see. It should be the moment of humanity's (re)awakening. It should be the moment of reorientation of our hearts to the love of others, the moment when one finds beauty, love, and peace in the world.

This essay was originally published in *The Imaginative Conservative*, 1 December 2018.

---

3. Tolstoy, *War and Peace*, 874.

21

Leo Tolstoy's *War and Peace*

The Odyssey of Love

As Prince Andrei lay dying beside Natasha and his sister, Princess Marya, he reflects inwardly, "Love? What is love?"[1] Love is the theme of all great literature, from Homer and Dante to Milton, Herbert, and Tennyson. It is the theme of all great philosophy, from Plato and Augustine to Schelling.

Love has been tied with literature from the beginning. The oldest work of extent literature, the *Epic of Gilgamesh*, wrestles with the question of love. The works of Homer run replete with the theme of love. The Bible obsessively concerns itself with love, the high point being the poetic works, namely the Psalms, and the wisdom literature, especially Sirach and the Song of Songs.

Given that the birth of literature is tied to lyric verse, and that the great works of ancient literature—being chiefly lyric poetry—were sung, it is unsurprising that the greatest works of literature have love as their central focus. Love, and the struggle for love, runs through the great poetry of the ages. "For smiles from reason flow, / To brute denied, and are of love the food; / Love, not the lowest end of human life," wrote Milton in *Paradise Lost*.[2] George Herbert also splendidly wrote, "Love took my hand, and smiling did reply / Who made the eyes but I? / Truth Lord, but I have marred them: let my shame / Go where it doth deserve. / And know you not, says Love, who bore the blame? / My dear, then I will serve. / You must sit down,

1. Tolstoy, *War and Peace*, 1058.
2. Milton, *Paradise Lost*, 192.

says Love, and taste my meat: / So I did sit and eat."[3] And perhaps most famously from Alfred Tennyson, "'Tis better to have loved and lost / Than never to have loved at all. /. . . / That God, which ever lives and loves, / One God, one law, one element, / And one far-off divine event, / To which the whole creation moves."[4]

Tolstoy's epic *War and Peace* deals with love as its chief feature. To ask its nature is to journey to the heart of something—the heart of the matter. The quest for wisdom and understanding, which often seems to drive the story and the characters, is tied to the struggle for love. For the highest wisdom is love, and the greatest heroic struggle is to find and consummate love. This is found in Homer, Dante, Austen, and so many others.

Homer's *Iliad* and *Odyssey* began the long tradition of Western heroic literature. As such, it is unsurprising that Tolstoy's epic should be "called Russia's *Iliad* and *Odyssey*"[5] and regularly be compared to Homer's classics. There is journey, battle, and filial homecoming. The sense of battle and struggle to find love and meaning throughout the text led C.S. Lewis to describe Tolstoy's work as "the greatest war book ever written."[6] In some ways, Tolstoy's novel is the culmination of over two millennia of development in the Western heroic literary tradition: the struggle through storm and war to find peaceful love at the end of it all.

War and Peace, in Russian, can also mean war and the world. The double significance is certainly visible even without a knowledge of Russian. World encompasses everything. And *War and Peace* certainly encompasses next to everything. Family. Scheming. Death. Courtship. Politics. Patriotism. Youth. Age. Everything associated with the world is front and center at various points of the story. By the story's end, however, all the struggles in the world eventually subside and culminate in the love through the marriages of Natasha Rostova with Pierre Bezukhov and Marya Bolkonsky with Nikolai Rostov, when they learn to let go of their worldly and empty ambitions and give the gift of themselves to one another as free gifts of each other to the beloved.

From Achilles to Christ: Andrei's War

Prince Andrei Bolkonsky is one of the main characters of Tolstoy's grand work and is, in my estimation, the dialectical contrast to Pierre. When

3. Herbert, "Love (III)."
4. Tennyson, *Major Works*, 220.
5. Tolstoy, *War and Peace*, xx.
6. Lewis, *Weight of Glory*, 51.

Andrei is introduced at Anna Pavlovna's party, he is a dashing man of ambition and success. He has a beautiful wife who is pregnant. He is to be General Mikhail Kutuzov's aide-de-camp for the upcoming 1805 campaign. He is described in the image of earthly success: "He was a very handsome young man, of medium height, with firm, clear-cut features."[7] Moreover, the highest members of Russian society are aware of Andrei's meteoric rise, and some think he'll one day become aide-de-camp even to the Tsar.

Andrei is introduced as the embodied ideal image of Russian high society, and this theme of an embodied image is something with which Tolstoy plays through Andrei as the story unfolds. Well-mannered and articulate, handsome and patriotic—Andrei stands in stark contrast to his bumbling and stumbling Jacobin-adoring friend Pierre, who, although the illegitimate son of a high society count, is an outcast of the Russian aristocracy by blood and by politics. Where Andrei knows when to hold his tongue, Pierre cannot help but leap into the conversation, to the shock and chagrin of others. Andrei has everything going for him. Indeed, Pierre sees in Andrei the "model of perfection" because "Andrei possessed in the highest degree just the very qualities [he] lacked, and which might be best described as strength of will. Pierre was always astonished at Prince Andrei's calm manner of treating everybody, his extraordinary memory, his extensive reading . . . but above all at his capacity for work and study."[8]

Despite external appearances, Andrei is an alienated man. The homelife, despite recognizing his wife as an excellent woman, does not fill his rapturous desires. Andrei wants, wills, excitement. That is what Pierre cannot understand, as to why Andrei is so eager for war in 1805. The family life weighs a man down, shackles one to a life of complacency, and drains the freedom for adventure and the thrills that come with it. In one of the many conversations Andrei and Pierre share, Andrei informs him, "Never, never marry, my dear fellow! That's my advice: never marry till you can say to yourself that you have done all you are capable of and until you have ceased to love the woman of your choice and have seen her plainly as she is . . . . Marry when you are old and good for nothing—or all that is good and noble in you will be lost."[9]

Although Andrei is, externally, the image of success, he is—in actuality, in the interior sense—a broken and empty man. The Andrei introduced in the opening pages of *War and Peace* is not a whole man. He is, in the Homeric tale, Achilles wanting the excitement and so-called glory and nobility

7. Tolstoy, *War and Peace*, 15.

8. Tolstoy, *War and Peace*, 31.

9. Tolstoy, *War and Peace*, 30.

offered in war rather than the contentment and simple life of marriage and family. Poised between war and homestead, like Achilles, Andrei chooses war and abandons his pregnant wife. The image of Achilles bears itself in the early Andrei for all to see, for Achilles also abandoned his family to fight in the Trojan War. Andrei, like Achilles at Troy, is at the helm leading the Russian army into the heart of Europe to confront the murderous villain Napoleon Bonaparte. Or at least he envisions himself in that role.

As the Russian army advances into central Europe, Andrei has dreams of his "Toulon" moment, where he will lead the Russian army to victory against their French adversary.[10] Napoleon is simultaneously villain and hero to Andrei. Napoleon is the great other, the oppositional foe that he, as a Russian, must defeat. Yet Napoleon also embodies and exudes everything for which Andrei yearns: a supposed brilliance, cunning, and heroic greatness.

There are various ironies about Andrei when he is out on campaign as opposed to enjoying the simple life of high society. In peaceful high society, he stands out among the other aristocrats with a successful career and a beautiful wife and is himself the ideal image of handsomeness. In the military ranks, however, he is alienated from himself and seeks to be anyone but himself. He doesn't stand out among the other officers, in which he is a faceless blur to all superiors besides Kutuzov. Rather than be Prince Andrei, he wishes to be Napoleon: "As soon as [Andrei] learned that the Russian army was in such a hopeless situation it occurred to him that it was he who was destined to lead it out of this position; that here was the Toulon that would lift him from the ranks of the obscure officers and offer him the first step to glory."[11]

Andrei's expectations for war glory commence in his first taste of battle at Schöngrabern. Although a relatively small encounter, when the dogs of war are loosed across the battlefield, Andrei cannot help but imagine his nihilistic dreams. "It has begun," Andrei thinks watching the cannon fire.[12] "Here it is . . . . But where and how will my Toulon present itself?"[13] While Schöngrabern did not turn out to be any Toulon for Andrei, the taste of battle was exciting and heroic for the young prince. He gleefully reports the salvific actions of Captain Tushin's artillery battery to Prince Bagration as the principal reason for why the Russians were able to hold off the French advance and retire in good order.

10. Tolstoy, *War and Peace*, 281.

11. Tolstoy, *War and Peace*, 173.

12. Tolstoy, *War and Peace*, 190.

13. Tolstoy, *War and Peace*, 190.

After Bagration's column, with which Andrei was present, reunites with Kutuzov, a tension over the coming battle with Napoleon spreads over the camp. Tolstoy, in his genius, presents the dialectic of war perfectly. In the war scenes, Tolstoy starts by presenting the perfect battle strategies and beautiful parade marches of an orderly sense of conflict, which suddenly vanish into chaos and confusion at the commencement of battle. It is in this tug of war of order and meaning, of chaos and confusion, that Andrei finds himself. On the eve of the Battle of Austerlitz, Andrei once again imagines his perfect Toulon moment that will win him renown and glory. "[Andrei]'s imagination pictured the battle, its loss, the concentration of fighting at one point, and the hesitation of all the commanders. And then that happy moment, that Toulon for which he had so long waited, presents itself to him at last . . . so he takes a regiment, a division . . . leads his division to the decisive point, and gains the victory alone."[14]

The Battle of Austerlitz is a disaster for the Russians and Austrians. Andrei is wounded when nihilistically replaying his dream. Having grabbed a standard and urging his comrades forward, he is struck from the back by a French bayonet and falls to the ground, looking up to the heavens. It is at this moment that Andrei experiences the beginning of his transformative pilgrimage. The chaos of battle and his dreams of glory disappear:

> Above him there was now nothing but the sky—the lofty sky, not clear yet still immeasurably lofty with grey clouds gliding slowly across it. "How quiet, peaceful, and solemn, not at all as I ran," thought Prince Andrei—"not as we ran, shouting, and fighting, not at all as the gunner and the Frenchman with frightened and angry faces struggled for the mop: how differently do those clouds glide across that lofty infinite sky! How was it I did not see that lofty sky before. And how happy I am to have found it at last! Yes! All is vanity, all falsehood, except that infinite sky. There is nothing, nothing, but that. But even it does not exist, there is nothing but quiet and peace. Thank God."[15]

Andrei's revelatory moment at Austerlitz is an unmistakable and archetypal encounter with what Edmund Burke called the sublime. It was more than just mere beauty that Andrei encountered as he gazed up to the sky—a theme that will be replayed several times by Tolstoy over the course of the book. He encountered, with awe-inspiring wonder, the sublime that overwhelms the individual to the point of death. In that moment, Andrei recognized the nakedness of his vanity and, ensnared by the sublime, lost

14. Tolstoy, *War and Peace*, 281.
15. Tolstoy, *War and Peace*, 299.

himself in a state of tranquility while a horrendously brutal battle raged around him. He found, however briefly and pain-induced, the joy and contentment he was recklessly pursuing on the battlefield and through the medium of earthly glory. In that moment Andrei did, in a sense, die in his encounter with the terrorizing beauty of the sublime, to be born anew.

From heroic man to maimed child moaning from his wounds, Andrei has—in fitting Tolstoyan irony—his encounter with his hero. Napoleon, that supposed great man of absolute spirit, is on the heights inspecting the dead right where Andrei fell wounded. But Andrei's encounter with the lofty and infinite sky has changed his perception of Napoleon. Andrei "knew it was Napoleon—his hero—but at that moment Napoleon seemed to him such a small and insignificant creature compared with what was passing now between himself and that lofty infinite sky with the clouds flying over it."[16] Napoleon, that significant and looming creature, is now insignificant as Andrei begins his transformation away from the pursuit of ego, vanity, and power.

Tolstoy also gives clues as to the problem that Andrei was facing—both internally and externally. Wounded, Andrei "was glad that people were standing near him, and only wished that they would help him and bring him back to life, which seemed to him so beautiful now that he had today learned to understand differently." Physically ill and needing attention from others, Andrei is bodily moved to relationships. Spiritually ill, or now having "learned to understand differently,"[17] Andrei's need for others is reflective of his beginning transformation from self-centered image-maker to relational animal made in the image of love and forgiveness. Andrei's physical ailment was related to his spiritual illness, which pushed him to the precipice of vainglorious idolatry, having put the self above all to the point of exclusion and renunciation of others. After all, Andrei left his pregnant wife and unborn child to achieve his Toulon moment, to etch his name in eternity as Achilles did.

This movement away from selfish and vain glory-seeker to a man who learns to love and forgives others is not immediately realized on the bloody slopes of the Pratzen Heights. Instead, it takes many more struggles—many more wars, so to speak—before Andrei achieves this total transformation and divinization. When Pierre visits Andrei at Bald Hills after their having being separated for nearly two years, Andrei has become a recluse hermit fighting a new internal struggle about what the experiences of Austerlitz meant.

16. Tolstoy, *War and Peace*, 310.
17. Tolstoy, *War and Peace*, 310.

When Pierre visits Andrei, he is shocked to see the "change in him." There is a double implication in the change Pierre sees. One, of course, is physical. The second change, perhaps the more profound of the two, is Andrei's interior character. Andrei has become a hermit-like monk dwelling in "prolonged concentration on some one thought."[18] Tolstoy makes explicitly clear that in this new meeting of Andrei and Pierre, it is as if they are both meeting each other for the first time, for both are changed men from when they last met. They spoke to each other, Tolstoy writes, "like people who do not know each other intimately."[19]

The defining moment of Pierre's visit for Andrei comes in their discussion over the meaning of life. When Pierre discusses living and loving others, Andrei is thrown into a dour disposition of reproach. Tolstoy plays with the contrast between the two so well in the unfolding dialogue. Pierre is convinced that he lived for himself, but now has found new meaning—true meaning—an earthly and spiritual joy, in loving and serving others. Andrei reproaches Pierre ever so gently and argues the opposite. He lived for others in his vain pursuit of glory, but now lives for himself and is happy. "I experienced the reverse," Andrei informs Pierre. "I lived for glory.—And after all what is glory? The same love of others, a desire to do something for them, a desire for their approval.—So I lived for others, and not almost but quite, ruined my life. And I have become calmer since I began to live only for myself."[20]

Tolstoyan irony runs deep in this critical moment of the story. Andrei is not yet aware that he lived for himself prior to Austerlitz and still lives for himself after Austerlitz but with a greater awareness of the beauty around him. The major difference is that he no longer pursues a self-glorifying vanity project, which he wrongly attributes to his wanting approval from others. In 1805, Andrei was the embodiment of that earthly creature who is moved by "the love of self . . . glories in itself . . . [and] seeks glory from men."[21]

As the conversation continues, this realization comes to the fore for the gentle reader: from new men who did not know each other, Andrei and Pierre grow ever more intimate as they look into each other's eyes and speak. The eyes are the window to the soul, and looking a person in the eye is a signification of intimacy and trust, of friendship and love. Eyes play a major role in Tolstoy's story, most explicitly seen in Natasha, but here given to Andrei and Pierre. As Pierre continually beseeches him, like a missionary

18. Tolstoy, *War and Peace*, 408.
19. Tolstoy, *War and Peace*, 409.
20. Tolstoy, *War and Peace*, 411.
21. Augustine, *City of God*, 477.

of God sent to a wayward soul struggling to find God on his own but unable to do so on his own power—much like Augustine's depiction of himself prior to his conversion in Milan in *Confessions*—the conversion of Andrei begins when he looks up at the sky again, the same sky to which he looked up when on his back at Austerlitz. "If there is a God and future life there is truth and good, and man's highest happiness consists in striving to attain them. We must live, we must love, and we must believe," Pierre tells Andrei before "point[ing] to the sky." As Andrei listened to Pierre, "he gazed with his eyes fixed on the red reflection of the sun gleaming on the blue waters. There was a perfect stillness."[22]

Andrei's movement away from vain glory-seeking began as he peered up to the lofty sky on the Pratzen Heights. But it took a sacramental person, a sort of missionary, an angel—Pierre—to make the annunciation to Andrei that the replacing of the self requires love and service to others. As Pierre departs, Tolstoy informs us that, "[Andrei's] meeting with Pierre formed an epoch in [his] life. Though outwardly he continued to live the same old way, inwardly he began a new life."[23] Andrei's meeting with Pierre at Bald Hills in 1807 is the directional reorientation of himself to Christ, others, and love itself. Struggling to find that directional guidance needed after having his empty vanity crushed at Austerlitz, it took Pierre to set Andrei on the course of the straight and true—though this course, this new life, on which Andrei is now will be equally difficult. Andrei's transformation, however, represents a great Tolstoyan achievement: the rebirth of Andrei away from the war-hungry and glory-seeking Achilles to a gentler, compassionate, and loving Christ figure.

Given the overlap of characters and their arcs, I do not wish to write about Andrei's well-known romance with Natasha. As such, I wish to move to the completion of Andrei's war from transitioning away from an image of Achilles to an image of Christ. Though it is important to state that his possible joyful and serendipitous life with Natasha was ruined by Anatole Kuragin, whom Andrei personally seeks out to kill in the months leading up to the Battle of Borodino, it is the eradication of this possible end life for Andrei that makes his transformation complete.

Andrei's transformative war is fittingly completed during a battle. For it is at the bloody fields of Borodino that Andrei's transformation from Achilles to Christ is consummated. On the eve of the battle, when Pierre visits him once more, Andrei's discussion with Pierre about the rules of war and the orders of battle is filled with the cynical venom of a man lost in the

22. Tolstoy, *War and Peace*, 416.
23. Tolstoy, *War and Peace*, 417.

whirlwind. Shunning the false glory of war, Andrei informs Pierre his new outlook of war and peace is "Take no prisoners, but kill and be killed!"[24] Andrei's statement, coupled with the reality of hunting for Anatole whilst trying to perform his duties as an officer, makes his moment of forgiveness on the bloody battlefield of Borodino even more incredible to witness.

After having been wounded as his regiment marches from their reserve positions to a new place on the battlefield, Andrei is taken to a field hospital where the screaming cries of the wounded pierce the air. As he is given a place to rest, he hears the whimpering of a familiar voice. Andrei has been placed right next to "the miserable, sobbing, enfeebled" Anatole who has just had his leg amputated.[25]

Given what has happened to Andrei because of Anatole, any lesser man would have been justified in taking revenge against the man who ruined his prospects of felicity and marriage. But rather than take revenge or embody the take-no-prisoners attitude of which he told Pierre, Andrei is overcome with love. "Prince Andrei could no longer restrain himself, and wept tender loving tears for his fellow men, for himself, and for his own and their errors." Andrei's war is completed at that moment, that moment when his heart sinks for his fellow brothers and sisters as he utters the unforgettable words of Christ-like forgiveness: "Compassion, love of our brothers, for those who love us and for those who hate us, love of our enemies; yes, that love which God preached on earth and which Princess Marya taught me and I did not understand—that is what made me sorry to part with life, that is what remained for me had I lived. But now it is too late. I know it!"[26]

It is here that Andrei completely gives himself over to God and Christ, becoming a literal image and mouthpiece of God in paraphrasing the Sermon on the Mount and having his ruptured relationships restored. The movement to forgiveness leading to love becomes the recurring theme at the end of Tolstoy's work, and Andrei embodies this reality better than anyone in the story. When Natasha meets him again, among the wounded being evacuated, she begs his forgiveness. Andrei, looking into Natasha's lively eyes—and eyes have been a major image throughout scenes of love and relationships throughout the book, as hitherto stated—tells her that he has already forgiven her.

Fittingly, Andrei's death is one of peace. It was the peace he found in becoming an image-bearer of the loving and forgiving Christ who loves and forgives those who do not know what they do. Moments before his death,

24. Tolstoy, *War and Peace*, 833.

25. Tolstoy, *War and Peace*, 874.

26. Tolstoy, *War and Peace*, 874.

surrounded by Natasha and Marya, the two woman who loved him, he ponders the meaning of love as he is surrounded by love. "Love is God," Andrei
tells himself, "and to die means that I, a particle of love, shall return to the
general and eternal source."[27]

The Pilgrim's Progress: Pierre's War

Pierre might be the most universal character of Tolstoy's work. This is not to
diminish Nikolai, who has many universal moments with which the reader
can identify, but there is something about Pierre that draws most, if not all,
readers to his predicament. From being an outcast to speaking out of turn,
to being opinionated, to pondering life's mystery, to experiencing the thrill
of lawlessness (in battle), to settling down into family life, Pierre's arc is one
through which most people go during their lifetime, which is why he is so
relatable.

In many ways, Pierre is the opposite of Andrei. He is, at the opening, the illegitimate son of a prominent aristocrat, which means he occupies
a muddled sphere in Russian society. He is neither fully accepted by the
aristocracy nor a serf; and with Russia lacking a bourgeois middle class,
his intermediate state of being cannot be in the middle class, as it could
be in other countries. Where Andrei is successful, handsome, and has
a family, Pierre is something of a travelling buffoon, not the most handsome of gentlemen (especially in comparison to Andrei), and is alone. As
such, Pierre spends his time in love with ideas and political abstractions
rather than in concrete human relationships. In many ways, Pierre is like
the young Saint Augustine, who was in love with the idea of love but unsure
how to actualize or concretize love in his life. At Anna Pavlovna's party, he is
a Jacobin humanitarian, incapable, like the Jacobins themselves, of helping
those he claims to love and whom he has never met nor spent time with. In
the excitement of conversation beckoning, with the other attendees critical
of Napoleon, Pierre jumps with joy to defend the French ruler: "Napoleon
is great because he rose superior to the Revolution, suppressed its abuses,
preserved all that was good in it—equality of citizenship, freedom of speech
and the press—and only for that reason did he obtain power."[28]

It becomes clear that while Andrei and Pierre are superficial contrasts
with each other, inside, they are very much alike. Like Andrei, Pierre is
alienated and estranged. Pierre is estranged from Russian high society; from
his family as an illegitimate son; from Hélène, his first wife; and, indeed,

27. Tolstoy, *War and Peace*, 1058.
28. Tolstoy, *War and Peace*, 21.

from himself, the world, and God. Throughout the story, Pierre struggles to find a home. Tolstoy brilliantly realizes this in that many of the scenes with Pierre he is away from home, out on a journey like a pilgrim, roaming from place to place in search for that home he never had.

The struggle in the world that Pierre fights is the struggle to make present, in incarnate form, the intoxicating love for abstract ideas that he has at the beginning of the story—and through this realization of love in the world rather than the realm of ideas, Pierre can find that home for which he is desperately yearning. The Russian attendees at Anna Pavlovna's party are down-to-earth; they see the embodied reality of the Terror, the Revolution, and Napoleon's conquest to expand the Revolution to the rest of Europe, but Pierre is altogether aloof from this reality. "What? Revolution and regicide a grand thing?" Anna Pavlovna retorts to Pierre in contempt and shock. "I am not speaking of regicide, I am speaking about ideas," Pierre boldly answers her.[29]

Pierre's estrangement from the world and himself goes as far as his imagining himself to be Napoleon. Again, the parallelism with Andrei is intermixed. Where Andrei wanted to instantiate Napoleon's greatness in himself prior to his transformative experience at Austerlitz, Pierre literally fantasizes himself as the Emperor of France and dictator of much of Europe. "But before Pierre—who at that moment imagined himself to be Napoleon in person to have just effected the dangerous cross of the Pas-de-Calais and captured London—could pronounce Pitt's sentence, he saw a well-built and handsome young officer entering his room."[30] When Pierre and Boris Drubetskaya (the officer) converse, Pierre openly admits to the Russian officer that he is rooting for the French emperor to win.

But Pierre's plight and estrangement from the world reach a threshold with the death of his father, Kiril Bezukhov. His family members, if you could call them that—Prince Vasili and Princess Katerina—are scheming to keep him out of the will of his dying father. Kiril's will, with all the authority it carries and from his own decree, legitimizes Pierre and passes down the family inheritance to him. The scheming of Vasili and Katerina fails. Pierre is legitimized.

The legitimization of Pierre propels him into a new world. The Russian aristocracy suddenly takes interest in him, not because of who Pierre is but because of the wealth and titles he carries. At the same time, Pierre's legitimization comes at the expense of his filial relationships. Vasili and Katerina, who were always distant to him, disappear in their anger. His father, who

29. Tolstoy, *War and Peace*, 21.
30. Tolstoy, *War and Peace*, 57.

loved him, but also kept his distance from him to maintain his reputation as a count while alive, is altogether gone. Pierre might have found new wealth and rights, but he is alone in a world ruptured by war.

With new wealth comes new temptations. Princess Hélène, the beautiful but scheming femme fatale in the epic, seduces Pierre to advance her social standing and wealth. Hélène wields her beauty as a seductive form of control, a lust to dominate through her charm and feminine mystique, which clouds Pierre's better judgement. In a room alone with her, Pierre falls under Hélène's smile and soothsaying charms that magnify her bodily beauty. "'So you have never before noticed how beautiful I am?' Hélène seemed to say." There is ambiguity here; "seemed to say" suggests that she may or may not have been speaking. Everything has become a blur to Pierre. Was she speaking to him in voice or in bodily invitation and gesture? Then Hélène pounced on him with her body-language, opening to Pierre and inviting him to be with her like the muses of Homeric antiquity. "You had not noticed that I am a woman? Yes, I am a woman who may belong to anyone—to you too," Hélène seductively tells Pierre with a "glance." Falling for her objectified beauty and mystique, "Pierre felt that Hélène not only could, but must, be his wife, and that it could not be otherwise."[31]

Pierre's falling for the temptations of Hélène marks his pivot toward the struggle for filial homecoming that dominates the rest of his character development. His relationship with Hélène quickly disintegrates when she berates him that she will never allow herself to bear his children. Her open infidelity, in carrying on a sexual relationship with Dolokhov, serves to further strain the relationship that they never had to begin with.

With his marriage falling apart and an utter feeling of meaninglessness engulfing him like a storm, Pierre falls into company with freemasons. Pierre's turn to freemasonry is the need for an anchor. Until now he has been rudderless and crashing about on the violent seas of strife and emotional rapture. He has long sought a meaningful life, first in the world of political ideas and then in (a failed) marriage. Nothing has brought him peaceful rest.

Freemasonry was the perfect synthesis for Pierre's wayfaring soul when he encounters the masonic stranger and is brought into the fellowship. It combines the two things in which he had, up till now, sought meaning: politics and family. Moreover, it wasn't a mere love for the idea of politics or family, but an actual instantiated reality of politics and family, though at the periphery of Pierre's life, that caused him to seek meaning in both. As a mason, Pierre could finally do good and help others as he dreamt

---

31. Tolstoy, *War and Peace*, 219.

the Jacobins and Napoleon were trying to do. The masons also served as the brotherhood, fraternity, and family that Pierre never had. The relational reality of the pursuit of truth and human nature is captured by the reality that to become a mason, one needs to nominate you, and in the stranger's reply on meeting Pierre for the first time: "No one can attain to truth by himself."[32]

It is a subtle moment in the story, not fully realized until the book's conclusion, but Pierre's turn to masonry is also his turning to God, from whom he had been estranged. Pierre spoke the language of piety and invoked Christ to suit his political agenda at Anna Pavlovna's party, but privately he was an atheist. While the intricacies of freemasonry initially inflame Pierre's appetite for knowledge and meaning, the most important change in Pierre through his encounter with freemasonry is his turning to God. For all his youth, virality, and wealth, Pierre is lost in a forest of darkness cloudier and murkier than when we first met him. The masonic stranger is an angelic messenger turning Pierre around; and Pierre, with newfound vigor in masonry, becomes that messenger to Andrei when they meet at Bald Hills in 1807.

The masons bring to Pierre's attention the problem with seeking a meaningful life purely out of carnality and the riches of the world. His swelling heart is enticed by the stranger's brief explanation of wisdom and truth in a very Augustinian moment of rapturous desire. "You are young, you are rich, you are clever, you are well educated. And what have you done with all these good gifts? Are you content with yourself and with your life?"[33] Pierre's standing in high society, his education, and his wealth have amounted to nothing but estranged wanderings like a pilgrim in endless desert sand. Furthermore, the language of pilgrimage is alluded to in Pierre's journey into the brotherhood: "The meeting was at an end, and on reaching home Pierre felt as if he had returned from a long journey on which he had spent dozens of years, had become completely changed, and had quite left behind his former habits and way of life."[34]

The complexity of masonry, however, doesn't satisfy Pierre. The esoteric philosophy, the fellowship among brothers, and the quasi-theological and political nature of the fraternity only serve to alienate Pierre yet again when he reaches the limit of what the masons can offer him. But the emphasis on relationships and the turning to God which was a prerequisite for membership linger in Pierre's burning heart. The masons, to this end, served

32. Tolstoy, *War and Peace*, 375.

33. Tolstoy, *War and Peace*, 377.

34. Tolstoy, *War and Peace*, 387.

as intermediaries to reorient Pierre to what he will eventually struggle to actualize in his life to have meaning: family. For family, through marriage, brings relationships, God (through the sacrament of marriage), and the joys of embodied and incarnational living to the fullness of life. From this perspective, the third time is the charm, as his failed marriage with Hélène and failed life as a brother with the masons prefigure Pierre's eventual successful marriage and family life with Natasha.

Pierre struggles with a wandering alienation in the moments leading up to the Battle of Borodino, following his disillusionment with the masons. Despite that disillusionment, he still ponders upon the mysteries of the masonic teachings and tries to convince himself of the meaning of the events and his place in the drama of the apocalypse. Pierre's alienation leads him into the classic *descensus ad inferos* as he stumbles onto the fields of the horrific battle; it is only through this descent into hellfire that he can be reborn and brought back to life.

There is a certain poetic irony and justice in Pierre's homecoming. He was introduced as a man who loved pure theory, soaring above the clouds as if a superior man to the rest of the Russian aristocracy, because of his theoretical high-mindedness that detached him from the world of personable relationships, from which he himself was estranged due to the circumstances of his birth. In joining the masons, as already discussed, he momentarily received a synthetic experience of practicable, personable relationships coupled with esoteric theory. But his disillusion with the masons was simultaneously a rupture with the faux relationality of the order and false theory offered by them. In a worse position now than before, he has crashed from the world of abstract theory into the world of violent materiality and battle. It took this pulling away the carpet of high-minded theory to cause Pierre to land back in the world of relationships—along with the help of Natasha, whom he soothed and comforted following Anatole's predatory advances on her.

This crash landing back into the world of relationships and descent into the maelstrom of Borodino begins with his chance, or preordained, encounter with Dolokhov. Dolokhov rushes to Pierre following a procession of the Holy Mother to ask for Pierre's forgiveness of their past encounters. "With tears in his eyes Dolokhov embraced Pierre and kissed him."[35] At long last, Pierre experiences a personable moment with his former enemy, and, like Christ, he is able to forgive and show mercy to the man with whom his unfaithful wife had illicitly carried on a sexual relationship. There is further

---

35. Tolstoy, *War and Peace*, 823.

poetic closure that it is Dolokhov who will save him from French captivity during Napoleon's retreat.

Following the Battle of Borodino, Pierre wanders aimlessly back into Moscow as the city burns. He is subsequently captured by the French as a prisoner, despite moments of personal heroism and sacrifice: his saving of the French officer and the endangered girl in the fire. Pierre, however, had to be broken in a sort of Babylonian captivity of his own; he had to be brought low, back down from the stratosphere of abstract idealism into the world of concrete relationships and the body. As Tolstoy writes concerning Pierre's transformative pilgrimage:

> In burnt and devastated Moscow Pierre experienced almost the extreme limits of privation of man can endure; but thanks to his physical strength and health, of which he had till then been unconscious, and thanks especially to the fact that the privations came so gradually that it was impossible to say when they began, he endured his position not only lightly but joyfully. And just at this time he obtained the tranquility and ease of mind he had formerly striven in vain to reach. He had long sought in different ways tranquility of mind, that inner harmony, which had so impressed him in the soldiers at the battle of Borodino. He had sought it in philanthropy, in Freemasonry, in the dissipations of town life, in wine, in heroic feats of self-sacrifice, and in romantic love for Natasha; he had sought it by reasoning—and all these quests and experiments had failed him. And now without thinking about it, he had found that peace and inner harmony only through the horror of death, through privation, and through what he recognized in Karataev.[36]

Pierre's having been brought low to the point of privation and his journey through hell and back are the last stage in his arrival at the shore of the meaningful life he had always sought. It was only through being imprisoned that Pierre could find the value of embodied life in the world and that tranquility he had longed for. "Life is everything," Pierre tells himself. "Life is God. Everything changes and moves and that movement is God. And while there is life there is joy in consciousness of the divine. To love life is to love God. Harder and more blessed than all else is to love this life in one's sufferings."[37]

The struggle and sojourning story of Pierre is the story of the pilgrim's progress. It is the perilous pilgrimage to something beyond the self,

36. Tolstoy, *War and Peace*, 1089.
37. Tolstoy, *War and Peace*, 1145.

something that binds heaven and earth, man and woman, human and dirt, together in splendid radiance and the grand waltz of life. It is the struggle to consummate love in the world, love others in the world, love the world, and love all the gifts before us—whether of flesh and blood or the inanimate objects that, taken in totality, constitute the wondrous beauty of the whole. The struggle to love life rather than be alienated from it is consummated in Pierre's marriage with Natasha, because the love of life, Tolstoy tells us through the union of Pierre and Natasha, is marriage. In marriage, Pierre ultimately does not follow Andrei's earlier advice, "Never, never marry, my dear fellow!"[38]

Therefore, it is through Pierre's marriage with Natasha and her wholesomeness in married life that the love of life after which Pierre always sought is made incarnate. The glow in both of their eyes, the tickling in their tongues, and the beatific charms in beholding one another was a long and arduous struggle for both, but especially for Pierre, whose entire journey brings him to this union. Tolstoy's genius with Pierre's struggles manifests itself in Pierre's arc over the course of the story; from his radical Jacobinism and failed marriage, to his descent into hell and his ascension to embodied life, sealed through the sacrament of marriage with Natasha and the birth of their children, Pierre's perilous journey was wandering east of Eden to finally finding that new Eden by story's end.

Blossoming to Life: Natasha's War

It goes without saying that the greatest achievement in *War and Peace* is the character of Natasha and her maturation into beauty and embodying a soulful life. It is, at times, a painful struggle—especially in her falling prey to the schemes of Anatole Kuragin, which destroys the planned marriage between her and Andrei. It is, at other times, a pleasant and heart-warming growth as she matures from that black-eyed little girl into a blossoming and fertile mother at story's end. From start to finish, the little seed that was Natasha withered away and grew into a wholesome and magnificent flower, one flush with fertility and life-giving power in a way that Hélène's exquisite body and breasts, but empty soul, never could.

There are two key features to Natasha that Tolstoy repeatedly emphasizes throughout the story: her voice and her eyes. Like the word of God, Natasha's voice has the power to awaken souls and bring them to life; on two occasions her voice sings out and lifts Nikolai and Andrei out of their suicidal and nihilistic stupors to a new appreciation of and for life. As Andrew

---

38. Tolstoy, *War and Peace*, 30.

Kaufman writes, Nikolai "has his moment of doubt and wants to put a gun to his head. But in that very instant, when he has been shaken to the core, he is lucky enough to hear Natasha sing, reminding him that sublime happiness and meaning are still available to him here and now, in the midst of his broken world."[39] Furthermore, Tolstoy also recourses to Natasha's eyes to bring out her liveliness. Eyes and voice, of course, emanate from the face; it is the face that is the seat of human subjectivity and not the objectified body below it, just as Roger Scruton brilliantly summarized: "The face shines in the world of objects with a light that is not of this world—the light of subjectivity."[40] As such, Natasha is revealed to us through the course of the story as the most personable, subjective, and lively of all the characters.

When we are introduced to Natasha, her mouth and eyes are the first features Tolstoy describes: "This black-eyed, wide-mouthed girl, not pretty but full of life, with childish bare shoulders which after her run heaved and shook her bodice, with black curls tossed backward, thin bare arms, little legs in lace-frilled drawers, and feet in low slippers—was just at that charming age when a girl is no longer a child, though the child is not yet a young woman."[41] There is a tremendous degree of foreshadowing going on in Tolstoy's introductory description of Natasha, and this foreshadowing establishes the genius of Tolstoy's incredible story, especially as it relates to the future maturation of Natasha through the unfolding of the story. Additionally, her introduction and contrast with Hélène—against whom she is intentionally dialectically paired—couldn't be starker.

Hélène is introduced as the maid of honor at Anna Pavlovna's party. One cannot miss her voluptuous and enticing body, which wins the eyes and hearts of the crowd. However, Hélène is never described as being "full of life."[42] More to the point, the focus of Hélène's womanhood is her body and not her soul; her womanhood is found in her breasts and shoulders rather than her face. Natasha's womanhood, or growth into womanhood, is found in her face—her subjectivity—which is doubly signified and represented through her voice of life and soulful eyes. Despite Hélène's unquestionable beauty, Hélène is a lifeless object in contrast to Natasha's pulsating and soulful being:

> The Princess Hélène smiled. She rose with the same unchanging smile with which she had first entered the room—the smile of a perfectly beautiful woman. With a slight rustle of her white

39. Kaufman, *Give War and Peace a Chance*, 56.

40. Scruton, *Face of God*, 49.

41. Tolstoy, *War and Peace*, 41.

42. Tolstoy, *War and Peace*, 41.

dress trimmed with moss and ivy, with a gleam of white shoulders, glossy hair and sparkling diamonds, she passed between the men who made way for her, not looking at any of them but smiling on all, as if graciously allowing each the privilege of admiring her beautiful figure and shapely shoulders, back, and bosom.[43]

Hélène's "unchanging smile" is the same smile "for everybody."[44] Hélène is everywhere described in the image and language of carnal beauty that Natasha lacks, but Hélène is never described as containing life: Natasha "kept looking round in turn at the rows of pomaded heads in the stalls and then at the semi-nude women in the boxes, especially at Hélène in the next box, who—apparently quite unclothed—sat with a quiet and tranquil smile."[45] Hélène's deadly charms and consuming appetite for scheming are nothing compared to Natasha's life-giving piety, which brings to her "the possibility of a new, clean life, and happiness."[46] Hélène may be a beautiful woman, but Tolstoy portrays Natasha as the true embodiment of feminine struggle and receptivity leading to motherhood that completes Natasha's embodiment of a life-filled and life-giving spirit. Natasha, struggle through hardship and temptations as she may—even lapsing into sin—has a soul of repentance, which provides her with a quickening spirit. Hélène, by contrast, has no spirit of repentance, and her drive for self-advancement leads to her eventual death, like all those who live for themselves and are ruled by the flesh.

Natasha's voice and eyes, as mentioned, are her two defining features on which Tolstoy focuses throughout her maturation into a life-bearing mother. Just as God's voice recalls to life in the biblical and Christian tradition, so too does Natasha's voice recall Nikolai to life. Just as God's voice draws humans to it, so too does Natasha's voice draw Andrei to her in love. Just as God's voice is the sound of vitality, so too does Natasha's voice triumphantly sound her resurrection before the presence of Pierre.

After having been swindled into serious debt by Dolokhov, Nikolai contemplates suicide because of his inability to pay off the debts and his shame in informing his father of his lack of virtue in matters relating to financial control and management. Returning home in a feeling of abject despair, depression, and loneliness, Nikolai is saved by the angelic voice of his sister singing in the room nearby. "In her voice there was a virginal

43. Tolstoy, *War and Peace*, 12.
44. Tolstoy, *War and Peace*, 471.
45. Tolstoy, *War and Peace*, 602.
46. Tolstoy, *War and Peace*, 707.

freshness, an unconsciousness of her own powers, and an as yet untrained velvety softness, which so mingled with her lack of art in singing that it seemed as if nothing in that voice could be altered without spoiling it."[47] Natasha's life-giving voice is the only thing that saves Nikolai at that moment.

Like the word of the Lord spoken by Old Testament prophets, Natasha's voice pierces into the center of Nikolai's dark depression and fills that empty void with a newness of life that is altogether a transcendent experience for him. Completely immersed in her heavenly singing, Nikolai's recalling to life leads him to becoming her cheerleader as she shifts pitches and octaves. "Now then, Natasha, now then, dearest! Now then, darling! How will she take that *si*? She's taken it! Thank God." Not only had Nikolai become hopeful in Natasha's singing success, he too became a participant in the song of life, "without noticing that he was singing, to strengthen the *si* he sang a second, a third below the high note."[48] This scene is one of particular beauty, an undeniable triumph of Tolstoy's literary ability and construction.

Following his conversation with Pierre, Andrei soon finds himself in the same house as Natasha and Sonya. He hears two female voices—again as if angels singing from on high: "Two girlish voices sang a musical passage—the end of some song." Moving from song to playful laughter, Andrei says, "For her I might as well not exist." But as Natasha keeps singing and laughing, that new life that was originally lit by Pierre is suddenly fueled by the voice of life emanating from Natasha: "In his soul there suddenly arose such an unexpected turmoil of youthful thoughts and hopes, contrary to the whole tenor of his life, that unable to explain his condition to himself he lay down and fell asleep at once."[49] As Andrei sleeps, he dreams of Natasha and her magnificent voice that eventually calls him to her during their grand waltz: "He stepped forward in the direction Pierre indicated. The despairing, dejected expression of Natasha's face caught his eye. He recognized her, guessed her feelings, saw that it was her first ball, remembered her conversation at the window, and with an expression of pleasure on his face, approached Countess Rostova."[50]

After being deceived and tempted by the Kuragins, Natasha's fall from innocence is a quintessential recapitulation of the Christian drama of the fall. Natasha's young innocence is shattered in being deceived by Anatole Kuragin and the prospective marriage with Andrei falls apart as a consequence. She falls into a doldrum. Though Sonya tries to comfort her, Natasha is not

47. Tolstoy, *War and Peace*, 367.
48. Tolstoy, *War and Peace*, 367.
49. Tolstoy, *War and Peace*, 451.
50. Tolstoy, *War and Peace*, 493.

truly recovered until she talks to Pierre about love and forgiveness. With Pierre by her side, she implores him to plead with Andrei to forgive her, "tell him . . . to for . . . forgive me."[51] Love, struggle, and forgiveness are now interconnected with Natasha and Andrei, and Andrei does indeed forgive Natasha when they meet again.

But this intermixing of love and forgiveness between Natasha and Andrei is sealed in her singing before Pierre which, as a matter of fact, also brings Pierre closer to her and will consummate the love Natasha originally sought in Andrei. Having come to visit the Rostovs, Pierre finds Natasha singing alone:

> The first person he saw in the house was Natasha. Even before he saw her, while taking off his cloak, he heard her. She was practicing sol-fa exercises in the music-room. He knew that she had not sung since her illness, and so the sound of her voice surprised and delighted him. He opened the door softly and saw her, in the lilac dress she had worn at church, walking about the room singing. She had her back to him when he opened the door, but when, turning quickly, she saw his broad, surprised face, she blushed and came rapidly to him.[52]

Natasha has recovered to life. She is singing again. She is blushing again. She is wholesome again. She is the matured image of that little girl who was introduced to us as being filled with love, ready to consummate her matured life and love—preferably with Andrei at this point, if given the chance, though, as we know, it is eventually sealed with Pierre.

Apart from singing, Natasha's eyes are also a major focus of Tolstoy's description of Natasha. Her eyes factor more prominently in the story than any other character's. As hitherto mentioned, she is introduced as that black-eyed girl full of life.

Natasha's happy face and her life-filled eyes are images that continually recur throughout the book. When Andrei asks Natasha to waltz, the "tremulous expression on Natasha's face, prepared either for despair or rapture, suddenly brightened into a happy, grateful, childlike smile . . . . Her face beamed with ecstatic happiness."[53] When Andrei asks Natasha if she loves him, he looks straight into her eyes while holding her hands—in that, the mystical experience, Andrei feels a pity for her childlike constitution that demands his watchful protection. Andrei becomes a man, filled now with a spirit of protectiveness, when Natasha declares her utmost love for

51. Tolstoy, *War and Peace*, 643.

52. Tolstoy, *War and Peace*, 716.

53. Tolstoy, *War and Peace*, 492.

him. Initiation and receptivity have merged in the hope for fatherhood and motherhood. Most of her encounters, especially with Andrei and Pierre, have her eyes or joyous smile and face front and center for all to behold.

After reconciling with Andrei before his death and now preparing for marriage with Pierre, Natasha's smile reappears and her "attentive eyes" lock with Pierre's and reveal the innermost secrets of her soul to his.[54] Indeed, the joyful and loving scenes between Natasha and Pierre focuses solely on their face and eyes. "From the moment they were alone and Natasha came up to him with wide-open happy eyes and quickly seizing his head pressed it to her bosom saying: 'Now you are all mine!'"[55] The final scene of Natasha is her joyful smile, her glittering eyes, her whole body filled with life.

In Natasha's maturation from little girl to wholesome woman who becomes a mother, the peace sought by Pierre and Natasha is sealed in their incarnate living with one another. It is in their participatory love, like the participatory love of the Trinity, that the meaning of life is found and consummated. As Natasha tells Pierre with a blushful smile, radiating with life, "I love you awfully . . . . Awfully, awfully!"[56]

The Odyssey of Love

Although *War and Peace* is nestled in real history, the real war in Tolstoy's epic is life itself. "Life, meanwhile—real life, with its essential interests of health and sickness, toil and rest, and its intellectual interests in thought, science, poetry, music, love, friendship, hatred, and passions—went on as usual, independently of and apart from political friendship or enmity with Napoleon Bonaparte and from all the schemes of reconstruction."[57] Real life is the center of the real war in *War and Peace*. The physical battles of the Napoleonic campaigns only serve to magnify the flesh and blood struggles of relationships that dominate the book and its many characters.

Andrew Kaufman is right to implore us to give *War and Peace* a chance. It is, at first glance, and even first read, an intimidating book. But it is well worth it to journey through it. It is a story of adventure, love, and struggle. It is a story of contrasts and foils. It is a story of cruelty, vindictiveness, and forgiveness. It is a story of heroism and tragedy. It is a story of two becoming one. The war for peace is the war for love. Tolstoy captures this dynamism so brilliantly in his story. C.S. Lewis goes so far as describing *War and Peace*

54. Tolstoy, *War and Peace*, 1198.

55. Tolstoy, *War and Peace*, 1264.

56. Tolstoy, *War and Peace*, 1267.

57. Tolstoy, *War and Peace*, 447.

as the "greatest war book ever written."[58] We might simply say it is one of the greatest books ever written.

Tolstoy's ability to craft his masterpiece with this dialectical advancement and enhancement in mind testifies to his and the work's genius. For a book set in the Napoleonic Wars, there is comparatively little dedicated to the spectacular battles of Austerlitz, Eylau, Friedland, and Borodino. The shadow of Napoleon and the wars against France loom over the story, but the ghost of Napoleon and the great battles and great men who pop up and just as quickly vanish pale in comparison to the struggles of Andrei, Pierre, Natasha, Nikolai, Marya, Sonya, Hélène, and others. The real war is in the world; and that world is one of flesh and blood relations. At the story's end, Tolstoy reveals to us the simplicity of wisdom. Meaningful life in love is right before us. Do we have the eyes to see and ears to hear?

This essay is adapted from an article originally published in *Voegelin View*, 24 May 2019.

---

58. Lewis, *Weight of Glory*, 51.

Afterword

IT IS MY SINCERE HOPE THAT THIS BOOK, WHICH SPANS NEARLY THREE MIL-
lennia of Western literature and some of the canonical great books, helps to
reveal a great theme that courses through our civilizational literature: love
(and how it is principally manifested through the grace of forgiveness).

Love is the great theme that defines great literature. It is not the prejudice of race, antiquity, or sex that characterizes the great books, though critics charge this to be the case. As witnessed in this tour, we find our great
poets, writers, and thinkers all struggling with the most central aspect of the
human condition: love.

What the Christian understands, as revealed by God through Christ,
is that man is created in love and for love. The object, the purpose, of life is
love itself. Love is what gives us nourishment, grounds our existence, and
governs our cosmos—as our short but hopefully resplendent tour of literature has conveyed. Love is what draws two creatures adrift together as one
flesh and binds them together in the maturation and growing in holiness
and upward ascent to the good things that the heavens hold. In love, we rise
together to take our seat in the realm of the white rose; without love, we tear
asunder and drift alone into the darkness of the ever-expanding void.

But how do we become united with others to enter the realm of the
white rose? As we witnessed with Achilles forgiving Priam, Dante and Virgil
forgiving each other, and Andrei forgiving Anatole, the greatest expression
of love in the great books seems to be forgiveness. Forgiveness is the greatest expression of love, and it is the particular love of forgiveness that brings
peace to the war-torn cosmos of Homer, allows Dante and Virgil to begin
their ascent to paradise, and brings forth Andrei's atonement—literally, harmony with the world at that one moment that he forgives Anatole and dies
in a condition of serene grace. (That is what atonement means: at one with
the cosmos.)

Many books and authors have not been included in this collection. I am aware that this is perhaps insufficient for all readers, but I hope the gentle reader can be touched by the Spirit of Love that moves literature and directs our sight to the heavenly stars and governs their movement. If our task, in teaching and reading, is to spread the good news of love and be transformed by love—to love God and neighbor and become more empathetic, forgiving, and compassionate persons made in that image of love—certainly, the wellspring of our literary tradition can do just that. And may we forgive those who destroy what they do not know.

Bibliography

For all translated material, I opted for widely accessible versions for ease of reader reference. In lieu of Robert Fagles's translations of Homer which my essays cited, I would recommend Richmond Lattimore to the interested reader.

Aeschylus. *The Oresteia*. Translated by Robert Fagles. New York: Penguin, 1979.

Aquinas. *The Summa Theologiae of St. Thomas Aquinas*. Translated by Fathers of the English Dominican Province. 2nd and rev. ed., 1920. New Advent (website). Edited by Kevin Knight. 2017. https://www.newadvent.org/summa/1020.htm.

Augustine. *The City of God*. Translated by Marcus Dods. New York: Modern Library, 2000.

————. *Confessions*. Translated by Henry Chadwick. New York: Oxford University Press, 2008.

Barrett, William. *Irrational Man*. New York: Anchor. 1990.

Dante. *The Divine Comedy*. In *The Portable Dante*, translated by Mark Musa, 1–586. New York: Penguin, 2003.

Dickens, Charles. *A Tale of Two Cities*. New York: Penguin, 2003.

————. *Great Expectations*. New York: Penguin, 2003.

Herbert, George. "Love (III)." Poetry Foundation (website). https://www.poetryfoundation.org/poems/44367/love-iii.

Herington, C.J. "Aeschylus: The Last Phase." *Arion: A Journal of Humanities and the Classics* 4, no. 3 (1965) 387–403.

Hesiod. *Theogony* and *Works and Days*. Translated by M.L. West. Oxford World's Classics. New York: Oxford University Press, 2008.

Homer. *The Iliad*. Translated by Robert Falges. New York: Penguin, 1998.

————. *The Odyssey*. Translated by Robert Fagles. New York: Penguin, 1997.

Horace. *The Complete Odes and Epodes*. Translated by David West. Oxford World's Classics. New York: Oxford University, 2008.

Kaufman, Andrew. *Give War and Peace a Chance*. New York: Simon and Schuster, 2014.

Keats, John. *Selected Poems*. New York: Penguin 2007.

Knox, Bernard. *The Oldest Dead White European Males: And Other Reflections on the Classics*. New York: W.W. Norton, 1994.

Lewis, C.S. *The Abolition of Man*. New York: HarperOne, 2001.

———. *The Weight of Glory*. New York: Harper Collins, 2001.

Milton, John. *Paradise Lost*. New York: Penguin, 2003.

Ovid. *Metamorphoses*. Translated by A.D. Melville. Oxford World's Classics. New York: Oxford University Press, 2008.

Pascal, Blaise. *Pensées*. Translated by A.J. Krailsheimer. New York: Penguin, 1995.

Scruton, Roger. *The Face of God*. New York: Continuum, 2012.

The Song of Roland. Translated by Glyn Burgess. New York: Penguin, 1990.

Shakespeare, William. *Antony and Cleopatra*. Edited by Barbara Everett. New York: Signet, 1998.

———. *Hamlet*. Edited by Barbara A. Mowat and Paul Werstine. Folger Shakespeare Library. New York: Washington Square, 1992.

———. *Henry V*. Edited by John Russell Brown. New York: Signet, 1998.

———. *Julius Caesar*. Edited by William and Barbara Rosen. New York: Signet, 1998.

———.*The Merchant of Venice*. Edited by Kenneth Myrick. New York: Signet, 1998.

———. *Richard III*. Edited by Mark Eccles. New York: Signet, 1998.

Sophocles. *The Complete Plays*. Translated by Paul Roche. New York: Signet, 2010.

Suetonius. *Suetonius*. Translated by C.J. Rolf. Vol. 2 of *Lives of the Caesars*. Loeb Classical Library 38. Cambridge, MA: Harvard University Press, 1998.

Swift, Jonathan. *Gulliver's Travels*. Edited by Claude Rawson and Ian Higgins. Oxford World's Classics. New York: Oxford University Press, 2008.

Tennyson, Alfred. *The Major Works*. New York: Oxford University Press, 2009.

Tolstoy, Leo. *War and Peace*. Translated by Louise and Aylmer Maude, revised by Amy Mandelker. Oxford World's Classics. New York: Oxford University Press, 2010.

Virgil. *The Aeneid*. Translated by Robert Fagles. New York: Penguin, 2010.

Wasserman, Steve. "Author Susan Sontag Dies." *Los Angeles Times*. 28 December 2004. https://www.latimes.com/local/obituaries/la-122804sontag_lat-story.html.

Subject Index

Author Index